REA

**DO NOT REMOVE
CARDS FROM POCKET**

H.P. Blavatsky at "Maycot," London, 1887

THE

OCCULT WORLD

OF

MADAME

BLAVATSKY

Reminiscences and Impressions
By Those Who Knew Her

Compiled and Edited by Daniel H. Caldwell

Impossible Dream Publications
P.O. Box 1844
Tucson, Arizona 85702
1991

Compilation Copyright 1991
by Daniel H. Caldwell

Library of Congress Cataloging-in-Publication Data

The Occult world of Madame Blavatsky : reminiscences and
impressions by those who knew her / compiled and edited by
Daniel H. Caldwell.
    p.   cm.
    Includes bibliographical references and index.
    ISBN 0-941657-04-3 : $13.95
    1. Blavatsky, H.P. (Helena Petrovna), 1831-1891.
2. Theosophists--Biography. I. Caldwell, Daniel H., 1949-   .
BP585.B6023   1991
299'.934'092--dc20
    [B]   91-36245
                                       CIP

Photo Credit: Original of computerized photograph on front
cover courtesy of ARCHIVES, Theosophical Society, P.O. Bin C,
Pasadena, CA 91109. Photo is by Sarony, N.Y., about 1877.

Printed in the United States of America

CONTENTS

"There are more things in heaven and earth, Horatio,
than are dreamt of in your philosophy."

William Shakespeare
Hamlet I, v, 166

INTRODUCTION

Here for the first time is the story of H.P. Blavatsky's life in the words of her contemporaries. Although not a biography *per se*, this book tells the story of Madame Blavatsky's eventful life with a special look at the "Occult World" in which she lived. These reminiscences by her relatives, acquaintances, friends, co-workers and enemies allow the reader to enter into the historical milieu of H.P.B.'s time and give a vivid portrayal of Madame Blavatsky's personality. The narratives are arranged in chronological order and include (1) striking word portraits of H.P.B.; (2) reminiscences giving insight into H.P.B.'s enigmatic character; (3) incidents that are sometimes humorous and witty; (4) accounts of psychic phenomena performed by Madame Blavatsky; and (5) descriptions of encounters with H.P.B.'s Masters.

Few individuals have been more misrepresented and slandered than Madame Blavatsky. Therefore, in selecting narratives for this book, only a few of the negative accounts have been used. There are several reasons for this decision. First and foremost, many of these hostile accounts are simply untrue. Those who would like to read some of the negative accounts should consult the following items in the bibliography: Marion Meade's biography (listed on p. 313) and the titles by Coulomb, Hodgson and Solovyov (listed under the heading "Major Attacks Against H.P.B and Their Rebuttals," pp. 315-316).

At the beginning of each narrative, the author, time-period, and place of the account are given. For biographical data on each narrator, refer to the section on "Biographical Sketches," pp. 329-335. If the reader is interested in other reminiscences of Madame Blavatsky, refer to the titles on pp. 314-315 in the bibliography.

The narratives have been transcribed verbatim from the original sources. Material not relevant to the narratives has been deleted; all deletions are indicated with ellipses (...). Explanatory notes added by the editor are enclosed within brackets. For consistency and readability, the spelling of people's names and geographical locations has been standardized. For people's names, the spelling used in H.P.B.'s *Collected Writings* (Vol. I and XV) has been adopted. No attempt has been made to standardize the variations in spelling between American and British usage (*e.g.,* color and colour).

The three appendices, especially "H.P.B. Speaks" and "Why Did Madame Blavatsky Perform Psychic Phenomena?," provide the reader with important material in the words of H.P.B. and her Masters. The bibliography is a useful 16-page listing of *in-print* books, audio cassettes and videos.

If readers have any questions or comments concerning the subject matter covered in this book, please address inquiries to the address below.

October, 1991   Daniel H. Caldwell

Impossible Dream Publications
P.O. Box 1844
Tucson, Arizona 85702
U.S.A.

ACKNOWLEDGMENTS

I would like to express my gratitude and appreciation to the following individuals who have helped me in my research on the life of Madame Blavatsky:

Dorothy Abbenhouse and Lakshmi Narayan of The Theosophical Society in America (Wheaton, Illinois); Grace F. Knoche, John van Mater, Kirby van Mater and Will Thackara of The Theosophical Society, International (Pasadena, California); Walter A. Carrithers, Jr. of The Blavatsky Foundation (Fresno, California); Joy Mills and Mary J. Schneider Kokochak of The Krotona Institute, School of Theosophy (Ojai, California); W. Emmett Small and Carmen Small of Point Loma Publications (San Diego, California); Richard Robb of Wizards Bookshelf (San Diego, California); Dara Eklund and Nicholas Weeks, Studio City, California; George E. Linton, Portland, Oregon; Henry and Maikka Van Thiel, Tucson, Arizona; Leona Sterba, Oklahoma City, Oklahoma; Anita Atkins, New York, New York; Michael Freeman of The H.P.B. Library, (Vernon, British Columbia, Canada); Ted G. Davy, Calgary, Alberta, Canada; Ernest and Rogelle Pelletier, Edmonton, Alberta, Canada; Leslie Price, London, England; Gregory Tillett, Petersham, New South Wales, Australia; and John Cooper, Bega, N.S.W., Australia.

Special thanks and appreciation to Mary Lessie Caldwell, Michelle B. Graye and Rick Remsburg of Tucson, Arizona for their help and support. Also appreciation to David M. Dunkle, David Yagla and Christopher Lewis for their discussions on my Blavatsky research.

I should like to dedicate this book to Virginia G. Hanson (1898-1991), author of *Masters and Men* and co-author of *Readers' Guide to The Mahatma Letters to A.P. Sinnett*. Virginia always gave me encouragement in my Theosophical studies.

H.P. BLAVATSKY'S LIFE AND WORK
A BRIEF SKETCH

H. P. Blavatsky (1831-1891) was one of the most extraordinary and controversial figures of the 19th century. The influence of her life, writings and teachings on world thought has been significant. The following quotations may help to indicate the extent of Madame Blavatsky's influence:

"...Helena Petrovna Blavatsky...is surely among the most original and perceptive minds of her time....Buried in the sprawling bulk of her two major books...there lies, in rudimentary form, the first philosophy of psychic and spiritual evolution to appear in the modern West....With all criticisms weighed up against her, HPB stands forth as a seminal talent of our time....Above all, she is among the modern world's trailblazing psychologists of the visionary mind. At the same historical moment that Freud, Pavlov, and James had begun to formulate the secularized and materialist theory of mind that has so far dominated modern Western thought, HPB and her fellow Theosophists were rescuing from occult tradition and exotic religion a forgotten psychology of the superconscious and the extrasensory....Madame Blavatsky may be credited with having set the style for modern occult literature."

Theodore Roszak, *The Unfinished Animal: The Aquarian Frontier and the Evolution of Consciousness*, New York, Harper and Row, 1975, pp. 118, 124-125.

―――――

"...Madame Blavatsky...stands out as the fountainhead of modern occult thought, and was either the originator and/or popularizer of many of the ideas and terms which have a century later been assembled within the New Age Movement. The Theosophical Society, which she cofounded, has been the major advocate of occult philosophy in the West and the single most important avenue of Eastern teaching to the West."

J. Gordon Melton, Jerome Clark and Aidan A. Kelly, editors, *New Age Almanac*, Detroit, Michigan, Gale Research Inc., 1991, p. 16.

―――――

"Theosophy occupies a central place in the history of new spiritual movements, for the writings of Blavatsky and some of her followers have had a great influence outside of her organization....The importance of Theosophy in modern history should not be underestimated. Not only have the writings of Blavatsky and others inspired several generations of occultists, but the movement had a remarkable role in the restoration to the colonial peoples of nineteenth century Asia their own spiritual heritage."

Robert S. Ellwood and Harry B. Partin, *Religious and Spiritual Groups in Modern America*, Englewood Cliffs, New Jersey, Prentice Hall, 1988, pp. 63, 79-80.

―――――

Helena Petrovna von Hahn was born at Ekaterinoslav, a town on the river Dnieper, in Southern Russia, on the 12th of August, 1831. She was the daughter of Colonel Peter von Hahn, and Helena de Fadeyev, a renowned novelist. On her mother's side, she was the granddaughter of the gifted Princess Helena Dolgorukov, a noted botanist and writer. After the early death of her mother in 1842, Helena was brought up in her maternal grandparents' house at Saratov, where her grandfather was Civil Governor.

Helena was an exceptional child, and at an early age was aware of being different from those around her. Her possession of certain psychic powers puzzled her family and friends. At once impatient of all authority, yet deeply sensitive, she was gifted in many ways. A clever linguist, a talented pianist and a fine artist, she was yet a fearless rider of half-broken horses, and always in close touch with nature. At a very early age she sensed that she was in some way dedicated to a life of service, and was aware of a special guidance and protection.

When almost eighteen, she married the middle-aged Nikifor V. Blavatsky, Vice-Governor of the Province of Yerivan', in a mood of rebellious independence and possibly with a plan to become free of her surroundings. The marriage, as such, meant nothing to her and was never consummated. In a few months she escaped and travelled widely in Turkey, Egypt, and Greece, on money supplied by her father.

On her twentieth birthday, in 1851, being then in London, she met the individual whom she had known in her psycho-spiritual visions from childhood---an Eastern Initiate of Rajput birth, the Mahatma Morya or M. as he became known in later years among Theosophists. He told her something of the work that was in store for her, and from that moment she accepted fully his guidance.

Later the same year, Helena embarked for Canada, and after adventurous travels in various parts of the U.S.A., Mexico, South America and the West Indies, went via the Cape and Ceylon to India in 1852. Her first attempt to enter Tibet failed. She returned to England via Java in 1853. In the Summer of 1854, she went to America again, crossing the Rockies with a caravan of emigrants, probably in a covered wagon.

In late 1855, she left for India via Japan and the Straits. On this trip she succeeded in entering Tibet through Kashmir and Ladakh, undergoing part of her occult training with her Master. In 1858 she was in France and Germany, and returned to Russia in the late Fall of the same year, staying a short time with her sister Vera at Pskov. From 1860 to 1865, she lived and travelled through the Caucasus, experiencing a severe physical and psychic crisis which placed her in complete control over her occult powers. She left Russia again in the Fall of 1865, and travelled extensively through the Balkans, Greece, Egypt, Syria and Italy and various other places.

In 1868 she went via India to Tibet. On this trip H.P.B. met the Master Koot Hoomi (K.H.) for the first time and stayed in his house in Little Tibet. In late 1870 she was back in Cyprus and Greece. Embarking for Egypt, she was shipwrecked near the island of Spetsai on July 4, 1871; saved from drowning, she went to Cairo where she tried to form a *Societe Spirite* which soon failed. After further travels through the Middle East, she returned for a short time to her relatives at Odessa, Russia in July, 1872. In the Spring of 1873, Helena was instructed by her Teacher to go to Paris, and on further direct orders from him, left for New York City where she landed July 7, 1873.

H.P. Blavatsky was then forty-two years old and in controlled possession of her many and most unusual spiritual and occult powers. In the opinion of the Mahatmas, she was the best available instrument for the work they had in mind, namely to offer to the world a new presentation, though only in brief outline of the age-old *Theosophia*, "The accumulated Wisdom of the ages, tested and verified by generations of Seers...," that body of Truth of which religions, great and small, are but as branches of the parent tree. Her task was to challenge on the one hand the entrenched beliefs and dogmas of Christian Theology and on the other the equally dogmatic materialistic view of the science of her day. A crack, however, had recently appeared in this twofold set of mental fortifications. It was caused by Spiritualism, then sweeping America. To quote Helena's own words: "I was sent to prove the phenomena and their reality, and to show the fallacy of the spiritualistic theory of spirits."

In October, 1874, H.P.B. was put in touch by her Teachers with Colonel Henry Steel Olcott, a man of sterling worth who had acquired considerable renown during the Civil War, had served the U.S. Government with distinction, and was at the time practicing law in New York. She also met William Quan Judge, a young Irish lawyer, who was to play a unique role in the future Theosophical work.

On September 7, 1875, these three leading figures, together with several others, founded a society which they chose to call The Theosophical Society, as promulgating the ancient teachings of Theosophy, or the Wisdom concerning the Divine which had been the spiritual basis of other great movements of the past, such as Neo-Platonism, Gnosticism, and the Mystery-Schools of the Classical world. The Inaugural Address by the President-Founder, Colonel Olcott, was delivered November 17, 1875, a date which is considered to be the official date of the founding of the Society. Starting from a generalized statement of objectives, namely, "to collect and diffuse a knowledge of the laws which govern the Universe," the Founders soon expressed them more specifically. After several minor changes in wording, the Objects stand today as follows:

1. To form a nucleus of the Universal Brotherhood of Humanity, without distinction of race, creed, sex, caste or color.

2. To encourage the study of Comparative Religion, Philosophy and Science.

3. To investigate unexplained laws of Nature, and the powers latent in man.

In September 1877, a powerful impact was made upon the reading and thinking public by the publication of H.P. Blavatsky's first monumental work, *Isis Unveiled*, which was issued by J.W. Bouton in New York City, the one thousand copies of the first printing being sold within ten days. The New York *Herald-Tribune* considered the work as one of the "remarkable productions of the century," many other papers and journals speaking in similar terms. *Isis Unveiled* outlines the history, scope and development of the Occult Sciences, the nature and origin of Magic, the roots of Christianity, the errors of Christian Theology and the fallacies of established orthodox Science, against the backdrop of the secret teachings which run as a golden thread through bygone centuries, coming up to the surface every now and then in the various mystical movements of the last two thousand years or so.

On July 8, 1878, H.P. Blavatsky was naturalized as a U.S. citizen, an event which received widespread publicity in various newspapers.

In December of the same year, H.P. Blavatsky and Colonel Olcott left for India via England. Arriving in Bombay in February, 1879, they established their Theosophical Headquarters in that city. Soon after landing, they were contacted by Alfred Percy Sinnett, then Editor of the Government paper, *The Pioneer* of Allahabad. This contact soon proved of the utmost importance.

After a tour of northwestern India, the Founders returned to Bombay and started, in October, 1879, their first Theosophical Journal, *The Theosophist* (still published today), with H.P. Blavatsky as Editor. The Society experienced then a rapid growth, and some very remarkable people were attracted to it both in India and elsewhere. During May-July, 1880 the Founders spent some time in Ceylon, where Colonel Olcott laid the foundations for his later work to stimulate the revival of Buddhism. They both took "Pancha Sila" or became officially Buddhists.

In September and October, 1880, H.P.B. and Colonel Olcott visited A.P. Sinnett and his wife Patience at Simla in northern India. The serious interest of Sinnett in the teachings and the work of the Theosophical Society prompted H.P. Blavatsky to establish a contact by correspondence between Sinnett and the two Adepts who were sponsoring the Society, Mahatmas K.H. and M. From this correspondence Sinnett wrote *The Occult World* (1881) and *Esoteric Buddhism* (1883), both of which had an enormous influence in generating public interest in Theosophy. The replies and explanations given by the Mahatmas to the questions by Sinnett are embodied in their letters from 1880 to 1885 and were published in 1923 as *The Mahatma Letters to A.P. Sinnett*. The original letters from these Teachers are the prized possession of the British Library where they can be viewed by special permission in the Department of Rare Manuscripts.

In May, 1882, a large estate was bought in southern India at Adyar, near Madras, and the Theosophical Headquarters were moved there at the end of the year. This center became soon the radiating point for a world-wide activity. Madame Blavatsky and Colonel Olcott engaged in trips to various outlying districts, founded Branches, received visitors, conducted an enormous correspondence with inquirers, and filled their Journal with most valuable and scholarly material the main purpose of which was to revitalize the dormant interest on the part of India in the spiritual worth of their own ancient Scriptures.

It is during this period that Colonel Olcott engaged in widespread mesmeric healings until February, 1884, when he left for London to petition the British Government on behalf of the Buddhists of Ceylon. H.P. Blavatsky, then in rather poor health, went to Europe with him.

After staying almost five months in Paris and London, H.P.B. visited the Gebhard family in Elberfeld, Germany during the late Summer and early Fall of 1884 and was busily engaged in writing her second work, *The Secret Doctrine*.

Meanwhile, a vicious attack on her by two of her staff members at Adyar, Alexis and Emma Coulomb, was rapidly building up. She returned to Adyar on December 21, 1884 to learn the details of the situation. She wished to sue the couple, already dismissed from Adyar for their gross libel on her concerning the supposed fraudulent production of psychic phenomena. H.P.B. was, however, overruled by a Committee of leading T.S. members, and in disgust resigned as Corresponding Secretary of the Society. On March 31, 1885, she left for Europe, never to return to Indian soil.

The Coulomb attack, as was later proved, had no solid foundation whatsoever. It was based on forged and partially forged letters, purporting to have been written by H.P. Blavatsky, with instructions to arrange fraudulent psychic phenomena of various kinds. A Christian missionary magazine in Madras published the most incriminating portions of these letters.

Meanwhile, the Society for Psychical Research (London) had appointed a special committee to investigate Madame Blavatsky's claims. Then in December, 1884, Richard Hodgson, a member of this S.P.R. committee, arrived in India to inquire into and report on the Coulombs' allegations. Based upon Hodgson's findings, the S.P.R. committee in its final report of December, 1885, branded Madame Blavatsky "one of the most accomplished, ingenious and interesting impostors in history." Mr. Hodgson also accused Madame Blavatsky of being a Russian spy. This "S.P.R.--Hodgson" Report has been the basis for most subsequent attacks on H.P. Blavatsky, as to her dishonesty, the non-existence of her Masters, and the worthlessness of Theosophy.

In 1963, Adlai Waterman, in his definitive work entitled *Obituary: The "Hodgson Report" on Madame Blavatsky*, analyzed and refuted Hodgson's contentions against Madame Blavatsky.[*]

This vicious attack had a most unfavorable effect on H.P. Blavatsky's health. Having left India for Europe, she settled first in Italy and then in August, 1885 at Wurzburg, Germany, where she worked on *The Secret Doctrine*. In July, 1886, she relocated to Ostend, Belgium, and in May of 1887, at the invitation of English Theosophists, she moved to a small house at Upper Norwood, London.

After her arrival in England, Theosophical activities immediately began to move rapidly. The Blavatsky Lodge was formed and started publicizing Theosophical ideas.

As H.P. Blavatsky had virtually lost control of *The Theosophist*, she founded in September, 1887 *Lucifer*, a monthly magazine designed, as stated on its title-page, "to bring to light the hidden things of darkness." Also in the same month, H.P.B. moved to 17 Lansdowne Road, Holland Park, London.

H.P.B. continued steadily to write her great work which was finally completed and published in two large volumes in October-December, 1888. Her indefatigable helpers in the transcription and editing of the MSS. were Bertram Keightley and Archibald

---

[*] [A copy of Waterman's book can be purchased for $6.50 (including postage and handling) from The Blavatsky Foundation, P.O. Box 1543, Fresno, California 93716.

Another recent refutation of some of Hodgson's charges against H.P.B. is Vernon Harrison's article entitled "J'Accuse: An Examination of the Hodgson Report of 1885," and published in **The Journal of the Society for Psychical Research**, London, April, 1986, pp. 286-310.

For more material on this controversy, consult pp. 315-316 in this volume.---Editor.]

Keightley, whose financial backing was also of immense assistance.

The Secret Doctrine was the crowning achievement of H.P. Blavatsky's literary career. Volume I is concerned mainly with the evolution of the Universe. The skeleton of this volume is formed by seven Stanzas, translated from the Secret Book of Dzyan, with commentary and explanations by H.P.B. Also in this volume is an extended elucidation of the fundamental symbols contained in the great religions and mythologies of the world. The second Volume contains a further series of Stanzas from the Book of Dzyan, which describe the Evolution of Humanity.

Also in October, 1888, Madame Blavatsky formed the Esoteric Section (or School) of the Theosophical Society for the deeper study of the Esoteric Philosophy by dedicated students, and wrote for them her three *E.S. Instructions.*

In 1889 H.P. Blavatsky published *The Key to Theosophy*, "a clear Exposition, in the form of Question and Answer, of the Ethics, Science and Philosophy for the study of which the Theosophical Society has been founded," and the devotional, mystical gem called *The Voice of the Silence*, containing selected excerpts translated from an Eastern scripture, *The Book of the Golden Precepts*, which she had learnt by heart during her training in the East.

In July, 1890, H.P.B. established the European Headquarters of the Theosophical Society at 19 Avenue Road, St. John's Wood, London. From this historic address H.P. Blavatsky died on May 8, 1891, during a severe epidemic of flu in England, and her remains were cremated at Woking Crematorium, Surrey.

Against the background of her writings and teachings, her life and character, her mission and occult powers, H.P. Blavatsky is destined to be recognized in time as the greatest Occultist in the history of Western civilization, a direct agent of the Trans-Himalayan Brotherhood of Adepts.[*]

---

[*][This sketch of H.P.B.'s life has been adapted (with additions and deletions) from a biographical article on H.P.B. written by Boris de Zirkoff and published in **Theosophia** (Los Angeles). Summer. 1968.---Editor.]

Chapter 1

RUSSIA

1831-1849

The Birth of Helena Petrovna Von Hahn[1]
August 12, 1831, Ekaterinoslav, Southern Russia

The baby [Helena Petrovna] was born on the night between
...[August 11 and 12, 1831]---weak, and apparently no denizen of
this world. A hurried baptism had to be resorted to, therefore, lest
the child died with the burden of original sin on her soul. The
ceremony of baptism in "orthodox" Russia is attended with all the
paraphernalia of lighted tapers, and "pairs" of god-mothers and
god-fathers, every one of the spectators and actors being furnished
with consecrated wax candles during the whole proceedings.
Moreover, every one has to stand during the baptismal rite, no one
being allowed to sit in the Greek religion, as they do in Roman
Catholic and Protestant Churches, during the church and religious
service. The room selected for the ceremony in the family
mansion was large, but the crowd of devotees eager to witness it
was still larger. Behind the priest officiating in the centre of the
room, with his assistants, in their golden robes and long hair, stood
the three pairs of sponsors and the whole household of vassals and
serfs. The child-aunt of the baby---only a few years older than
her niece aged twenty-four hours---placed as "proxy" for an absent
relative, was in the first row....Feeling nervous and tired of
standing still for nearly an hour, the child settled on the floor
unperceived by the elders, and became probably drowsy in the
over-crowded room on that hot...day. The ceremony was nearing
its close. The sponsors were just in the act of renouncing the Evil

One and his deeds, a renunciation emphasized in the Greek Church by thrice spitting upon the invisible enemy, when the little lady, toying with her lighted taper at the feet of the crowd, inadvertently set fire to the long flowing robes of the priest....The result was an immediate conflagration, during which several persons---chiefly the old priest---were severely burnt. That was ...[a] bad omen, according to the superstitious beliefs of orthodox Russia; and the innocent cause of it---the future Mme. Blavatsky ---was doomed from that day in the eyes of all the town to an eventful life, full of...trouble....

Nadyezhda A. de Fadeyev[2]
(H.P.B.'s aunt)
1831-1849, Russia

...From her earliest childhood she was unlike any other person. Very lively and highly gifted, full of humour and of most remarkable daring; she struck everyone with astonishment by her self-willed and determined actions. Thus in her earliest youth and hardly married, she disposed of herself in an angry mood, abandoning her country, without the knowledge of her relatives or husband, who, unfortunately was a man in every way unsuited to her, and more than thrice her age....Her restless and very nervous temperament, one that led her into the most unheard of, ungirlish mischief; her unaccountable---especially in those days - --attraction to, and at the same time fear of, the dead; her passionate love and curiosity for everything unknown and mysterious, weird and fantastical; and, foremost of all, her craving for independence and freedom of action---a craving that nothing and nobody could control; all this, combined with an exuberance of imagination and wonderful sensitiveness, ought to have warned her friends that she was an exceptional creature, to be dealt with and controlled by means as exceptional. The slightest contradiction brought on an outburst of passion, often a fit of convulsion. Left alone with no one near her to impede her liberty of action, no hand to chain her down or stop her natural impulses, and thus arouse to fury her inherent combativeness, she would spend hours and days quietly whispering, as people thought, to herself, and narrating, with no one near her, in some dark corner, marvellous tales of travels in bright stars and other worlds, which her governess described as "profane gibberish;" but no sooner would the governess give her a distinct order to do this or the other thing than her first impulse was to disobey. It was enough to forbid her doing a thing to make her do it, come what would. Her nurse, as indeed other members of the family, sincerely believed the child possessed "the seven spirits of rebellion." Her governesses were martyrs to their task, and never succeeded in bending her resolute will, or influencing by anything but kindness her indomitable, obstinate, and fearless nature.

Spoilt in her childhood by the adulation of dependents and the devoted affection of relatives, who forgave all to "the poor, motherless child"---later on, in her girlhood, her self-willed temper made her rebel openly against the exigencies of society. She would submit to no sham respect for or fear of the public opinion. She *would* ride at fifteen, as she had at ten, any Cossack horse on a man's saddle! She would bow to no one, as she would recede before no prejudice or established conventionality. She defied all and everyone. As in her childhood, all her sympathies and attractions went out towards people of the lower class. She had always preferred to play with her servants' children rather than with her equals, and as a child had to be constantly watched for fear she should escape from the house to make friends with ragged street boys. So, later on in life, she continued to be drawn in sympathy towards those who were in a humbler station of life than herself, and showed as pronounced indifference to the "nobility" to which by birth she belonged.

23

Vera P. de Zhelihovsky[3]

(H.P.B.'s sister)
1842-1846, Saratov, Russia
(where H.P.B.'s maternal grandparents lived)

Helena...was a precocious child, and from her earliest youth attracted the attention of all with whom she came in contact. Her nature was quite intractable to the routine demanded by her instructors, she rebelled against all discipline, recognized no master but her own good will and her personal tastes. She was exclusive, original, and at times bold even to roughness....

When her mother was dying, although her eldest daughter was only eleven years old, she was filled with well-founded apprehensions for her future, and said:

"Ah well! perhaps it is best that I am dying, so at least I shall be spared seeing what befalls Helena! Of one thing I am certain, her life will not be as that of other women, and that she will have much to suffer."....

...At the death of our mother, we went to live with her parents....The great country mansion...occupied by us at Saratov, was an old and vast building, full of subterranean galleries, long abandoned passages, turrets, and most weird nooks and corners....It looked more like a medieval ruined castle than a building of the past century. The man who took care of the estate for the proprietors...had been known for his cruelty and tyranny....The legends told of his ferocious and despotic temper, of unfortunate serfs beaten by him to death, and imprisoned for months in dark subterranean dungeons, were many and thrilling....Our heads were full of stories about the ghosts of the martyred serfs, seen promenading in chains during nocturnal hours...and other stories that left us children and girls in an agony of fear whenever we had to cross a dark room or passage. We had been permitted to explore, under the protection of half-a-dozen male servants and a quantity of torches and lanterns, those awe-inspiring "Catacombs."...Still Helena would not remain satisfied with one solitary visit, nor with a second either. She had selected the uncanny region as...a safe refuge where she could avoid her lessons. A long time passed before her secret was found out, and whenever she was found missing, a deputation of strong-bodied servant men...was despatched in search of her....She had erected for herself a tower out of old broken chairs and tables in a corner under an iron-barred window, high up in the ceiling of the vault, and there she would hide for hours, reading a book known as "Solomon's Wisdom," in which every kind of popular legend was taught. Once or twice she could hardly be found in those damp subterranean corridors, having in her endeavours to escape detection, lost her way in the labyrinth. For all this she was not in the least daunted or repentant, for, as she assured us, she was never there alone, but in the company of "beings" she used to call her little "hunch-backs" and playmates.

Intensely nervous and sensitive, speaking loud, and often walking in her sleep, she used to be found at nights in the most out-of-way places, and to be carried back to her bed profoundly asleep. Thus she was missed from her room one night when she was hardly twelve, and the alarm having been given, she was searched for and found pacing one of the long subterranean corridors, evidently in deep conversation with someone invisible for all but herself. She was the strangest girl one has ever seen, one with a distinct dual nature in her, that made one think there were two beings in one and the same body; one mischievous, combative, and obstinate---everyway graceless; the other...mystical and metaphysically inclined....No schoolboy was ever more uncontrollable or full of the most unimaginable and daring pranks...as she was. At the same time, when the paroxysm of mischief-making had run its course no old scholar could be more assiduous in his study, and she could not be prevailed to give up her books, which she would devour night and day as long as the impulse lasted. The enormous library of her grandparents seemed then hardly large enough to satisfy her cravings....

Fancy, or that which we all regarded in these days as fancy, was developed in the most extraordinary way, and from her earliest childhood, in my sister Helena. For hours at times she used to narrate to us younger children, and even to her seniors in years, the most incredible stories with the cool assurance and conviction of an eyewitness, and one who knew what she was talking about. When a child, daring and fearless in everything else, she got often scared into fits through her own hallucinations. She felt certain of being persecuted by what she called "the

25

terrible glaring eyes" invisible to everyone else, and often attributed by her to the most inoffensive inanimate objects; an idea that appeared quite ridiculous to the bystanders. As to herself, she would shut her eyes tight during such visions, and run away to hide from the ghostly glances thrown on her by pieces of furniture or articles of dress, screaming desperately, and frightening the whole household. At other times she would be seized with fits of laughter, explaining them by the amusing pranks of her invisible companions....Every locked door notwithstanding, Helena was found several times during the night hours in those dark apartments in a half-conscious state, sometimes fast asleep, and unable to say how she got there from our common bedroom on the top story. She disappeared in the same mysterious manner in daytime also. Searched for, called and hunted after, she would be often discovered, with great pains, in the most unfrequented localities; once it was in the dark loft, under the very roof, to which she was traced, amid pigeons' nests, and surrounded by hundreds of those birds. She was "putting them to sleep" (according to the rules taught in "Solomon's Wisdom"), as she explained. And, indeed, pigeons were found, if not asleep, still unable to move, and as though stunned, in her lap at such times.

...For her all nature seemed animated with a mysterious life of its own. She heard the voice of every object and form, whether organic or inorganic; and claimed consciousness and being, not only for some mysterious powers visible and audible for herself alone in what was to every one else empty space, but even for visible but inanimate things such as pebbles, mounds and pieces of decaying phosphorescent timber...

...At about...[6.6 miles] from the Governor's villa there was a field, an extensive sandy tract of land, evidently once upon a time the bottom of a sea or a great lake, as its soil yielded petrified relics of fishes, shells, and teeth of some (to us) unknown monsters. Most of these relics were broken and mangled by time, but one could often find whole stones of various sizes on which were imprinted figures of fishes and plants and animals of kinds now wholly extinct, but which proved their undeniable antediluvian origin. The marvellous and sensational stories that we, children and schoolgirls, heard from Helena...were countless.

26

I well remember when stretched at full length on the ground, her chin reclining on her two palms, and her two elbows buried deep in the soft sand, she used to dream aloud, and tell us of her visions, evidently clear, vivid, and palpable as life to her!...How vividly she described their past fights and battles on the spot where she lay, assuring us she saw it all; and how minutely she drew on the sand with her finger the fantastic forms of the long dead sea monsters, and made us almost see the very colours of the fauna and flora of those dead regions. While listening eagerly to her descriptions of the lovely azure waves reflecting the sunbeams playing in the rainbow lights on the golden sands of the sea bottom, of the coral reefs and stalactite caves, of the sea-green grass mixed with the delicate shining anemones,...our imagination galloped off with her fancy to a full oblivion of the present reality. She never spoke in later years as she used to speak in her childhood and early girlhood. The stream of her eloquence has dried up, and the very source of her inspiration is now seeming lost! She had a strong power of carrying away her audiences with her, of making them see actually, if even vaguely, that which she herself saw....Once she frightened all of us youngsters very nearly into fits. We had just been transported into a fairy world, when suddenly she changed her narrative from the past to the present tense, and began to ask us to imagine that all that which she had told us of the cool blue waves with their dense populations, was around us, only invisible and intangible, so far...."Just fancy! A miracle!" she said; "the earth suddenly opening, the air condensing around us and rebecoming sea waves....Look, look...there, they begin already appearing and moving. We are surrounded with water ...amid the mysteries and the wonders of a submarine world!..."

She had started from the sand, and was speaking with such conviction, her voice had such a ring of real amazement, horror, and her childish face wore such a look of a wild joy and terror at the same time, that when, suddenly covering her eyes with both hands, as she used to do in her excited moments, she fell down on the sand, screaming at the top of her voice, "There's the wave...it has come!...The sea, the sea, we are drowning!"...Everyone one of us fell down on our faces, as desperately screaming and as fully convinced that the sea had engulfed us, and that we were no more!...

Nadyezhda A. de Fadeyev[4]
Spring & Summer, 1849, Russia

...[Helena] cared not whether she should get married or not. She had been simply defied one day by her governess to find any man who would be her husband, in view of her temper and disposition. The governess, to emphasise the taunt, said that even the old man [Nikifor V. Blavatsky] she had found so ugly, and had laughed at so much, calling him "a plumeless raven"---that even he would decline her for a wife! That was enough: three days after she made him propose, and then, frightened at what she had done, sought to escape from her joking acceptance of his offer. But it was too late. Hence the fatal step. All she knew and understood was---when *too late*---that she had been accepting, and was now forced to accept---a *master* she cared nothing for, nay, that she hated; that she was *tied* to him by the law of the country, hand and foot. A "great horror" crept upon her, as she explained it later; one desire, ardent, unceasing, irresistible, got hold of her entire being, led her on, so to say, by the hand, forcing her to act instinctively, as she would have done if, in the act of saving her life, she had been running away from a mortal danger. There had been a distinct attempt to impress her with the solemnity of marriage, with her future obligations and her duties to her *husband*, and married life. A few hours later, at the altar, she heard the priest saying to her:---"Thou shalt honour and obey thy husband," and at this hated word, "shalt," her young face...was seen to flush angrily, then to become deadly pale. She was overheard to mutter in response, through her set teeth---"Surely, I *shall* not."

And surely she has not. Forthwith she determined to take the law and her future life into her own hands, and---she left her "husband" for ever, without giving him any opportunity to ever even think of her as *his wife*.

Thus Mme. Blavatsky abandoned her country at seventeen, and passed ten long years in strange and out-of-the-way places, in Central Asia, India, South America, Africa, and Eastern Europe.

Chapter 2

TRAVELS AROUND THE WORLD

HOME TO RUSSIA

1849-1873

Countess Constance Wachtmeister[5]
1851, London

...During her childhood...[Madame Blavatsky] had often seen near her an Astral form, that always seemed to come in any moment of danger, and save her just at the critical point. H.P.B. had learnt to look upon this Astral form as a guardian angel, and felt that she was under His care and guidance.

...In London, in 1851..., she was one day out walking when, to her astonishment, she saw a tall Hindu in the street with some Indian princes. She immediately recognized him as the same person that she had seen in the Astral. Her first impulse was to rush forward to speak to him, but he made her a sign not to move, and she stood as if spellbound while he passed on. The next day she went into Hyde Park for a stroll, that she might be alone and free to think over her extraordinary adventure. Looking up, she saw the same form approaching her, and then her Master told her that he had come to London with the Indian princes on an important mission, and he was desirous of meeting her personally, as he required her co-operation in a work which he was about to undertake. He then told her how The Theosophical Society was to be formed, and that he wished her to be the founder. He gave her a slight sketch of all the troubles she

29

would have to undergo, and also told her that she would have to spend three years in Tibet to prepare her for the important task....H.P.B. decided to accept the offer made to her and shortly afterwards left London for India.

Vera P. de Zhelihovsky[6]
Christmas Day, 1858---Spring, 1859, Pskov, Russia

...Madame Blavatsky returned to Russia [in 1858]. After her return..., she first came and settled herself in...Pskov, where...I was living....We were not expecting her to arrive for some weeks to come, but, curiously enough, no sooner did I hear her ring at the door-bell than I jumped up, knowing that she had arrived. As it happened there was a party going on that evening in my father-in-law's house, in which I was living. His daughter was to be married that very evening, the guests were seated at table and the ringing of the door-bell was incessant. Nevertheless I was so sure it was she who had arrived that, to the astonishment of everyone, I hurriedly rose from the wedding feast and ran to open the door, not wishing the servants to do so.

We embraced each other, overcome with joy, forgetting for the moment the strangeness of the event. I took her at once to my room, and that very evening I was convinced that my sister had acquired strange powers. She was constantly surrounded, awake or asleep, with mysterious movements, strange sounds, little taps which came from all sides---from the furniture, from the window-panes, from the ceiling, from the floor, and from the walls. They were very distinct and seemed intelligent into the bargain; they tapped once, and three times for "yes," twice for "no."

My sister asked me to ask them a mental question. This I did, selecting a question as to a fact only known to myself. I recited the alphabet, and the reply I received was so true and so precise that I was positively astounded. I had often heard talk of spirit-rapping, but never before had I had an opportunity of testing their knowledge.

Before long the whole town was talking of the "miracles"

which surrounded Madame Blavatsky. The not only intelligent, but even clairvoyant answers given by these invisible forces, which operated night and day, without any apparent intervention on her part, all round her, struck more astonishment and wonder into the minds of the curious than even the movement of inanimate objects, which apparently gained or lost their weight, which phenomena she directly produced by merely fixing her eyes on the object selected....

It is impossible to give in detail even a portion of what was produced in the way of such phenomena during the stay of Mme. Blavatsky amongst us in the town of Pskov....

The following...took place in the presence of many eye-witnesses....

As usual, those nearest and dearest to her were, at the same time, the most sceptical as to her occult powers. Her brother Leonid and her father stood out longer than all against evidence, until at last the doubts of the former were greatly shaken by the following fact.

The drawing-room...was full of visitors. Some were occupied with music, others with cards, but most of us, as usual, with phenomena. Leonid...did not concern himself with anything in particular, but was leisurely walking about, watching everybody and everything....He stopped behind the back of his sister's chair, and was listening to her narratives of how some persons, who called themselves mediums, made light objects become so heavy that it was impossible to lift them; and others which were naturally heavy became again remarkably light.

"And you mean to say that you can do it?" ironically asked the young man of his sister.

"Mediums can, and I have done it occasionally; though I cannot always answer for its success," coolly replied Mme. Blavatsky.

"But would you try?" asked somebody in the room; and immediately all joined in requesting her to do so.

"I will try," she said, "but I beg of you to remember that I promise nothing. I will simply fix this chess-table, and try....He who wants to make the experiment, let him lift it now, and then try *again* after I shall have fixed it."

"After you shall have fixed it?" said a voice, "and what then?

Do you mean to say that you will not touch the table at all?"

"Why should I touch it?" answered Mme. Blavatsky, with a quiet smile.

Upon hearing the extraordinary assertion, one of the young men went determinedly to the small chess-table, and lifted it up as though it were a feather.

"All right," she said. "Now kindly leave it alone, and stand back!"

The order was at once obeyed, and a great silence fell upon the company. All, holding their breath, anxiously watched for what Mme. Blavatsky would do next. She apparently, however, did nothing at all. She merely fixed her large blue eyes upon the chess-table, and kept looking at it with an intense gaze. Then, without removing her gaze, she silently, with a motion of her hand, invited the same young man to remove it. He approached, and grasped the table by its leg with great assurance. The table *could not be moved*!

He then seized it with both his hands. The table stood as though screwed to the floor.

Then the young man, crouching down, took hold of it with both hands, exerting all his strength to lift it by the additional means of his broad shoulders. He grew red with the effort, but all in vain! The table seemed rooted to the carpet, and would not be moved. There was a loud burst of applause. The young man, looking very much confused, abandoned his task...and stood aside.

Folding his arms in quite a Napoleonic way, he only slowly said, "Well, this is a good joke!"

"Indeed, it is a good one!" echoed Leonid.

A suspicion had crossed his mind that the young visitor was acting in secret confederacy with his sister, and was fooling them.

"May I also try?" he suddenly asked her.

"Please do, my dear," was the laughing response.

Her brother upon this approached, smiling, and seized, in his turn, the diminutive table by its leg with his strong muscular arm. But the smile instantly vanished, to give place to an expression of mute amazement. He stepped back a little and examined again very carefully the, to him, well-known chess table. Then he gave it a tremendous kick, but the little table did not even budge.

Suddenly applying to its surface his powerful chest he

32

enclosed it within his arms, trying to shake it. The wood cracked, but would yield to no effort. Its three feet seemed screwed to the floor. Then Leonid Hahn lost all hope, and abandoning the ungrateful task, stepped aside, and frowning exclaimed but these two words, "How strange!" his eyes turning meanwhile with a wild expression of astonishment from the table to his sister....

The loud debate had meanwhile drawn the attention of several visitors, and they came pouring in from the drawing-room into...where we were...Many of them old and young, tried to lift up, or even to impart some slight motion to, the obstinate little chess table. They failed, like the rest of us.

Upon seeing her brother's astonishment, and perchance desiring finally to destroy his doubts, Mme. Blavatsky, addressing him with her usual careless laugh, said, "Try to lift the table now, once more!"

Leonid...approached the little thing very irresolutely, grasped it again by the leg, and, pulling it upwards, came very nearly to dislocating his arm owing to the useless effort: the table was lifted like a feather this time!...

Vera P. de Zhelihovsky[7]
Spring, 1859, St. Petersburg, Russia

...Mme. Blavatsky...left Pskov with her father and sister.... Living in a hotel...they had come to St. Petersburg....All their forenoons were occupied with business, their afternoons and evenings with making and receiving visits, and there was no time for, or even mention of, phenomena.

One night they received a visit from two old friends of their father; both were old gentlemen....Baron M-----, the other the well-known K-----w. Both were much interested in recent spiritualism and were, of course, anxious to see something.

After a few successful phenomena, the visitors declared

themselves positively delighted, amazed and quite at a loss what to make of Mme. Blavatsky's powers. They could neither understand nor account, they said, for her father's indifference in presence of such manifestations. There he was, coolly laying out his "*grande patience*"[*] with cards, while phenomena of such a wonderful nature were occurring around him. The old gentleman, thus taken to task, answered that it was all bosh, and that he would not hear of such nonsense; such occupation being hardly worthy of serious people, he added. The rebuke left the two old gentlemen unconcerned. They began, on the contrary, to insist that Col. Hahn should, for old friendship's sake, make an experiment, before denying the importance, or even the possibility of his daughter's phenomena. They offered him to test the *intelligences* and their power by writing a word in another room, secretly from all of them, and then asking the raps to repeat it. The old gentleman, more probably in the hope of a failure that would afford him the opportunity of laughing at his two old friends, then out of a desire to humour them, finally consented. He left his cards, and proceeding into an adjoining room, wrote a word on a bit of paper, after, which conveying it to his pocket, he returned to his *patience*, and waited silently, laughing behind his gray moustache.

"Well, our dispute will now be settled in a few moments," said K-----w. "What shall you say, however, old friend, if the word written by you is correctly repeated? Will you not feel compelled to believe in such a case?"

"What I might say, *if* the word were correctly guessed, I could not tell at present," he sceptically replied. "One thing I could answer, however, from the time I can be made to believe your alleged spiritism and its phenomena, I shall be ready to believe in the existence of the devil.., sorcerers, and witches---in the whole paraphernalia---in short, of old women's superstitions; and you may prepare to offer me as an inmate of a lunatic asylum."

Upon delivering himself thus, he went on with his *patience*, and paid no further attention to the proceedings. He was an old

---

[*]["Patience"---A game of solitaire: any of various card games played by one person.---Editor.]

"Voltarian," as the positivists who believed in nothing, are called in Russia. But we, who felt deeply interested in the experiment, began to listen to the loud and unceasing raps coming from a plate brought there for the purpose.

The younger sister was repeating the alphabet; the old general marked the letters down; while Mme. Blavatsky did nothing at all---apparently....

By the means of raps and alphabet we got *one word*, but it proved such a strange one, so grotesquely absurd as having no evident relation to anything that might be supposed to have been written by her father, that all of us who had been in the expectation of some complicated sentence looked at each other, dubious whether we ought to read it aloud. To our question, whether it was all, the raps became more energetic in the affirmative. We had several *triple* raps, which meant in our code ---Yes!...yes, yes, yes!!!

Remarking our agitation and whispering, Madame B.'s father looked at us over his spectacles, and asked---

"Well! Have you any answer? It must be something very elaborate and profound indeed!"

He arose and, laughing in his moustache, approached us....

"We only got *one* word."

"And what is it?"

"*Zaitchik!*"

It was a sight indeed to witness the extraordinary change that came over the old man's face at this *one* word! He became deadly pale. Adjusting his spectacles with a trembling hand, he stretched it out while hurriedly saying---

"Let me see it! Hand it over. Is it really so?"

He took the slips of paper, and read in a very agitated voice, ---"Zaitchik. Yes, zaitchik; so it is. How very strange!"

Taking out of his pocket the paper he had written upon in the adjoining room, he handed it in silence to his daughter and guests.

They found on it both the question offered and the answer that was anticipated. The words read thus---

"What was the name of my favourite war-horse which I rode during my first Turkish campaign?" and lower down, in parenthesis, ("Zaitchik.")....

This solitary word, *Zaitchik*, had an enormous effect upon the old gentleman. As it often happens with inveterate sceptics, once that he had found out that there was indeed *something* in his eldest daughter's claims, and that it had nothing to do whatever with deceit or juggling, having been convinced of this one fact, he rushed into the region of phenomena with all the zeal of an ardent investigator. As a matter of course, once he believed he felt no more inclined to doubt his own reason.

Having received from Mme. Blavatsky one correct answer, her father became passionately fond of experimenting with his daughter's powers....

Vera P. de Zhelihovsky[8]
1859-1865, Rugodevo, and then later at Tiflis, and other parts of the Caucasus, Russia

In the early part of 1859...Mme. Blavatsky went to live with her father and sister in a country house...at Rugodevo....

[But] the quiet life of the sisters at Rugodevo was brought to an end by a terrible illness which befell Mme. Blavatsky. Years before, perhaps during her solitary travels in the steppes of Asia, she had received a remarkable wound. We could never learn how she had met with it. Suffice to say that the profound wound re-opened occasionally, and during that time she suffered intense agony, often bringing on convulsions and a death-like trance. The sickness used to last from three to four days, and then the wound would heal as suddenly as it had re-opened, as though an invisible hand had closed it, and there would remain no trace of her illness. But the affrighted family was ignorant at first of this strange peculiarity, and their despair and fear were great indeed. A physician was sent for...; but he proved of little use, not so much indeed through his ignorance of surgery, as owing to a remarkable phenomenon which left him almost powerless to act through sheer terror at what he had witnessed. He had hardly examined the wound of the patient prostrated before him in complete unconsciousness, when suddenly he saw a large, dark hand between his own and the wound he was going to anoint. The gaping wound was near the heart, and the hand kept slowly moving at several intervals from the neck down to the waist. To make his terror worse, there began suddenly in the room such a terrific noise, such a chaos of noises and sounds from the ceiling, the floor, window-panes, and every bit of furniture in the apartment, that he begged he might not be left alone in the room with the insensible patient.

In the spring of 1860 both sisters left Rugodevo for the Caucasus, on a visit to their grandparents, whom they had not seen for long years....The three weeks' journey...to Tiflis...[was performed] in a coach with post horses....

Mme. Blavatsky resided at Tiflis less than two years, and not more than three in the Caucasus. The last year she passed roaming about in Imeretia, Georgia, and Mingreliya...and...along the coasts of the Black Sea....

Her occult powers, all this while, instead of weakening, became every day stronger, and she seemed finally to subject to her direct will every kind of manifestation. The whole country was talking of her. The superstitious...nobility began very soon to regard her as a magician, and people came from afar off to consult her about their private affairs. She had long since given up communication through raps, and preferred---what was a far more rapid and satisfactory method---to answer people either verbally or by means of direct writing. At times, during such process, Mme. Blavatsky seemed to fall into a kind of coma, or magnetic sleep, with eyes wide open, though even then her hand never ceased to move, and continued this writing. When thus answering to mental questions, the answers were rarely unsatisfactory. Generally they astonished the querists---friends and enemies.

Meanwhile sporadic phenomena were gradually dying away in her presence. They still occurred, but very rarely, though they were always very remarkable. We give one.

It must, however, be explained, that some months previous to that event, Mme. Blavatsky was taken very ill....No doctor could understand her illness....Soon after the commencement of that illness, she began---as she repeatedly told her friends---"to lead a

H.P. Blavatsky in 1848

double life."...This is how she herself describes that state:---

"Whenever I was called by name, I opened my eyes upon hearing it, and was myself, my own personality in every particular. As soon as I was left alone, however, I relapsed into my usual, half-dreamy condition, and became *somebody else*....I had simply a mild fever that consumed me slowly but surely, day after day, with entire loss of appetite, and finally of hunger, as I would feel none for days, and often went a week without touching any food whatever, except a little water, so that in four months I was reduced to a living skeleton. In cases when I was interrupted, when in my other *self*, by the sound of my present name being pronounced, and while I was conversing in my dream-life---say at half a sentence either spoken by me or those who were with my second *me* at the time,---and opened my eyes to answer the call, I used to answer very rationally, and understood all, for I was never delirious. But no sooner had I closed my eyes again than the sentence which had been interrupted was completed by my other self, continued from the word, or even half the word, it had stopped at. When awake, and *myself*, I remembered well *who I was* in my second capacity, and what I had been and was doing. When *somebody else, i.e.,* the personage I had become, I know I had no idea of who was H.P. Blavatsky! I was in another far-off country, a totally different individuality from myself, and had no connection at all with my actual life."

Such is Mme. Blavatsky's analysis of her state at that time. She was residing then at Ozurgety, a military settlement in Mingreliya, where she had bought a house. It is a little town, lost among the old forests and woods, which, in those days, had neither roads nor conveyances, save of the most primitive kind....The only physician of the place, the army surgeon, could make nothing of her symptoms; but as she was visibly and rapidly declining, he packed her off to Tiflis to her friends. Unable to go on horseback, owing to her great weakness, and a journey in a cart being deemed dangerous, she was sent off in a large native boat along the river---a journey of four days to Kutais---with four native servants only to take care of her.

...In that solitary boat, on a narrow river, hedged on both sides by centenarian forests, her position must have been precarious.

The little stream they were sailing along was, though navigable, rarely, if ever, used as a means of transit....As they were gliding slowly along the narrow stream, cutting its way between two steep and woody banks, the servants were several times during three consecutive nights frightened out of their senses by seeing, *what they swore was their mistress*, gliding off from the boat, and across the water in the direction of the forests, while the body of that same mistress was lying prostrate on her bed at the bottom of the boat. Twice the man who towed the canoe, upon seeing the "form," ran away shrieking, and in great terror. Had it not been for a faithful old servant who was taking care of her, the boat and the patient would have been abandoned in the middle of the stream. On the last evening, the servant swore he saw two figures, while the third---his mistress, in flesh and bone---was sleeping before his eyes. No sooner had they arrived at Kutais, where Mme. Blavatsky had a distant relative residing at that place, than all the servants, with the exception of the old butler, left her, and returned no more.

It was with great difficulty that she was transported to Tiflis. A carriage and a friend of the family were sent to meet her; and she was brought into the house of her friends apparently dying.

...One afternoon, very weak and delicate still, after the illness just described, Mme. Blavatsky came in to her aunt's, N.A. de Fadeyev's, room. After a few words of conversation, remarking that she felt tired and sleepy, she was offered to rest upon a sofa. Hardly had her head touched her cushion when she fell into a profound sleep. Her aunt had quietly resumed some writing she had interrupted to talk with her niece, when suddenly soft but quite audible steps in the room behind her chair made her rapidly turn her head to see who was the intruder, as she was anxious that Mme. Blavatsky should not be disturbed. The room was empty! There was no other living person in it but herself and her sleeping niece, yet the steps continued, audibly, as though of a heavy person treading softly, the floor creaking all the while. They approached the sofa, and suddenly ceased. Then she heard stronger sounds, as though someone was whispering near Mme. Blavatsky, and presently a book placed on a table near the sofa was seen by N.A de Fadeyev to open, and its pages kept turning to and fro, as if an invisible hand were busy at it. Another book was snatched from the library shelves, and flew in that same direction.

More astonished than frightened---for everyone in the house had been trained in and become quite familiar with such manifestations---N.A. de Fadeyev arose from her arm-chair to awaken her niece, hoping thereby to put a stop to the phenomena; but at the same moment a heavy arm-chair moved at the other end of the room, and rattling on the floor, glided toward the sofa. The noise it made awoke Mme. Blavatsky, who, upon opening her eyes, enquired of the invisible presence what was the matter. A few more whisperings, and all relapsed into quietness and silence, and there was nothing more of the sort during the rest of the evening.

...As soon as she was restored to life and health, she left the Caucasus, and went to Italy. Yet it was before her departure from the country in...[1865] that the nature of her powers seems to have entirely changed....At what time this complete change in her occult powers was wrought we are unable to say, as she was far away from our observation, and spoke of it but rarely---never unless distinctly asked in our correspondence to answer the question....And we believe her statements with regard to her powers to have been entirely true when she wrote to tell us, "Now...[in 1865] I shall never be subjected to external influences." *It is not H.P.B. who was from that time forth victim to "influences" which would have without doubt triumphed over a less strong nature than was hers; but, on the contrary, it is she who subjected these influences---whatever they may be---to her will.*

Nadyezhda A. de Fadeyev[9]
November 11, 1870, Odessa, Russia

...I [will] narrate...what happened to me in connection with a certain note, received by me phenomenally when my niece was at the other side of the world, and not a soul knew where she was ---which grieved us greatly. All our researches had ended in nothing. We were ready to believe her dead, when---I think it was about the year 1870...I received a letter from him, whom I believe you call Kouth-humi [Koot Hoomi]---which was brought to me in the most incomprehensible and mysterious manner, by a messenger of Asiatic appearance, *who then disappeared before my very eyes.* This letter...begged me not to fear anything, and ...announced that she was in safety....*

...My niece spoke of...[these Mahatmas] to me, and at great length, years ago. She wrote me that she had again met and renewed her relations with several of them, even before she wrote her *Isis [Unveiled]*...If I, who have ever been, and hope ever to continue, to be a fervent Christian, believe in the existence of these men---although I may refuse to credit *all* the miracles they attribute to them---why should not others believe in them? For the existence of at least one of them, *I can certify*. Who, then, could have written me this letter to reassure me at the moment when I had the greatest need for such comfort, unless it had been one of those adepts mentioned? *It is true that the handwriting is not known to me*; but the manner in which it was delivered to me was phenomenal, that none other than an adept in occult science could have effected it. It promised me the return of my niece, ---and the promise was duly fulfilled....

Vera P. de Zhelihovsky[10]
Oct., 1871---April, 1872, Egypt

In 1871 Mme. Blavatsky wrote from Cairo to tell her friends that she had just returned from India, and had been wrecked...near [Septsai, an island in the Gulf of Nauplia, Greece]....She had...determined to establish a *Societe Spirite* for the

----

*[This letter from Koot Hoomi is preserved in the archives of The Theosophical Society, Adyar, Madras, India. For a facsimile of the letter and background information, see pp. 3-5 in **Letters from The Masters of the Wisdom**, Second Series, transcribed and annotated by C. Jinarajadasa, Adyar, Madras, India, The Theosophical Publishing House, 1977.---Editor.]

investigation of mediums and phenomena according to Allan Kardec's theories and philosophy,* since there was no other way to give people a chance to see for themselves how mistaken they were. She would first give free play to an already established and accepted teaching and then, when the public would see that nothing was coming out of it, she would offer her own explanations. To accomplish this object, she said, she was ready to go to any amount of trouble,---even to allowing herself to be regarded for a time as a helpless medium. "They know no better, and it does me no harm---for I will very soon show them the difference between a passive medium and an active doer," she explains.

A few weeks later a new letter was received. In this one she showed herself full of disgust for the enterprise, which had proved a perfect failure. She had written, it seems, to England and France for a medium, but without success. *En desespoir de cause*, she had surrounded herself with amateur mediums---French female spiritists....

"They steal the society's money," she wrote, "they drink like sponges, and I now caught them cheating most shamefully our members, who come to investigate the phenomena, by bogus manifestations. I had very disagreeable scenes with several persons who held me alone responsible for all this. So I gave orders that their fees of membership should be returned to them and I will bear myself the costs and moneys laid out for hire of the premises and the furniture used. My famous *Societe Spirite* has not lasted a fortnight---it is a heap of ruins---majestic, but as suggestive as those of the Pharaoh's tombs....To wind up the comedy with a drama, I got nearly shot by a madman---a Greek clerk who had been present at the only two public seances we held, and got possessed, I suppose, by some vile spook."

She broke all connection with the "mediums," shut up her *Societe*, and went to live in Boulak near the Museum....The sceptics who had, moved by idle curiosity, visited the *Societe* and

---

*[Allan Kardec (1804-1869), the father of Spiritism (Spiritualism) in France. His most famous work **Le Livre des Esprits** (The Spirits' Book), first published in 1856, expounded a theory of human life and destiny in which the doctrine of "reincarnation" was a prominent feature.---Editor.]

witnessed the whole failure, made capital of the thing: ridiculing the idea of phenomena, they had as a natural result declared such claims to be fraud and charlatanry all round. Conveniently mixing up the whole truth, they even went the length of maintaining that instead of paying the mediums and the expenses of the Society, it was Mme. Blavatsky who had herself been paid, and had attempted to palm off juggler tricks as genuine phenomena. The groundless inventions and rumours thus set on foot by her enemies...did not prevent Mme. Blavatsky from pursuing her studies, and proving to every honest investigator, that her extraordinary powers of clairvoyance and clairaudience were *facts*, and independent of mere physical manifestations, over which she possessed an undeniable control....

A gentleman...Mr. G. Yakovlef who happened to visit Egypt at that time wrote to his friends the most enthusiastic letters about Madame Blavatsky. Thus he wrote...in a letter we have in our possession: "She is a marvel, an unfathomable mystery....That which she produces is simply phenomenal....Once I showed her a closed medallion containing the portrait of one person and the hair of another, an object which I had had in my possession but a few months, which was made at Moscow, and of which very few know, and she told me without touching it, 'Oh! it is your god-mother's portrait and your cousin's hair...Both are dead,' and she proceeded forthwith to describe them, as though she had both before her eyes....How *could* she know!"...

Further on he speaks of visiting [Madame Blavatsky]...in a hotel of Alexandria....They remained...sitting on a sofa and having a chat together. Before the sofa there stood a little teapoy, on which the waiter had placed for Mr. Yakovlef a bottle of liqueur, some wine, a small wine-glass, and a tumbler. As he was carrying the...[wine-glass] with its contents to his mouth, without any visible cause, the glass broke in his hand into many pieces. She laughed, appearing overjoyed, and made the remark that she hated liqueurs and wine, and could hardly tolerate those who used them too freely....

"You do not mean to infer that it is *you* who broke my wine-glass...? It is simply an accident....The glass is very thin; it was perhaps cracked, and I squeezed it too strongly....! I lied purposely, for I had just made the mental remark that it seemed very strange

and incomprehensible, the glass being very thick and strong....
But I wanted to draw her out."

"She looked at me very seriously, and her eyes flashed. 'What
will you bet,' she asked, 'that I do it again?'"

" 'Well, we will try on the spot. If you do, I will be the first
to proclaim you a true magician. If not, we will have a good
laugh at you or your spirits tomorrow at the Consulate...' And
saying so, I half filled the tumbler with wine and prepared to
drink it. But no sooner had the glass touched my lips than I felt
it shattered between my fingers, and my hand bled, wounded by
a broken piece in my instinctive act at grasping the tumbler
together when I felt myself losing hold of it...."

Disgusted with the failure of her spiritist society...Mme.
Blavatsky soon went home *via* Palestine, and lingered for some
months longer, making a voyage to Palmyra [an ancient city of
Syria] and other ruins, whither she went with Russian friends....At
the end of 1872, she returned in her usual way without warning,
and surprised her family at Odessa....

Emma Coulomb[11]
1872, Cairo, Egypt

In the year 1872 one day as I was walking through the street
called "Sekke el Ghamma el harmar"---"the street of the red
mosque"---in Cairo, Egypt, I was roused from my pensive mood by
something that brushed by me very swiftly. I looked up and saw
a lady. "Who is that lady?" I asked a passer-by. "She is that
Russian Spiritist who calls the dead and makes them answer your
questions." This news was to me tidings of great joy, as I was just
mourning for the death of my dear and only brother, whom I had
recently lost. The idea of being able to hear his voice was for me
heavenly delight. I was told that if I asked the Secretary of her
Spiritualistic Society to introduce me to her he would do so (he
was a Greek gentleman of my acquaintance). I was introduced,
and found her very interesting and very clever. My first essay
at the spirits was not succesful; I neither saw nor heard anything

but a few raps. Having shown my disappointment to the Secretary of the Society, I was told that the spirits did not like to appear in a room which had not been purified and not exclusively used for the purpose, but if I would return in a few days I would see wonders, as they were preparing a closet where nothing else but seances was to be done. I went to see the closet, and saw that it was lined with red cloth, all over the four sides and also the ceiling, with a space between the wall and the cloth of about three inches. I was so ignorant of these things at the time that I formed no malicious idea of it. I called again when the closet was ready, but what was my surprise when, instead of finding the kind spirits there to answer our questions, I found a room full of people, *all alive*, and using most offensive language towards the founder of the Society, saying that she had taken their money and had left them only with this, pointing at the space between the wall and the cloth, where several pieces of twine were still hanging which had served to pull through the ceiling a long glove stuffed with cotton, which was to represent the materialized hand and arm of some spirit. I went away, leaving the crowd as red as fire, ready to knock her down when she came back. Later on I met her again, and I asked her how she came to do such a thing; to which she answered that it was Madame Sebire's doings (this was a lady who lived with Madame Blavatsky), so I let this matter drop. I saw that she looked very unhappy. I called on her the next day....Our acquaintance continued all the while she remained in the country.

...To my knowledge Madame Blavatsky while in Cairo never lived in an hotel. I have known her in three different apartments. The first was in "Sekke el Ghamma el harmar," the second at "Abdeen," and the third at "Kantara el dick." In "Abdeen" she had opened her apartment to the public, who went there to consult her spirits, and where the *fiasco* of the materialized hand and arm took place....

She [then] left Cairo for Russia....

Countess Lydia A. de Pashkov[12]
Spring, 1872, Lebanon

I was once traveling between Baalbek and the river Orontes, and in the desert I saw a caravan. It was Mme. Blavatsky's. We camped together. There was a great monument standing there near the village of Dair Mar Maroon. It was between Lebanon and the Anti-Lebanon [Mountains]. On the monument were inscriptions that no one could ever read. Mme. Blavatsky could do strange things with the spirits, as I knew, and I asked her to find out what the monument was.

We waited until night. She drew a circle and we went in it. We built a fire and put much incense on it. Then she said many spells. Then we put on more incense. Then she pointed with her wand at the monument and we saw a great ball of white flame on it. There was a sycamore tree near by; we saw many little flames on it. The jackals came and howled in the darkness a little way off. We put on more incense. Then Mme. Blavatsky commanded the spirit to appear of the person to whom the monument was reared. Soon a cloud of vapor arose and obscured the little moonlight there was. We put on more incense. The cloud took the indistinct shape of an old man with a beard, and a voice came, as it seemed, from a great distance, through the image. He said the monument was once the altar of a temple that had long disappeared. It was reared to a god that had long since gone to another world. "Who are you?" asked Mme. Blavatsky, "I am Hiero, one of the priests of the temple," said the voice. Then Mme. Blavatsky commanded him to show us the place as it was when the temple stood. He bowed, and for one instant we had a glimpse of the temple and of a vast city filling the plain as far as the eye could reach. Then it was gone, and the image faded away. Then we built up big fires to keep off the jackals and went to sleep.

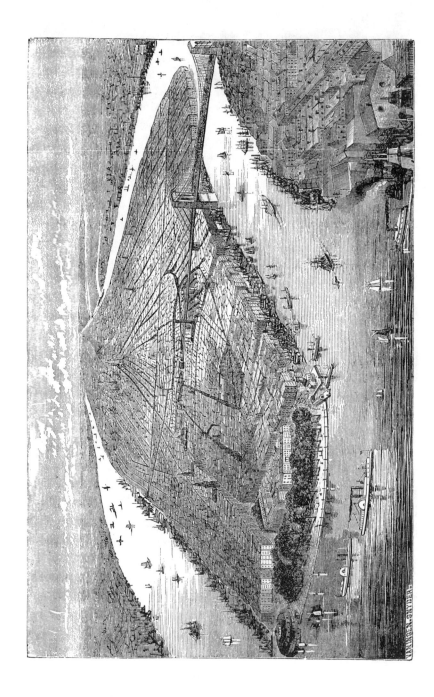

VAN INGEN SNYDER

Chapter 3

NEW YORK

1873-1878

Anna Ballard[13]

July, 1873, New York City

My acquaintanceship with Mme. Blavatsky dates...back...[to]
July, 1873, at New York, not more than a week after she landed.
I was then a reporter on the staff of the *New York Sun*, and had
been detailed to write an article upon a Russian subject. In the
course of my search after facts the arrival of this Russian lady
was reported to me by a friend, and I called upon her; thus
beginning an acquaintance that lasted several years. At our first
interview she told me she had had no idea of leaving Paris for
America until the very evening before she sailed, but why she
came or who hurried her off she did not say. I remember
perfectly well her saying with an air of exultation, "I have been
in Tibet." Why she should think that a great matter, more
remarkable than any other of the travels in Egypt, India, and
other countries she told me about, I could not make out, but she
said it with special emphasis and animation....

Elizabeth G.K. Holt[14]

Aug., 1873---June, 1874, New York City

...It was hard...for respectable women workers of small means to find a fitting place in which to live; so it happened that some forty of them launched a small experiment in co-operative living. They rented a new tenement house, 222 Madison Street....It was a street of small two-storey houses occupied by their owners, who were proud of their shade-trees, and kept their front and back yards in order....

My mother and I had spent the summer of 1873 at Saratoga. In order to be ready for school when it opened, I was sent home in August to the Madison Street house, where we had a friend who would take me under her protection; and there I found Mme. Blavatsky. She had a room on the second floor, and my friend had a duplicate room next to her, so that they became very friendly neighbours. Being a co-operative family, we all knew one another familiarly, and kept a room next the street-door as a common sitting room or office, a meeting-place for members, and a place where mail and messages were cared for.

Mme. Blavatsky sat in the office a large part of her time, but she seldom sat alone; she was like a magnet, powerful enough to draw round her everyone who could possibly come. I saw her, day by day, sitting there rolling her cigarettes and smoking incessantly. She had a conspicuous tobacco pouch, the head of some fur-bearing animal, which she wore round the neck. She was certainly an unusual figure. I think she must have been taller than she looked, she was so broad; she had a broad face and broad shoulders; her hair was a lightish brown and crinkled like that of some negroes. Her whole appearance conveyed the idea of power....

Madame referred often to her life in Paris....Later she gave practical demonstration that she had ability in the arts. I had a piano, and Madame sometimes played, usually because somebody pressed her to do so.

She described their past life to the people who asked her to do so, and these accounts must have been accurate, they made such a profound impression. I never heard that she told them their future....She was considered to be a Spiritualist, though I never heard her say she was one....When my friend, Miss Parker, asked Madame to put her in communication with her dead mother, Madame said it was impossible, as her mother was absorbed in higher things and had progressed beyond reach. The spirits she spoke about continually were the *diaki*, tricksy little beings, evidently counterparts of the fairies of Irish folk-lore, and certainly non-human from her description of them....

I never looked upon Madame as an ethical teacher. For one thing, she was too excitable; when things went wrong with her, she could express her opinion about them with a vigour which was very disturbing....

In mental or physical dilemma, you would instinctively appeal to her, for you felt her fearlessness, her unconventionality, her great wisdom and wide experience and hearty good will---her sympathy with the underdog.

An instance of this kind comes to mind. Undesirable people were beginning to move into the street, and the neighbourhood was changing rapidly. One evening one of our young girls, coming home late from work, was followed and greatly frightened; she flung herself breathless into a chair in the office. Madame interested herself at once, expressed her indignation in most vigorous terms, and finally drew from some fold in her dress a knife (I think she used it to cut her tobacco, but it was sufficiently large to be a formidable weapon of defence) and said she had *that* for any man who molested her.

At this time Madame was greatly troubled about money; the income she had received regularly from her father in Russia had stopped, and she was almost penniless....Some of the more conservative people in our house suggested that she was, after all, an adventuress, and the want of money was only what might be expected; but my friend, Miss Parker, whom she took with her to the Russian Consul, assured me that she was really a Russian Countess, that the Consul knew of her family, and had promised to do all he could to get in touch with them and find out what was the difficulty. I may say here that the holding up of her income was caused by the death of her father and the consequent time required to settle up his affairs....

...She had a long table in her private room and I saw her for days, perhaps weeks, steadily writing page after page of manuscript....

Shortly after this and while Madame was still without income she met and became intimate with a French lady, a widow, whose name I have forgotten....

At this time she lived a short distance away in Henry Street. She offered to share her home with H.P.B. until the latter's money difficulties had passed. This offer was accepted, and Madame left our house. Many of our people, however, and notably Miss Parker, kept in close touch with her....

Shortly after this Madame received money from Russia, and moved to the north-east corner of 14th Street and Fourth Avenue. The house was very unpretentious, with a liquor saloon on the street floor, and the two upper floors let as furnished rooms. To this house Miss Parker took me....There I found Madame in a poorly furnished top-floor room; her bed was an iron cot, and beside her bed on a table was a small cabinet with three drawers.

Madame was in a state of great excitement. Earlier in the day her room had been on fire; she said it had been purposely set on fire to rob her. After the fire was out, and the firemen and curious strangers had gone, she found that her valuable watch and chain had been stolen. When she complained to the proprietor of the saloon, who was her landlord, he intimated that she had never had a watch to lose. She told us that she asked "Them" to give her some proof which she could show her landlord and convince him that she really had lost her property; immediately there appeared before her a sheet of paper all grey with smoke except for white spots, the size and shape of a watch and chain, indicating that after the fire had darkened the paper, the watch and chain had been lifted from it, revealing the white spots which they had covered.

...I had always heard the "They" and "Them" explained by the people who were round her, as referring to her "Spirit Guides"; naturally I thought she spoke of them. I knew nothing of Occultism....

...My visit to H.P.B. was the last time I saw her....

Henry S. Olcott[15]
October, 1874, Chittenden, Vermont

One day, in the month of July, 1874, I was sitting in my law-office thinking over a heavy case in which I had been retained by the Corporation of the City of New York, when it occurred to me that for years I had paid no attention to the Spiritualist movement....I went around the corner to a dealer's and bought a copy of the *Banner of Light*. In it I read an account of certain incredible phenomena, *viz.*, the solidification of phantom forms, which were said to be occurring at a farm-house in the township of Chittenden, in the State of Vermont, several hundred miles distant from New York. I saw at once that, if it were true that visitors could see, even touch and converse with, deceased relatives who had found means to reconstruct their bodies and clothing so as to be temporarily solid, visible, and tangible, this was the most important fact in modern physical science. I determined to go and see for myself. I did so, found the story true, stopped three or four days, and then returned to New York. I wrote an account of my observations to the *New York Sun*, which was copied pretty much throughout the whole world....A proposal was then made to me by the Editor of the *New York Daily Graphic* to return to Chittenden in its interest, accompanied by an artist to sketch under my orders, and to make a thorough investigation of the affair. The matter so deeply interested me that I made the necessary disposition of office engagements, and on September 17th was back at the "Eddy Homestead," as it was called from the name of the family who owned and occupied it. I stopped in that house of mystery, surrounded by phantoms and having daily experiences of a most extraordinary character, for about twelve weeks....Meanwhile, twice a week there appeared in the *Daily Graphic* my letters about the "Eddy ghosts," each one illustrated with sketches of spectres actually seen by the artist, Mr. Kappes, and myself, as well as by every one of the persons---sometimes as many as forty---present in the "seance-room." It was the publication of these letters which drew Madame Blavatsky to Chittenden, and so brought us together.

I remember our first day's acquaintance as if it were yesterday....It was a sunny day and even the gloomy old farm-house looked cheerful. It stands amid a lovely landscape, in a valley bounded by grassy slopes that rise into mountains covered to their very crests with leafy groves. This was the time of the "Indian Summer," when the whole country is covered with a faint bluish haze....and the foliage of the beeches, elms, and maples, touched by early frosts, has been turned from green into a mottling of gold and crimson that gives the landscape the appearance of being hung all over with royal tapestries....

The dinner hour at Eddy's was noon, and it was from the entrance door of the bare and comfortless dining-room that Kappes and I first saw H.P.B. She had arrived shortly before noon with a French Canadian lady, and they were at table as we entered. My eye was first attracted by a scarlet Garibaldian shirt the former wore, as in vivid contrast with the dull colours around. Her hair was then a thick blond mop, worn shorter than the shoulders, and it stood out from her head, silken-soft and crinkled to the roots, like the fleece of a Cotswold ewe. This and the red shirt were what struck my attention before I took in the picture

The Eddy Homestead

The Dining Room at the Eddys

of her features. It was a massive Calmuck face, contrasting in its suggestion of power, culture, and imperiousness, as strangely with the commonplace visages about the room as her red garment did with the grey and white tones of the walls and woodwork and the dull costumes of the rest of the guests. All sorts of cranky people were continually coming and going at Eddy's to see the mediumistic phenomena, and it only struck me on seeing this eccentric lady that this was but one more of the sort. Pausing on the door-sill, I whispered to Kappes, "Good gracious! look at *that* specimen, will you." I went straight across and took a seat opposite her to indulge my favourite habit of character-study. The two ladies conversed in French, making remarks of no consequence ....Dinner over, the two went outside the house and Madame Blavatsky rolled herself a cigarette, for which I gave her a light as a pretext to enter into conversation. My remark having been made in French, we fell at once into talk in that language. She asked me how long I had been there and what I thought of the phenomena; saying that she herself was greatly interested in such things, and had been drawn to Chittenden by reading the letters in the *Daily Graphic*: the public were growing so interested in these that it was sometimes impossible to find a copy of the paper on the book-stalls an hour after publication, and she had paid a dollar for a copy of the last issue. "I hesitated before coming here," she said, "because I was afraid of meeting that Colonel Olcott." "Why should you be afraid of him, Madame?" I rejoined. "Oh! because I fear he might write about me in his paper." I told her that she might make herself perfectly easy on that score, for I felt quite sure Col. Olcott would not mention her in his letters unless she wished it. And I introduced myself. We became friends at once. Each of us felt as if we were of the same social world, cosmopolitans, free-thinkers, and in closer touch than with the rest of the company....It was the voice of common sympathy with the higher occult side of man and nature; the attraction of soul to soul, not that of sex to sex....

Strolling along with my new acquaintance, we talked together about the Eddy phenomena and those of other lands. I found she had been a great traveller and seen many occult things and adepts in occult science, but at first she did not give me any hint as to the existence of the Himalayan Sages or of her own powers. She spoke of the materialistic tendency of American Spiritualism, which was a sort of debauch of phenomena accompanied by comparative indifference to philosophy. Her manner was gracious and captivating, her criticisms upon men and things original and witty. She was particularly interested in drawing me out as to my own ideas about spiritual things and expressed pleasure in finding that I had instinctively thought along the occult lines which she herself had pursued. It was not as an Eastern mystic, but rather as a refined Spiritualist that she talked. For my part I knew nothing then, or next to nothing, about Eastern philosophy, and at first she kept silent on that subject.

The seances of William Eddy, the chief medium of the family, were held every evening in a large upstairs hall, in a wing of the house, over the dining-room and kitchen...At the farther end of the seance-hall...was a narrow closet...in which William Eddy would seat himself to wait for the phenomena. He had no seeming control over them, but merely sat and waited from them to sporadically occur. A blanket being hung across the doorway, the closet would be in perfect darkness. Shortly after William had entered the cabinet, the blanket would be pulled aside and forth would step some figure of a dead man, woman or child...temporarily solid and substantial, but the next minute resolved back into nothingness or invisibility. They would occasionally dissolve away while in full view of the spectators.

Up to the time of H.P.B.'s appearance on the scene, the figures which had shown themselves were either Red Indians, or Americans or Europeans akin to the visitors. But on the first evening of her stay spooks of other nationalities came before us. There was a Georgian servant boy from the Caucasus; a Mussulman merchant from Tiflis; a Russian peasant girl, and others....The advent of such figures in the seance-room of those poor, almost illiterate Vermont farmers, who had neither the money to buy theatrical properties, the experience to employ such if they had had them, nor the room where they could have availed of them, was to every eye-witness a convincing proof that the apparitions were genuine. At the same time they show that a strange attraction to call out these images from what Asiatics call the Kama-loka attended Madame Blavatsky. It was long afterwards that I was informed that she had evoked them by her own developed and masterful power....

H.P.B. tried her best to make me suspect the value of William Eddy's phenomena as proofs of the intelligent control of a medium by spirits; telling me that, if genuine, they must be the double of the medium escaping from his body and clothing itself with other appearances; but I did not believe her. I contended that the forms were of too great diversities of height, bulk, and appearance to be a masquerade of William Eddy; they must be what they seemed, *viz.*, the spirits of the dead. Our disputes were quite warm on occasions, for at that time I had not gone deep enough into the question of the plastic nature of the human Double to see the force of her hints, while of the Eastern theory of Maya I did not know its least iota. The result, however, was, as she told me, to convince her of my disposition to accept nothing on trust and to cling pertinaciously to such facts as I had, or thought I had acquired. We became greater friends day by day, and by the time she was ready to leave Chittenden she had accepted from me the nick-name "Jack," and so signed herself in her letters to me from New York. When we parted it was as good friends likely to continue the acquaintance thus pleasantly begun....

Henry S. Olcott[16]

Nov., 1874---April, 1875, New York City & then later at Philadelphia, Pennsylvania

In November, 1874, when my researches were finished [at Chittenden, Vermont], I returned to New York and called upon...[H.P.B.] at her lodgings at 16 Irving Place, where she gave me some seances of table-tipping and rapping, spelling out messages of sorts, principally from an invisible intelligence calling itself "John King"....I thought it a veritable John King then, for its personality had been as convincingly proved to me, I fancied, as anybody could have asked. But now, after seeing what H.P.B. could do in the way of producing *mayavic* (*i.e.*, hypnotic) illusions and in the control of elementals, I am persuaded that "John King" was a humbugging elemental, worked by her like a marionette

58

and used as a help towards my education. Understand me, the phenomena were real, but they were done by no disincarnate *human* spirit...She kept up the illusion for months...and I saw numbers of phenomena done as alleged by John King....

An experiment [was] made by H.P.B., with myself as a passive agent...after my coming to her house in Philadelphia....She was tipping tables for me, with and without the contact between her hands and the table; making loud and tiny raps---sometimes while holding her hand six inches above the wood, and sometimes while resting her hand upon mine as it lay flat upon the table; and spelling out messages to me from the pretended John King which, as rapped out by the alphabet, I recorded on scraps of paper....At last some of these messages relating to third parties seemed worth keeping so one day, on my way home, I bought a reporter's note-book, and, on getting to the house, showed it to her and explained its intended use. She was seated at the time and I standing. Without touching the book or making any mystical pass or sign, she told me to put it in my bosom. I did so, and after a moment's pause she bade me take it out and look within. This is what I found: inside the first cover, written and drawn on the white lining paper in lead pencil:---

"JOHN KING,

HENRY DE MORGAN,
his book.

4th of the Fourth month in A.D. 1875."

Underneath this, the drawing of a Rosicrucian jewel; over the arch of the jewelled crown, the word FATE; beneath which is her name, "Helen," followed by what looks...like 99, something smudged out, and then a simple + [etc.]....I have the book on my table as I write, and my description is taken from the drawing itself. One striking feature of this example of psycho-dynamics is the fact that no one but myself had touched the book after it was purchased; I had had it in my pocket until it was shown to H.P.B., from the distance of two or three feet, had myself held it in my bosom, removed it a moment later when bidden, and the precipitation of the lead-pencil writing and drawing had been done while the book was inside my waist-coat. Now the writing inside the cover of the book is very peculiar...It is a quaint and quite individual handwriting, not like H.P.B.'s, but identical with that in all the written messages I had from first to last from "John King." H.P.B. having, then, the power of precipitation, must have transferred from her mind to the paper the images of words traced in this special style of script; or, if not she, but some other expert in this art did it, then that other person must have done it in that same way---*i.e.*, have first pictured to himself mentally the images of those words and that drawing, and then precipitated; that is, made them visible on the paper, as though written with a lead pencil....

Little by little, H.P.B. let me know of the existence of Eastern adepts and their powers, and gave me by a multitude of phenomena the proofs of her own control over the occult forces of nature....

William Q. Judge[17]
Aug., 1875---1878, New York City

My first acquaintance with H.P. Blavatsky began in the winter of the year...[1875]. She was then living in apartments in Irving Place, New York City....She had several rooms *en suite*. The front rooms looked out on Irving Place, and the back upon the garden. My first visit was made in the evening, and I saw her there among a large number of persons who were always attracted to her presence. Several languages were to be heard among them, and Mme. Blavatsky, while conversing volubly in Russian, apparently quite absorbed, would suddenly turn round and interject an observation in English into a discussion between other persons upon a different topic to the one she was engaged with. This never disturbed her, for she at once returned to her Russian talk, taking it up much where it had been dropped.

Very much was said on the first evening that arrested my attention and enchained my imagination. I found my secret thoughts read, my private affairs known to her. Unasked, and certainly without any possibility of her having inquired about me,

William Q. Judge

she referred to several private and peculiar circumstances in a way that showed at once that she had a perfect knowledge of my family, my history, my surroundings, and my idiosyncrasies....

The next day I thought I would try an experiment with Mme. Blavatsky. I took an ancient scarabaeus that she had never seen, had it wrapped up and sent to her through the mails by a clerk in the employment of a friend. My hand did not touch the package, nor did I know when it was posted. But when I called on her at the end of the week the second time, she greeted me with thanks for the scarabaeus. I pretended ignorance. But she said it was useless to pretend, and then informed me how I had sent it, and where the clerk had posted it. During the time that elapsed between my seeing her and the sending of the package no one had heard from me a word about the matter.

Very soon after I met her, she moved to 34th Street, and while there I visited her very often. In those rooms I used to hear the raps in furniture, in glasses, mirrors, windows and walls, which are usually the accompaniment of dark "spiritist" seances. But with her they occurred in the light, and never except when ordered by her. Nor could they be induced to continue once that she ordered them to stop. They exhibited intelligence also, and would at her request change from weak to strong, or from many to few at a time.

She remained in 34th Street only a few months, and then removed to 47th Street....

After she had comfortably settled herself in 47th Street, where, as usual, she was from morning till night surrounded by all sorts of visitors, mysterious events, extraordinary sights and sounds continued to occur. I have sat there many an evening, and seen in broad gas light, large luminous balls creeping over the furniture, or playfully jumping from point to point, while the most beautiful liquid bell sounds now and again burst out from the air of the room. These sounds often imitated either the piano or a gamut of sounds whistled by either myself or some other person. While all this was going, H.P. Blavatsky sat unconcernedly reading or writing at "Isis Unveiled."

...Precipitation of messages or sentences occurred very frequently, and I will relate one which took place under my own hand and eyes, in such a way as to be unimpeachable for me.

I was one day, about four o'clock, reading a book...that had just been brought in by a friend of Colonel Olcott. I was sitting some six feet distance from H.P. Blavatsky, who was busy writing. I had carefully read the title-page of the book, but had forgotten the exact title. But I knew that there was not one word of writing upon it. As I began to read the first paragraph, I heard a bell sound in the air, and looking, saw that Mme. Blavatsky was intently regarding me.

"What book do you read?" said she.

Turning back to the title-page, I was about to read aloud the name, when my eye was arrested by a message written in ink across the top of the page which, a few minutes before, I had looked at, and found clean. It was a message in about seven lines, and the fluid had not yet quite dried on the page---its contents were a warning about the book. I am positive that when I took the volume in my hand not one word was written in it....

About any object that might be transported mysteriously around her room, or that came into it through the air by supermundane means, there always lingered for a greater or less space of time a very peculiar though pleasant odour. It was not always the same. At one time it was sandal-wood mixed with what I thought was otto of roses; at another time some unknown Eastern perfume, and again it came like the incense burnt in temples.

One day she asked me if I would care to smell again the perfume. Upon my replying affirmatively, she took my handkerchief in her hand, held it for a few moments, and when she gave it back to me it was heavy with the well known odour. Then in order to show me that her hand was not covered with something that would come off upon the handkerchief, she permitted me to examine both hands. They were without perfume. But after I had convinced myself that there was no perfumery or odoriferous objects concealed in her hands, I found from one hand beginning to exhale one peculiar strong perfume, while from the other there rolled out strong waves of incense....

...One evening I was in a hurry to copy a drawing I had made, and looked about on the table for a paper-cutter with which to rub the back of the drawing so as to transfer the surplus carbon to a clean sheet.

As I searched, it was suggested by some one that the round smooth back of a spoon bowl would be the best means, and I arose to go to the kitchen at the end of the hall for a spoon. But Mme. Blavatsky said, "Stop, you need not go there; wait a moment." I stopped at the door, and she, sitting in her chair, held up her left hand. At that instant a large table-spoon flew through the air across the room from out of the opposite wall and into her hand. No one was there to throw it to her, and the dining-room from which it had been transported was about thirty feet distant; two brick walls separating it from the front room....

My office was at least three miles away from her rooms. One day, at about 2 P.M., I was sitting in my office engaged in reading a legal document, my mind intent on the subject of the paper. No one else was in the office, and in fact the nearest room was separated from me by a wide opening, or well, in the building, made to let light into the inner chambers. Suddenly I felt on my hand a peculiar tingling sensation that always preceded any strange thing to happen in the presence of H.P.B., and at that moment there fell from the ceiling upon the edge of my desk, and from there to the floor, a triangularly-folded note from Madame to myself....The message was in her handwriting, and was addressed to me in her writing across the printed face....

Rev. James H. Wiggin[18]
Late Aug., 1875, New York City

...Rosicrucianism claims that a brotherhood of occultists has existed and still exists, reaching perfection in the far East;...that in the fraternity's archives are preserved grand records of truths about men and nature;...that Rosicrucians can work what are falsely called miracles, by their knowledge of the true essence of things;...that human bodies can disappear and reappear at will; that they can float in the air;...that all nature is subject to their decrees through their knowledge of divine laws....

It is a little startling to find oneself associating with those who possess, or claim to possess, such powers....Of late Rosicrucianism has been brought to the front by the advent in the [United] States of a Russian baroness, Madame H.P. De Blavatsky.....I was kindly bidden by my friend Mr. [Charles] Sotheran, of the *American Bibliopolist*, to meet both Madame and...Colonel [Olcott] the following evening in [46] Irving Place....

Col. Olcott is well known as the author of "People from Another World"....His experience as a lawyer and a war detective might be supposed to guard him against deception....

Judge M., of New Jersey, represented the judicial mind, and his poetic wife graces any gathering.

There was present also a Boston gentleman....

The centre of the group was Madame De Blavatsky, who is certainly a most original and interesting woman to meet. The journals have complained of her cigarettes....Madame speaks English with a strong accent, but with remarkable fluency and accuracy, distinguishing nicely its delicacies and quickly understanding its allusions....Her fantastic Rosicrucian jewel...she wore about her neck. She is perhaps forty years old, strong-built, brusque and generous appearing. Interesting were the stories she had to relate about her residence in Asia and Africa....Marvellous were her narratives of her attempts at commerce, selling a cargo for cocoanuts which the unseaworthy ship could not bring away. Strange sights had she seen among the tribes of sorcerers in Africa....The Phallic element in religions; the souls of flowers; recent wonders among the mediums;...Nature's duality; Romanism; Gravitation; the Carbonari; jugglery;...the literature of magic--- were among the topics of animated discussion lasting till after midnight.

If Madame Blavatsky can indeed bring order out of the chaos of modern spiritism she will do the world a service. Col. Olcott declares that till he met her he had no philosophy which could adequately explain the contradictory phenomena he witnessed....

Eugene Rollin Corson[19]
Sept.---Oct., 1875, Ithaca, New York

My father's [Hiram Corson's] acquaintance and correspondence with Mme. Blavatsky came about in this way. On July 15th, 1874, my sister died, my father's only daughter, and the blow to him was very great. In the religion of the Churches he found no comfort, and he turned to spiritualism for some sign and assurance of the continued existence of his child. In the end he believed that this sign had come to him, and the assurance of his daughter's continued life became very strong....

H.P.B.'s appearance in this country first became generally known after her visit to the Eddy brothers in Chittenden, Vermont, when she published her experiences at the seances of these mediums....My father [then] wrote to her....

Her letters...had so increased his interest in her, that he and my mother invited her to be their guest at their home in Ithaca. My father at that time was professor of Anglo-Saxon and English literature at Cornell University, and had been there since 1870. He was a fine scholar, of wide interests, and had become a great authority and teacher, and especially on English poetry....My mother, who was French, herself a fine scholar of the most varied interests, became interested in spiritualism in a moderate way only; it never possessed her as it did my father. She had accepted the loss of her daughter with great composure and resignation, and her interest in H.P.B. was more in the woman herself than in her doctrines and mission. My mother, however, was not interested in occultism; on the contrary, she was greatly opposed to it....

...H.P.B. arrived in Ithaca...about September 17th, 1875....At that time my father had a cottage known as the Richardson Cottage, on Heustis Street....At the time when H.P.B. visited Ithaca the weather is usually fine. In October there is the Indian Summer; the trees have put on their autumn tints, the mornings and nights are crisp and frosty, with a pleasant warmth in the middle of the day, with the distant hills and lake bathed in the late summer haze....Ithaca proper is in the valley at the foot of Cayuga Lake, and is built up on the east, west, and south hills, with the outskirts heavily wooded. My father's home was on the east hill....On this hill the University stands, an imposing array of noble buildings....

...My father in a letter dated October 2nd, 1875 [writes]: "Mme. B. is still with us. She gives us a good deal of trouble, and we get very little from her in return, for she is occupied wholly with her own work. I had expected we should have some [spiritualistic] 'sittings' together; but she is not only not disposed, but is decidedly opposed to anything of the kind. She is a smart woman, but ignorant of all the graces and amenities of life. She is a great Russian bear."...

One day my father said to her: "It is a pity, Madame, for you not to see the beauties around you. I want to give you a carriage drive that you may see the University buildings and the lovely country." She finally consented to go, but my father begged her not to smoke in the carriage because the people were not used to it, and it would give them a bad impression and might cause comment, especially with a staid university professor. To this she also reluctantly consented. But before the drive was over, Madame said she would have to smoke a cigarette, she could not stand it a minute longer, and begged that she might get out of the carriage and sit on a stone on a side of the road and smoke in comfort. If the country people took her for a gypsy, why not, what harm would it do? So there sat the author of *Isis Unveiled* and the *Secret Doctrine*, satisfied with her own thoughts and oblivious of everything around her, even the waiting horses and coachman and the carriage with its occupants. Perhaps it was less the tobacco she wanted than the desire to be alone with herself and her own thoughts. When the cigarettes were finished she returned to the carriage and they continued on their drive.

My father dwelt especially on this incident as showing the woman's preoccupation. As he repeatedly said to me: "Never have I seen such an intense creature, intense in her purpose, intense in her endeavour; nothing around her mattered; though the heavens fall she would keep on her way."

It has always been a regret of my life that I did not meet her at that time....I was in Philadelphia studying medicine....[so] I have to rely on what my father and mother told me subsequently....

In her dress she wore mostly a loose wrapper with a sort of embroidered jacket, as my mother described it to me, with the cigarette papers in one pocket and the tobacco in the other. My father, who was a great smoker himself and a judge of tobacco, thought her brand a cheap kind; perhaps her lack of money accounted for it. The cigarettes were countless, and the flowerpots were full of the stubs....

She spent her time at her desk, writing, writing, writing most of the day and way into the night, carrying on a huge correspondence by long letters. Here she started *Isis Unveiled*, writing about twenty-five closely written foolscap pages a day....

On one occasion she asked...[my father] for a Greek word on some text in the New Testament, and when...[he] said he could not remember it but would look it up for her at once, she said to him, half irritated and half joking: "You school-boy! Why, don't you know it?" My father got the Greek for her, and she went on with her writing....

My mother described to me how H.P.B. would sit down at the piano and improvise with great skill, showing a remarkable efficiency for one who played but at odd times as the spirit might move her....

H.P.B.'s phenomena with a few exceptions were not a feature of her visit. She showed the raps as produced by her will-power sometimes through a stack of hands, and again on different parts of the room. My father was familiar with this phenomenon in the seance room through the ordinary medium, but was much more impressed when produced by conscious will-power. On another occasion he had asked if she could place me and tell what I was doing, then a student of medicine in Philadelphia, and she gave him an accurate account of where I was and what was taking place. It happened to be that I was visiting my preceptor on Green Street. She said I was much under his influence, which was true....On another occasion she caused a heavy table to rise up in the air without touching it, and she repeatedly said that this was all due to her will-power, and was not to be classed with the ordinary mediumistic phenomena....

...H.P.B. left our home for New York after a visit of a month....[In] a letter from my father...he writes: "Mme. B. has gone. Though there were many things unpleasant in her stay with us, altogether we enjoyed her visit. She is a very remarkable woman, a woman of a frantic intensity. I never knew such a worker. She would write from morning until midnight often, without stopping longer than to take dinner and make a cigarette. She smoked two hundred cigarettes in a day. Beardsley has taken some magnificent pictures of her. I shall send you one as soon as they are ready...."[*]

---

[*] [In 1910, Professor Hiram Corson related the following account: "She continually filled me with amazement and curiosity as to what was coming next. She had a profound knowledge of everything, and her method of work was most unusual. She would write in bed, from nine o'clock in the morning, smoking innumerable cigarettes, quoting long verbatim paragraphs from dozens of books of which I am perfectly certain there were no copies at that time in America, translating easily from several languages, and occasionally calling out to me, in my study, to know how to turn some old-world idiom into literary English....She herself told me that she wrote...[down quotations from books] as they appeared to her eyes on another plane of objective existence, that she clearly saw the page of the book, and the quotation she needed, and simply translated what she saw into English....The hundreds of books she quoted were certainly not in my library...and if her quotations were from memory, then it was an even more startling feat than writing them from the ether...." **The Path** [Hale, England], July, 1910, pp. 9, 4.---Editor.]

H.P. Blavatsky, 1875, Ithaca, New York

Henry S. Olcott[20]
Sept.---Nov., 1875, New York City

...[On September 7, 1875,] a group of ladies and gentlemen agreed, upon my motion, to form a body, which became in due course the Theosophical Society....The meeting...was an informal gathering of friends and acquaintances...in Madame Blavatsky's parlour [at 46, Irving Place], to listen to Mr. George H. Felt's explanation of a certain alleged discovery by him of the Lost Canon of Proportion [of the Egyptians], by use of which the peerless architects of [Egypt and] Greece had built their temples and forums. His lecture, illustrated by a set of very fine colored drawings, was tenfold heightened in interest by his assertion that he had not only found, on reading the hieroglyphs, that the elemental spirits were largely used in the [Egyptian] temple mysteries, but he had even deciphered the *mantrams* by which they were subjugated, had practically tested them, and found them efficacious. In the company present were several old Spiritualists, myself included, of open mind, who were ready and willing to investigate this subject....As for myself, I had acquired a full conviction of...[the] existence...[of elemental spirits] and of the power of man to subjugate them, from seeing many phenomena produced by Madame Blavatsky....I had also come to know of the existence of initiated magical adepts in Egypt, India and certain other parts of the world. The chance, therefore, of being able, with Mr. Felt's help and without dragging in the names of either of my Teachers, to throw such a flood of light upon the problem of psychical phenomena, at once suggested itself to my mind; so I wrote on a slip of paper a line or two asking H.P.B. if she thought it a good idea to propose the formation of such a Society, got Mr. Judge to pass it over to her to the opposite side of the room, and, upon her nodding assent, rose and, after making some remarks about the lecture and lecturer, asked if the company present would join me in organizing a society of research in the department covered by Mr. Felt's alleged discovery. I dwelt upon the materialistic tendencies of the age and the desire of mankind to get absolute proof of immortality; pointing to the enormous spread of the spiritualistic movement as the best evidence of the fact, and hinting at the possibility of our being helped in our philanthropic work by the Teachers, from whom H.P.B. had learnt what she knew, if we seriously and unselfishly set ourselves to study....

My views as to the necessity of such a society...receiving general assent, a motion was made by Mr. Judge and adopted...that I be elected chairman of the meeting, and on my motion Mr. Judge was elected secretary. A committee to frame Bye-laws was chosen....An adjourned meeting was held on the...[8th] and another on the...[13th] September following, at which latter, the Bye-laws Committee reported progress, and the name of "The Theosophical Society" was adopted. Other meetings were held on the 16th and 30th October, at which the Bye-Laws were considered and adopted, subject of final revision: at a final meeting, on the 17th November, they were formally adopted as revised, the President delivered his Inaugural Address and the Society was launched as

70

a perfected organization. The officers had been elected at the meeting of October 30th, and were

President, H. S. Olcott;

Vice-Presidents, Dr. S. Pancoast and G.H. Felt;

Corresponding Secretary, H.P. Blavatsky;

Recording Secretary, John Storer Cobb;

Treasurer, H.J. Newton;

Librarian, Charles Sotheran;

Councillors, Rev. J.H. Wiggin, R.B. Westbrook, Emma Hardinge Britten, Dr. C.E. Simmons, Herbert D. Monachesi;

Counsel to the Society: W. Q. Judge.

...The originally declared objects of the Theosophical Society were the study of occult science and esoteric philosophy, in theory and practice, and the popularisation of the facts throughout the world. The original Preamble says: "...(the Founders) hope that by going deeper than modern science has hitherto done into the Esoteric philosophies of ancient times, they may be enabled to attain for themselves and other investigators, proof of the existence of an 'Unseen Universe,' the nature of its inhabitants, if such there be, and the laws which govern them and their relations with mankind." In a word, our hope was to acquire this occult knowledge with the aid of Mr. Felt and H.P.B. That our ideas were eclectic and non-sectarian is clearly shown in the second paragraph of our Preamble:

"Whatever may be the private opinions of its members, *the Society has no dogmas to enforce, no creed to disseminate.* It is formed neither as a Spiritualistic schism, nor to serve as the foe or friend of any sectarian or philosophic body. Its only axiom is the omnipotence of truth, its only creed a profession of unqualified devotion to its discovery and propagation. In considering the qualifications of applicants for membership, it knows neither race, sex, color, country nor creed."

...Our first bitter disappointment was the failure of Mr. Felt to fulfil his promises. With difficulty I got him to give one or two more lectures, but he never showed us so much as the wag of the tail of a vanishing elemental. H.P.B., then working night and day upon her first book, "Isis Unveiled," soon refused to even attend our meetings, let alone do so much at them as make the smallest phenomenon---though she was continually astounding her visitors with them at her own house....

...The above is a plain, unvarnished narrative of the beginnings of the Theosophical Society as it appears from the outside....I got no "order" to make the Society....The provocation of the suggestion lay in my long-felt and practical interest in psychical science, now fanned into a hot flame by H.P.B.'s phenomena, my fresh contact with Eastern adepts, and the apparently easy means of contributing enormously, with Mr. Felt's help and H.P.B.'s participation, to the current knowledge of the astral world and its races. The idea sprang up in my mind as naturally and spontaneously as possible, as such ideas do usually occur in one's every-day experience. But a deeper problem lies back of this mental fact. Did the thought of forming...the Theosophical Society, really spring from my own brain, or was it put there *ab extra*, by some master of thought transference?...[*]

The Seal of
The Theosophical Society

---

[*] [In a note dated "July. 1875." in her Scrapbook. H.P.B. writes: **"Orders** received from India direct to establish a philosophico-religious Society and choose a name for it---also to choose Olcott." And in another note from the same Scrapbook. H.P.B. specifically states: "M[orya] brings orders to form a Society---a secret Society like the Rosicrucian Lodge. He promises to help." See H.P.B.'s **Collected Writings**. Vol. I. pp. 94, 73.---Editor.]

Henry S. Olcott[21]
Summer, 1875---Sept., 1877, New York City

One day in the Summer of 1875, H.P.B. showed me some sheets of manuscript which she had written, and said: "I wrote this last night 'by order,' but what the deuce it is to be I don't know. Perhaps it is for a newspaper article, perhaps for a book, perhaps for nothing: anyhow, I did as I was ordered." And she put it away in a drawer, and nothing more was said about it for some time. But in the month of September...she went...on a visit to her new friends, Professor and Mrs. Corson, of Cornell University, and the work went on. She wrote me that it was to be a book on the history and philosophy of the Eastern Schools and their relations with those of our times. She said she was writing about things she had never studied and making quotations from books she had never read in all her life: that, to test her accuracy, Prof. Corson had compared her quotations with classical works in the University Library, and had found her to be right. Upon her return to town, she was not very industrious in this affair, but wrote only spasmodically...., but a month or two after the formation of the Theosophical Society, she and I took two suites of rooms at 433 West 34th St., she on the first and I on the second floor, and thenceforward the writing of *Isis* went on without break or interruption until its completion in the year 1877.

In her whole life she had not done a tithe of such literary labour, yet I never knew even a managing daily journalist who could be compared with her for dogged endurance or tireless working capacity. From morning till night she would be at her desk, and it was seldom that either of us got to bed before 2 o'clock A.M. During the daytime I had my professional duties to attend to, but always, after an early dinner we would settle down together to our big writing-table and work, as if for dear life, until bodily fatigue would compel us to stop. What an experience!...

She worked on no fixed plan, but ideas came streaming through her mind like a perennial spring which is ever overflowing its brim....Higgledy-piggledy it came, in a ceaseless rivulet, each paragraph complete in itself and capable of being excised without harm to its predecessor or successor....

Her own manuscript was often a sight to behold; cut and patched, re-cut and re-pasted, until if one held a page of it to the light, it would be seen to consist of, perhaps, six, or eight, or ten slips cut from other pages, pasted together, and the text joined by interlined words or sentences....

I corrected every page of her manuscript several times, and every page of the proofs; wrote many paragraphs for her, often merely embodying her ideas that she could not then...frame to her liking in English; helped her to find out quotations, and did other purely auxiliary work: the book is hers alone, so far as personalities on this plane of manifestation are concerned, and she must take all the praise and the blame that it deserves....Then, whence did H.P.B. draw the materials which compose *Isis*, and which cannot be traced to accessible literary sources of quotation? *From the Astral Light*, and by her soul-senses, from her Teachers ---the "Brothers," "Adepts," "Sages," "Masters," as they have been variously called. How do I know it? By working two years with her on *Isis* and many more years on other literary work.

To watch her at work was a rare and never-to-be-forgotten experience. We sat at opposite sides of one big table usually, and I could see her every movement. Her pen would be flying over the page, when she would suddenly stop, look out into space with the vacant eye of the clairvoyant seer, shorten her vision as though to look at something held invisible in the air before her, and begin copying on her paper what she saw. The quotation finished, her eyes would resume their natural expression, and she would go on writing until again stopped by a similar interruption. I remember well two instances when I, also, was able to see and even handle books from whose astral duplicates she copied quotations into her manuscript, and which she was obliged to "materialise" for me, to refer to when reading the proofs, as I refused to pass the pages for the "strike-off" unless my doubts as to the accuracy of her copy were satisfactory....It was when we were living at 302 West 47th street---the once-famous "Lamasery," and the executive headquarters of the Theosophical Society. I said: "I cannot pass this quotation, for I am sure it cannot read as you have it." She said: "Oh don't bother; it's right; let it pass." I refused, until finally she said: "Well, keep still a minute and I'll try to get it." The far-away look came into her eyes, and presently she pointed to a far corner of the room, to an *etagere* on which were kept some curios, and in a hollow voice said: "There!" and then came to herself again. "There, there; go look for it over there!" I went, and found the two volumes wanted, which, to my knowledge, had not been in the house until that very moment. I compared the text with H.P.B.'s quotation, showed her that I was right in my suspicions as to the error, made the proof correction and then, at her request, returned the two volumes to the place on the *etagere* from which I had taken them. I resumed my seat and work, and when, after awhile, I looked again in that direction, the books had disappeared! After my telling this (absolutely true) story, ignorant sceptics are free to doubt my sanity; I hope it may do them good. The same thing happened in the case of the *apport* of the other book, but this one remained, and is in our possession at the present time.

The "copy" turned off by H.P.B. presented the most marked dissemblances at different times. While the handwriting bore one peculiar character throughout, so that one familiar with her writing would always be able to detect any given page as H.P.B.'s, yet, when examined carefully, one discovered at least three or four variations of the one style, and each of these persistent for pages together, when it would give place to some other of the calligraphic variants....The style which had been running through the work of, perhaps, a whole evening or half an evening, would suddenly give place to one of the other styles which would, in its turn, run through the rest of an evening....One of these H.P.B. handwritings was very small, but plain; one bold and free; another plain, of medium size, and very legible; and one scratchy and hard to read, with its queer, foreign-shaped a's and x's and e's. There was also the greatest possible difference in the English of these various styles. Sometimes I would have to make several corrections in each line, while at others I could pass many pages with scarcely a fault of idiom or spelling to correct. Most perfect of all were the manuscripts which were written for her while she was sleeping. The beginning of the chapter on the civilisation of Ancient Egypt (vol. i, chap. xiv) is an illustration. We had stopped work the evening before at about 2 A.M. as usual, both too tired to stop for our usual smoke and chat before parting; she almost fell asleep in her chair while I was bidding her good-night, so I hurried off to my bedroom. The next morning, when I came down after my breakfast, she showed me a pile of at least thirty or forty pages of beautifully written H.P.B. manuscript, which, she said, she had had written for her by----well, a Master, whose name has never yet been degraded like some others. It was perfect in every respect, and went to the printers without revision.

Now it was a curious fact that each change in the H.P.B. manuscript would be preceded, either by her leaving the room for a moment or two, or by her going off into the trance or abstracted state, when her lifeless eyes would be looking beyond me into space, as it were, and returning to the normal state almost immediately. And there would also be a distinct change of personality, or rather personal peculiarities, in gait, vocal expression, vivacity of manner, and, above all, in temper....

...H.P.B....would leave the room one person and...return to it another. Not another as to visible change of physical body, but another as to tricks of motion, speech, and manners; with different mental brightness, different views of things, different command of English orthography, idiom, and grammar, and different---very, *very* different command over her temper; which, at its sunniest, was almost angelic, at its worst, the opposite....

...Did she write *Isis* in the capacity of an ordinary spiritual medium....? I answer, Assuredly not....I have known mediums of all sorts---speaking, trance, writing, phenomena-making, medical, clairvoyant, and materialising; have seen them at work, attended their seances and observed the signs of their obsession and possession. H.P.B.'s case resembled none of them. Nearly all they did she could do; but at her own will and pleasure, by day or by night, without forming "circles," choosing the witnesses, or imposing the usual conditions. Then, again, I had ocular proof that at least some of those who worked with us were living men, from having seen them in the flesh in India after having seen them in the astral body in America and Europe; from having touched and talked with them....

...One of these *Alter Egos* of hers, one whom I have since personally met, wears a full beard and long moustache that are twisted, Rajput fashion, into his side whiskers. He has the habit of constantly pulling at his moustache when deeply pondering: he does it mechanically and unconsciously. Well, there were times when H.P.B.'s personality had melted away and she was "*Somebody else*" when I would sit and watch her hand as if pulling at and twisting a moustache that certainly was not growing visibly on H.P.B.'s upper lip, and the far-away look would be in the eyes, until presently resuming attention of passing things, the moustached Somebody would look up, catch me watching him, hastily remove the hand from the face and go on with the work of writing. Then there was another Somebody, who disliked English so much that he never willingly talked with me in anything but French: he had a fine artistic talent and a passionate fondness for mechanical invention. Another one would now and then sit there, scrawling something with a pencil and reeling off for me dozens of poetical stanzas which embodied, now sublime, now humourous ideas. So each of the several Somebodies had his peculiarities distinctly marked, as recognisable as those of any of our ordinary acquaintances or friends. One was jovial, fond of good stories and witty to a degree; another, all dignity, reserve, and erudition. One would be calm, patient, and benevolently helpful, another testy and sometimes exasperating. One Somebody would always be willing to emphasise his philosophical or scientific explanations of the subjects I was to write upon, by doing phenomena for my edification, while to another Somebody I dared not even mention them. I got an awful rebuke one evening. I had brought home a while before two nice, soft pencils, just the thing for our desk work, and had given one to H.P.B. and kept one myself. She had the very bad habit of borrowing pen-knives, pencils,...and other articles of stationery and forgetting to return them: once put into her drawer or writing-desk, there they would stay, no matter how much of a protest you might make over it. On this particular evening, the artistic Somebody was sketching...on a sheet of common paper and chatting with me about something, when he asked me to lend him another pencil. The thought flashed into my mind, "If I once lend this nice pencil it will go into her drawer and I shall have none for my own use." I did not say this, I only thought it, but the Somebody gave me a mildly sarcastic look, reached out to the pen-tray between us, laid his pencil in it, handled it with his fingers of that hand for a moment, and lo! a dozen pencils of the identical make and quality! He said not a word, did not even give me a look, but the blood rushed to my temples and I felt more humble than I ever did in my life. All the same, I scarcely think I deserved the rebuke, considering what a stationery-*annexer* H.P.B. was!

Now when either of these Somebodies was "on guard," as I used to term it, the H.P.B. manuscript would present the identical peculiarities that it had on the last occasion when he had taken his turn at the literary work....If you had given me in those days any page of *Isis* manuscript, I could almost certainly have told you by which Somebody it had been written. Where, then, was H.P.B.'s self at those times of replacement?...As I understood it, she herself had loaned her body as one might one's typewriter, and had gone off on other occult business that she could transact in her astral body; a certain group of Adepts occupying and manoeuvreing the body by turns. When they knew that I could distinguish between them, so as to even have invented a name for each by which H.P.B. and I might designate them in our conversation in their absence, they would frequently give me a grave bow or a friendly farewell nod when about to leave the room and give place to the next relief-guard. And they would sometimes talk to me of each other as friends do about absent third parties, by which means I came to know bits of their several personal histories; and would also speak about the absent H.P.B., distinguishing her from the physical body they had borrowed from her....*

---

*[In a letter to her sister Vera, Madame Blavatsky writes: "**Someone** comes and envelops me as a misty cloud and all at once pushes me out of myself, and then I am not 'I' any more---Helena Petrovna Blavatsky---but someone else. Someone strong and powerful, born in a totally different region of the world; and as to myself it is almost as if I were asleep, or lying by not quite conscious,---not in my own body but close by, held only by a thread which ties me to it. However, at times I see and hear everything quite clearly: I am perfectly conscious of what my body is saying and doing---or at least its new possessor. I even understand and remember it all so well that afterwards I can repeat it and even write down **his** words....At such a time I see awe and fear on the faces of Olcott and others, and follow with interest the way in which **he** half-pityingly regards them out of my own eyes and teaches them with my physical tongue. Yet not with my mind but his own, which enwraps my brain like a cloud...." **The Path** [New York], Dec., 1894, p. 266. For more on this subject, consult Geoffrey A. Barborka's **H.P. Blavatsky, Tibet and Tulku**, Adyar, Madras, India, The Theosophical Publishing House, 1966.---Editor.]

Alexander Wilder[22]
Autumn, 1876---Sept., 1877, New York City

...In the autumn of 1876...I had been editing several publications for Mr. J.W. Bouton, a bookseller in New York....Other engagements and associations had been laid aside....

On a pleasant afternoon..., I was alone in the house. The bell was rung, and I answered at the door. Colonel Henry S. Olcott was there with an errand to myself....He had been referred to me by Mr. Bouton. Madame Blavatsky had compiled a work upon occult and philosophic subjects, and Mr. Bouton had been asked in relation to undertaking its publication....Mr. Bouton...meant that I should examine the work, and I agreed to undertake the task.

It was truly a ponderous document and displayed research in a very extended field....In my report to...[Mr. Bouton], I stated that the manuscript was the product of great research, and that so far as related to current thinking, there was a revolution in it, but I added that I deemed it too long for remunerative publishing.

Mr. Bouton, however, presently agreed to publish the work....He placed the manuscript again in my hands, with instructions to shorten it as much as it would bear. This was a discretionary power that was far from agreeable. It can hardly be fair that a person acting solely in behalf of the publisher should have such authority over the work of an author. Nevertheless, I undertook the task. While abridging the work, I endeavored in every instance to preserve the thought of the author in plain language, removing only such terms and matter as might be regarded as superfluous, and not necessary to the main purpose. In this way, enough was taken out to fill a volume of respectable dimensions....

Colonel Olcott was very desirous that I should become acquainted with Madame Blavatsky. He appeared to hold her in high regard closely approaching to veneration, and to consider the opportunity to know her a rare favor for any one. I was hardly able to share his enthusiasm. Having a natural diffidence about making new acquaintances, and acting as a critic upon her manuscript, I hesitated for a long time. Finally, however, these considerations were passed over and I accompanied him to their establishment in Forty-seventh Street.

It was a "flat," that unhomelike fashion of abode that now extends over populous cities, superseding the household and family relationship wherever it prevails. The building where they lived had been "transmogrified" for such purposes, and they occupied a suite of apartments on an upper floor. The household in this case comprised several individuals, with separate employments. They generally met at meal-time, together with such guests from elsewhere as might happen to be making a visit....

The study in which Madame Blavatsky lived and worked was arranged after a quaint and very primitive manner. It was a large front room, and being on the side next the street, was well lighted. In the midst of this was her "den," a spot fenced off on three sides by temporary partitions, writing desk and shelves for books. She had it as convenient as it was unique. She had but to reach out an arm to get a book, paper or other article that she might desire, that was within the enclosure....In this place Madame Blavatsky reigned supreme, gave her orders, issued her judgments, conducted her correspondence, received her visitors and produced the manuscript of her book.

She did not resemble in manner or figure what I had been led to expect. She was tall, but not strapping; her countenance bore the marks and exhibited the characteristics of one who had seen much, thought much, traveled much, and experienced much....Her appearance was certainly impressive, but in no respect was she coarse, awkward, or ill-bred. On the other hand she exhibited culture, familiarity with the manners of the most courtly society and genuine courtesy itself. She expressed her opinions with boldness and decision, but not obtrusively. It was easy to perceive that she had not been kept within the circumscribed limitations of a common female education; she knew a vast variety of topics and could discourse freely upon them.

...I have heard tell of her profession of superhuman powers and of extraordinary occurrences that would be termed miraculous. I, too, believe, like Hamlet, that there are more things in heaven and earth than our wise men of this age are willing to believe. But Madame Blavatsky never made any such claim to me. We always discoursed of topics which were familiar to both, as individuals on a common plane. Colonel Olcott often spoke to me as one who enjoyed a grand opportunity, but she herself made no

*The Lamasery, 47th St and 8th Ave,
New York City*

The Salon in the Lamasery

affectation of superiority. Nor did I ever see or know of any such thing occurring with anyone else.

She professed, however, to have communicated with personages whom she called "Brothers," and intimated that this, at times, was by the agency, or some means analogous to what is termed "telepathy."...I have supposed that an important condition for ability to hold such intercourse was abstinence from artificial stimulation such as comes from the use of flesh as food, alcoholic drink and other narcotic substances. I do not attach any specific immorality to these things, but I have conjectured that such abstemiousness was essential in order to give the mental powers full play, and to the noetic faculty free course without impediment or contamination from lower influence. But Madame Blavatsky displayed no such asceticism. Her table was well furnished, but without profusion, and after a manner not differing from that of other housekeepers. Besides, she indulged freely in the smoking of cigarettes, which she made as she had occasion. I never saw any evidence that these things disturbed, or in any way interfered with her mental acuteness or activity.

At my first visit, her reception was courteous and even friendly. She seemed to become acquainted at once. She spoke of the abridgements which I had made of her manuscript, extolling what I had done far beyond what it deserved. "What had been taken out was 'flapdoodle,'" she declared. My judgment, certainly, had not been so severe as that....

...While she was engaged in the work, she had many books relating to the various topics, evidently for consultation. There were Jacolliot's works on India, Bunsen's *Egypt*, Ennemoser's *History of Magic* and others. I had myself written papers upon a variety of subjects for the *Phrenological Journal* and other periodicals, and she had procured many of them. We often discussed the topics, and their various characteristics, for she was a superior conversationalist and at home on every matter about which we discoursed. She spoke the English language with the fluency of one perfectly familiar with it, and who thought in it. It was the same to me as though talking with any man of my acquaintance. She was ready to take the idea as it was expressed, and uttered her own thoughts clearly, concisely and often forcibly. Some of the words which she employed had characteristics which indicated their source. Any thing which she did not approve or hold in respect she promptly disposed of as "flapdoodle." I have never heard or encountered the term elsewhere. Not even the acts or projects of Colonel Olcott escaped such scathing, and in fact he not unfrequently came under her scorching criticism. He writhed under it, but, except for making some brief expression at the time, he did not appear to cherish resentment....

Several individuals have written letters, as though I knew something that would discredit...the genuineness of the originality of *Isis Unveiled*....The manuscript which I handled I am very sure was in the handwriting of Madame Blavatsky herself. Anybody who was familiar with her, would, upon reading the first volume of *Isis Unveiled*, not have any difficulty in recognizing her as the author....Besides, a full third, or even more, of what was published, was written by Madame Blavatsky after Mr. Bouton had set about putting the work in type. She was by no means expert in preparing her material. She patched and changed, making a very large bill for "alterations." Indeed, she never actually finished the work, the publisher declared to me, till he told her that she must stop....

She always treated me with courtesy. When her work was most urgent, or she had been wearied with visitors, she commanded the woman at the door to turn off all callers. That prohibition was repeatedly spoken to me, but as she heard my voice, she would call out to admit me. This occurred when the call was not a matter of business. She was ready in conversation, and was at home on any topic....Few persons in any walk of life are as well supplied with material for discourse. Even Colonel Olcott, who was by no means inferior or commonplace, was not her equal except in his own profession.

Believing that the main body of the work would not be sufficiently attractive to purchasers, I urged her to include in it accounts of the marvellous things which she had observed in India. But this she invariably declined to do, saying that it was not permitted by "the Brothers." That was a tribunal that I could not question; my wisdom in the matter was that of the market-place. But she was always ready to hear what I had to say, whether in relation to her work, or to philosophic questions, or to subjects of everyday life. When the printer had placed everything in type, I was employed to prepare the index....

The work was finally completed, and *Isis Unveiled* was duly issued [in September, 1877]....

Henry S. Olcott[23]
March, 1877, New York City

...Putting aside...[H.P.B.'s] actions, habits of thought, masculine ways, her constant asseverations of the fact...putting these aside, I have pumped enough out of her to satisfy me that the theory long since communicated by me to you was correct---she is a man, a very old man, and a most learned and wonderful man. Of course *she* knows just what my impressions are for she reads my thoughts like a printed page (and others' thoughts) and it seems to me *she* is not dissatisfied, for our relations have insensibly merged into those of Master and pupil. There is not a trace left of the old *sabreur* Blavatsky ("Jack" as I nicknamed her to her great delight) so far as I am concerned. Now she is all sobriety, dignity, stern self-repression. Before others she is as of old, but the moment their backs are turned she is *Mejnour* and I the neophyte....

I say Isis [H.P.B.] is a man. Let me add that *she* is (in my opinion) a Hindu man. At any rate, this thing happened to-night after my sister and her husband had gone home: Isis was leaning back in her chair, fooling with her hair, and smoking a cigarette. She got one lock in her fingers and pulled it, and fingered it in an absent way---talking the while, when lo! the lock grew visibly darker and darker until, presto! it was as black as coal. I said nothing until the thing was done, when suddenly catching her hand I asked her to let me have this neat specimen of miracle-making as a keepsake. You ought to have seen her face when she saw what she had done in her brown study. But she laughed good-naturedly, called me a sharp Yankee, and cut off the lock and gave it to me....I will send you a bit of it as a talisman...Mind you, this was cut off of Isis' head in my sight and under the full blaze of the chandelier. This one lock showed against the blonde silky and crinkled hair of Blavatsky's head like a skein of black

84

sewing-silk upon a light-brown cloth. Now what this teaches me is just this---The Blavatsky shell is a shell, tenanted by a copper-coloured Hindu Solon or Pythagoras, and in this moment of abstraction his own hair---previously there only in its astral condition...became materialized and now stays so. Mind you these are my private speculations....

Why, I can't tell you the number and variety of exhibitions of magical power she has given me and others during the past four months. They exceed all I had seen before. She has done her wonders before 4, 5, and 8 persons, some of them comparative strangers. On Monday night, in the presence of Dr. Billing, Dr. Marquette, Mr. and Miss Monachesi, Mr. Curtis...and myself these things happened in full light; she made the music of a musical-box to be heard in the air. At first faint and far, far away, it grew louder and louder until it sounded as if the box were floating around the room and playing at full force. Then it died away again, again approached, and then suddenly ceased. She carelessly put out her hand, and withdrawing it showed us a long string of those perfumed Oriental beads, whose fragrance filled the room. Holding them in one hand, she asked me if I wanted some, and at once pulled *duplicates* off, one by one, until she had given me 27. I strung them and after handling them awhile laid them on my writing-table (beyond her reach a good way) for a moment while I filled a pipe and upon taking them up again, there was a Turkish coin strung on the string with them! Still holding her own original necklace she pulled off (materialized) a bead mounted in gold as a scarf-pin, and upon our drawing lots Monachesi got it and has it now. The four of the party happening to sit so they could look out of the window into the street (a room in second story of house), saw pass the window *on the outside* the forms of two men. *One of them was a Brother I know well*, and whose portrait was materialized instantly for me some months ago. The other was a younger Brother---an advanced pupil who can travel in his [astral] double.

O'Sullivan (J.L.) has been here *en route* to Paris, and made "Mme.'s" acquaintance and even stayed all night once with us. In his presence she materialized, on two different occasions, handkerchiefs of a beautifully fine and delicate Chinese silk crepe with a satin striped border. In the corner, marked in ink,

85

was the name of a certain Brother in the Ancient Zenzar character. I was present, both times. I wish you might have seen O'Sullivan's consternation: he jumped for the hdkfs like a trout at a fly, and carried one off as a trophy....The original handkerchief was materialized two weeks ago Sunday in the presence of a French artist named Harrisse. We three were talking of the delicate fabrics of the Chinese, and Harrisse said that their crepes were much finer than those of Lyons. "Did you ever see their handkerchiefs, Madame?" he asked. "Oh! yes---see, here is one!" she replied, quietly grabbing the very article out of the *Astral Wardrobe*! This specimen I retained for myself, chiefly because it was strongly impregnated with the Lodge perfume....

I saw a splendid exhibition of will-power recently. Isis and I were alone after dinner, in the parlor, when she bade me turn the gas very low and sit quiet at the other side of the room. I made the light very dim, and upon looking at her through the gloom in a few minutes I saw beside her dark figure (she was dressed in a dark gown) *a man's figure in white*, or light robes, and with a shawl wound in Eastern fashion about his head. She told me to look away for a moment, and then to turn up the gas. *She sat there with the very shawl transferred to her own head*, and no one else visible but us two. She gave me the shawl. It was powerfully perfumed with the familiar odor. *In one corner was worked the name of the same Brother above alluded to, and in the same Zensar character.* It is on his portrait, in my bedroom.

Henry S. Olcott[24]
1877, New York City

Our evening's work on *Isis* was finished, I had bade good-night to H.P.B., retired to my own room, closed the door as usual, sat me down to read and smoke, and was soon absorbed in my book....All at once, as I read with my shoulder a little turned from the door, there came a gleam of something white in the right-hand corner of my right eye; I turned my head, dropped my book in astonishment, and saw towering above me in his great stature an

Master Morya

Oriental clad in white garments, and wearing a head-cloth or turban of amber-striped fabric, hand-embroidered in yellow floss-silk. Long raven hair hung from under his turban to the shoulders; his black beard, parted vertically on the chin in the Rajput fashion, was twisted up at the ends and carried over the ears; his eyes were alive with soul-fire; eyes which were at once benignant and piercing in glance....He was so grand a man, so imbued with the majesty of moral strength, so luminously spiritual, so evidently above average humanity, that I felt abashed in his presence, and bowed my head and bent my knee as one does before a god or a god-like personage. A hand was lightly laid on my head, a sweet though strong voice, bade me be seated, and when I raised my eyes, the Presence was seated in the other chair beyond the table. He told me he had come at the crisis when I needed him; that my actions had brought me to this point; that it lay with me alone whether he and I should meet often in this life as co-workers for the good of mankind; that a great work was to be done for humanity, and I had the right to share in it if I wished; that a mysterious tie, not now to be explained to me, had drawn my colleague [H.P.B.] and myself together; a tie which could not be broken, however strained it might be at times. He told me things about H.P.B. that I may not repeat, as well as things about myself, that do not concern third parties....At last he rose, I wondering at his great height and observing the sort of splendour in his countenance---not an external shining, but the soft gleam, as it were, of an inner light---that of the spirit. Suddenly the thought came into my mind: "What if this be but hallucination; what if H.P.B. has cast a hypnotic glamour over me? I wish I had some tangible object to prove to me that he has really been here; something that I might handle after he is gone!" The Master smiled kindly as if reading my thought, untwisted the *fehta* [turban] from his head, benignantly saluted me in farewell and ---was gone*: his chair was empty; I was alone with my emotions! Not quite alone, though, for on the table lay the embroidered head-cloth; a tangible and enduring proof that I had not been "overlooked," or psychically befooled, but had been face to face with one of the Elder Brothers of Humanity....To run and beat at H.P.B.'s door and tell her my experience, was the first natural impulse, and she was as glad to hear my story as I was to tell it. I returned to my room to think, and the gray morning found me still thinking and resolving....I have been blessed with meetings with this Master and others since then....

---

*[Colonel Olcott elsewhere describes how the Master Morya left his room: "When I asked him to leave me some tangible evidence that I had not been the dupe of a vision, but that he had indeed been there, he removed from his head the **puggri** [turban] he wore, and giving it to me, vanished from my sight...." H.S. Olcott, **Theosophy, Religion and Occult Science**, London, 1885, p. 123.---Editor.]

Emily Kislingbury[25]
Autumn, 1877, New York City

My earliest acquaintance with H.P.B. dates from the autumn of the year 1877, when I took advantage of a three months' leave of absence from my duties in England to seek her out in New York. The Spiritualist movement, with which I was officially connected, was at that time in full swing, and the appearance of Col. Olcott's book, *People from the Other World*, was making a great stir....The part of the book which attracted me however, was that in which Col. Olcott related the appearance on the scene of the Russian lady lately arrived from the East, and whose explanation of the phenomena was widely different from that generally received. As soon as I learned the address of Madame Blavatsky from the American Spiritualist journals, I wrote to her, and it was in consequence of our correspondence that I was induced to visit America.

Our first introduction was a singular one. I was staying at some distance from...where H.P.B. was then residing, and one afternoon, soon after my arrival, I went to call on her. After ringing three times in vain, I was about to turn away in despair, when the door was opened by H.P.B. herself! Having already exchanged photographs, recognition was mutual, and my welcome the heartiest imaginable. We went up to the flat on the second floor....I could not remain then, for I was leaving New York the next day on a little tour to Niagara and elsewhere; but on my return three weeks later, I spent five weeks with H.P.B. until I finally left for England.

Just at that time *Isis Unveiled* was going through the press, and many were the happy hours I spent correcting proof-sheets and discussing the problems put forward in that marvelous book....

Various instances of H.P.B.'s psychical powers occurred while I was with her, but most of these are difficult to record, are in fact incommunicable....One instance is of mesmeric power exerted upon myself. I was reading, in a position from which I could see into a mirror on the opposite side of the room, and I remarked to Madame Blavatsky that the wall which was reflected in the mirror appeared to be moving up and down. She said, "That is an atmospheric effect," and went on reading her Russian newspaper.

I then began to look at the mirror intently, and I saw Madame Blavatsky look at me once or twice. I was aware that she had her eye on me, but that was all. I continued to gaze, and presently the mirror became clouded and I saw distinctly, though momentarily, two different scenes. The first was that of a sea in motion, covered with ships, and might have been a port or harbor. This faded out, like a dissolving view, and was succeeded by a picture representing a group of men in Eastern costume, turbans and long garments, such as is worn by Hindoos. The men seemed as if alive and conversing together. When I told Madame Blavatsky what I had seen, she said, "That is right; that is what I wished you to see; I am sorry I did not write it down, that you might have had the proof to carry away with you."...

It required no special insight to perceive that communication was constantly kept up with some distant or invisible minds. Frequent signals of various kinds were heard even at the dinner-table, when H.P.B. would immediately retire to her own apartment. So familiar were these sounds as well as the terms "Masters," and "Brothers," that when in after years so much controversy as to their reality took place, even among those calling themselves Theosophists, it never occurred to me to doubt their existence....

Princess Helene von Racowitza[26]
May, 1878, New York City

Accompanied by my husband, I pulled the bell of Madame Blavatsky's flat. The door was opened by a neat little negress, who, showing all her teeth in a broad grin, pointed with her hand to a door closed by dark Indian curtains, through which the sound of lively conversation reached us. We went in unannounced and were greeted with a loud joyous shout of welcome by H.P.B.---as Madame Blavatsky always liked best to be called.

She sat at her writing table in a large, comfortable armchair, which seemed as much a part of her as the flowing garments....A samovar stood beside her, from which she continually supplied her guests with the fragrant Russian national beverage, while just as perpetually her beautiful hands never ceased for a moment to roll between their graceful fingers delicate cigarettes for herself and all present, for H.P.B. was almost more inseparable from her box of finely-cut Turkish tobacco than from her Indian garments, and whenever she changed her seat, which seldom happened, the little negress had to carry it after her. Around her sat or reclined eight or ten people, men and women of all ages and apparently belonging to every possible class of society....

As we entered, a man of very distinguished appearance was just relating to a small group his latest experiences from the "spirit-world." He was a former Ambassador of the United States, well known for his personal charm, who was then living wholly for the occult sciences. All these people...sat or reclined in comfortable, careless attitudes on the low divans and cushions or on small seats, made up of boxes and chests, covered with Indian cloths and rugs.

These, with a variety of idols and oriental *bric-a-brac*, formed the furnishing of the room....In it there reigned a hum and buzz of conversation in various languages, and clouds of incense and tobacco smoke, streaming from oriental incense sticks and the Russian cigarettes which everyone present was smoking, so that it needed a few moments of becoming accustomed to it, before eye and ear could clearly make out what was going on....

We were instantly, as...[H.P.B.] expressed it, quite crazy for one another. She declared that I impressed her as if a bit of sunshine had got loose and were shining straight into her heart; while I found myself at once entirely under the spell of this marvellous woman. Outwardly she was quite unusually corpulent and indeed never spoke of herself otherwise than as "an old hippopotamus." But that made not the smallest unpleasant impression; she always wore loose flowing garments of a sort of Indian cut---a kind of flowing robe, which concealed the entire figure, leaving only the really ideally beautiful hands free....

Her head, standing out from the usually dark-coloured woollen garments, was equally full of character, even though far sooner to be called ugly than beautiful. A genuinely Russian type: broad forehead, short, thick nose, prominent cheek bones, thin, clever, ever mobile mouth with beautiful, small teeth, brown, quite curly hair, almost like a negro's, then still without a single silver

91

thread in it, yellowish complexion, and---a pair of eyes, such as I have never elsewhere seen---light blue, almost water-grey, but with a look so deep, so piercing, so compelling, as if they gazed into the inmost being of things, and at times with an expression as if directed far, far above and beyond all earthly things; large, long, wonderful eyes, that lit up the whole of that most singular face. ...To give this bodily picture is easy---but how shall I begin to describe the wonderful woman herself, how give an idea of her nature, her power, her character---of what she could do!

She was a mixture of the most heterogeneous qualities....In conversation she possessed a charm which none could withstand, and which probably lay for the most part in her keen and living appreciation of everything great and noble, and in her bubbling enthusiasm, mated with an original, often somewhat pungent humour, and a way of expressing herself which often drove into the most comical despair her Anglo-Saxon friends, who as all the world knows are rather given to prudery in the use of words.

Her contempt, nay rebellion, against all society forms and formalities made her sometimes of purpose put on a coarseness not usual with her; and she hated and battled against the conventional lie with the heroic courage of a true Don Quixote. Yet whoever came to her poor and ragged, hungry and needing comfort, could be certain of finding a heart so warm and hand so freely and generously open as could be found with no other cultured human being however "good-mannered" he might be....

The New York Daily Graphic[27]
Dec. 10, 1878, New York City

Helen P. Blavatsky...is...leaving America, as she says, forever. A very damp reporter found his way into the pleasant French flat at Eighth avenue and Forty-seventh street this morning, and his ring was answered by a colored servant, who expressed serious doubts as to whether his mistress would see any one at so early an hour. The interviewer was, however, ushered into a breakfast room, which was in a very disordered condition, and invited to a

H.P. Blavatsky in 1876

seat on a vacant stool. The disorder was a necessary result of
yesterday's auction sale, and the only semblance of occupancy left
were an uncleared breakfast table and three human occupants.
Colonel Olcott...sat at the table busily making memoranda in a
note-book and burning his handsome moustache with a half-

finished cigar that struggled ineffectually to reach beyond the outskirts of his beard.

...When the reporter was finally ushered into Mme. Blavatsky's own room, he found that lady seated at the end of a letter and tobacco laden table, twisting a fragrant cigarette from a quantity of loose tobacco of a famous Turkish brand. The room was the inner temple of the Lamasery, which has become so widely known in recent years....

The reporter said: "And so you are going to leave America?"

"Yes, and the Lamasery where I have spent so many happy, happy hours. I am sorry to leave these rooms, although there is little to regret about them now," glancing about at the bare floors and walls, "but I am glad to get away from your country. You have liberty, but that is all, and of that you have too much, too much!"

...The reporter...asked Mme. Blavatsky: "How with your dislike for America did you come to abandon your Russian citizenship and become a resident of New York?"

"Ah, you have liberty. I had none. I could not be protected by Russian consuls so I will be protected by American consuls...."

"When shall you leave?"...

"I know neither the time nor the vessel, but it will be very soon....I am going first to Liverpool and London, where we have branch theosophical societies....Then...I shall go direct to Bombay....Oh! how glad I shall be to see my dear Indian home again!" and as she arose and wrapped a morning gown of strange design about her, she looked very much the Oriental priestess which she claims she is---not.

Chapter 4

INDIA

1879-1884

Charles C. Massey[28]
Jan., 1879, Norwood, near London

...One evening in January, 1879...I had come down to Norwood
by train, and found a company of...some half-dozen persons
assembled in the dining-room of Dr. and Mrs. Billing's house.
Madame Blavatsky was not in the room when I entered, but
joined us very shortly afterwards. I had hung up my over-coat in
the hall outside....Madame Blavatsky turned to me, and asked if I
would like to name some article for myself to be produced then
and there....Having for some time been in want of a card-case---a
want I had certainly not mentioned to any one present, or, I
believe, to anyone at all,---I named that article....

...I...[was] immediately afterwards dissatisfied with that
particular article I had named, as a test...[and] wished to substitute
another choice, but was told I was too late. I was to go into the
hall, and put my hand in the pocket of my overcoat. Be it
observed---and this I can state most positively---that *no one* but
myself left the room after I had asked for the card-case, and I
went out into the hall as directed, unaccompanied by anyone.
The hall was just outside the room, which had no other door than
the one I went out at. I at once put my hand into the pocket of
my overcoat, and there, sure enough, was an ivory card-case,
which I still have. It was a large, square, lady's card-case, not the
small oblong one used by men....The card-case was not in my
pocket when I entered the house....Madame Blavatsky was "not

H.P. Blavatsky

prepared" for my desire....I have long regarded the incident as inexplicable (except by occult power) on the facts present to my recollection.

Henry S. Olcott[29]
Jan., 1879, London

The most striking incident of our stay in London was the meeting of a Master by three of us as we were walking down Cannon Street. There was a fog that morning so dense that one could hardly see across the street, and London appeared at its worst. The two who were with me saw him first, as I was next to the curb, and just then my eyes were otherwise occupied. But when they uttered an exclamation, I turned my head quickly and met the glance of the Master as he looked back at me over his shoulder. I did not recognise him for an acquaintance, but I recognised the face as that of an Exalted One; for the type once seen can never be mistaken....We three friends kept together in the City and went together back to Dr. Billing's house, yet on entering we were told by both Mrs. Billing and H.P.B. that the Brother had been there and mentioned that he had met us three---naming us ---in the City. Mrs. Billing described him as a very tall and handsome Hindu, with a peculiarly piercing eye which seemed to look her through. For the moment she was so staggered that she could not say a word, but the stranger said: "I wish to see Madame Blavatsky," and moved towards the door of the room where she sat. Mrs. Billing opened it for him and bade him enter. He did so, and walked straight towards H.P.B., made her an Oriental salutation, and began speaking to her in a tongue the sounds of which were totally unfamiliar to Mrs. Billing....

George Wyld[30]
Jan., 1879, Norwood near London

...It was in 1879 that, at a dinner party at the house of Mr. Billing, I first met Madame Blavatsky and Colonel Olcott. As I left the house, accompanied by a friend, he asked me what my impression was as to the character of Madame, and my reply was: "She seems to me quite the Kalmuck, and my impression is that she might have been a worn-out actress from some suburban theatre in Paris." But her undoubtedly mediumistic powers, her striking personality, her cleverness and humour, and her evidently kindly instincts interested me; and so out of curiosity, and interest, and belief in her promises, I joined her "Theosophical" Society, and after some two years, I became the President of the British Branch.

On one occasion when I was dining with her at the Billing's, I observed that she and Colonel Olcott ate very freely of animal food; and this startled me, for she had always taught us that those who eat animal food were never admitted to the higher circles of the occult societies, and I thought to myself, "I wonder if that woman is altogether an impostor." As I asked myself this question, she knocked on her plate with her knife, and when I looked at her she said, "Not quite so bad as that, doctor;" and we both good-humoredly laughed at the comicality of the situation. I think it was also at the same dinner party that she suddenly turned round on Colonel Olcott, who sat a few places from her, engaged in the consumption of animal food, and in an angry and loud voice exclaimed: "You baboon!" This shocked me, for Colonel Olcott was, although very credulous, yet an intelligent, self-denying and kindly man. After dinner was over I took him aside and asked him what Madame Blavatsky meant by so coarsely addressing him at the table, and his reply was: "Dr. Wyld, her conduct is part of my training; and I do not believe there is another man in the United States who would submit as I do to the continual insults I receive at her hands."

On another occasion I was sitting at her side on the drawing-room stairs when she again and again cried out and jumped about; and on my asking her what it all meant, she said: "They won't let me alone!" and when I asked: "Who won't let you alone?"

98

she answered: "These Mahatmas are always pinching me to attract my attention!" Lastly, on one occasion when, with a most refined and interesting woman, I was in her society, and the lady asked her what her views as to the nature of Jesus Christ were, she answered: "Madame, I have not the honour of the gentleman's acquaintance."

I do not idly record these experiences, but because I think it right that her irreverence and vulgarities should be known. For, although she knew some curious Eastern occult secrets of psychical origin, yet it has always seemed to me a marvellous thing how any refined and thoughtful man or woman could *continue* to believe in this queer woman who smoked so incessantly, as an inspired expounder of the highest spiritual secrets of the human race....

Henry S. Olcott[31]
Feb.---July, 1879, Bombay, India

...On the 17th [of January]...we left...for Liverpool, after a delightful stay of a fortnight [in England] with and among our kind friends and colleagues....The next day we passed at the Great Western Hotel, Liverpool, and at 5 p.m. embarked on the "Speke Hall" in a downpour of rain. The vessel was dirty and disagreeable to see; and what with that, and the falling of rain, the smell of damp tapestries and carpets in the saloon and cabins, and the forlorn faces of our forty fellow-passengers, all equally disgusted as ourselves, it was a wretched omen for our long voyage out to India....

...Meanwhile H.P.B. was making it lively for the servants and her fellow-passengers who, with one or two exceptions, were shocked by her ironclad language...[and] outraged by her religious heterodoxy....The ship being struck by a tremendous sea, H.P.B. was pitched against a leg of the dining-table...got her knee badly bruised ...[and was] laid up in her cabin with her lame knee....

At the rate of 250 to 300 miles a day, we sailed up the Mediterranean, past Gibraltar, past Algiers, on to Malta....Port Said

[Egypt] was reached on 2nd February...and then came...two days and nights in the Suez Canal...[We] emerged into the Red Sea and began the third and final stage of our sea-pilgrimage to the Land of Desire....That night the moon paved with silver the waters of the Gulf of Suez, and we felt as if we were sailing on a dream-sea. Nothing of moment happened until the 12th, when a flue burst in the boiler, and we had to stop for repairs....On the 15th [of February], at noon, [we] were but 160 miles away from...[the Bombay lights], and the next morning entered Bombay Harbor. ...Before sunrise I was on deck...and as we steamed rapidly towards our anchorage, revelled in the panorama of the Harbor that was spread before me. Elephanta, ahead of us, was the first locality we asked to be shown us, for it was the type and visible representative of that Ancient India....Alas! as one turned towards promontory of the Malabar Hill the dream was dispelled. The India we saw there was one of sumptuous bungalows, framed in the luxury of English flower-gardens, and surrounded with all the signs of wealth gained in foreign commerce....

The ship's anchor was hardly dropped before we were boarded by three Hindu gentlemen in search of us. All seemed strangers to us, but when they pronounced their names I opened my arms and pressed them to my breast....We went ashore...in their bunder-boat and landed on the Apollo Bunder. The first thing I did on touching land was to stoop down and kiss the granite step; my instinctive act of pooja!....

...The noonday Bombay sun of mid-February is a surprise to a Western visitor, and we had time to feel its full power before Mr. Hurrychund came....

The streets of Bombay charmed us with their strikingly Oriental character. The tall apartment-houses in stucco, the novel dresses of the motley Asiatic population, the quaint vehicles...all these vivid impressions filled us with delight.

Before leaving New York, I had written Hurrychund to engage for us a small, clean house in the Hindu quarter....We were taken to a house...on Girgaum Back Road, standing in a comparatively forlorn compound, and adjoining his glass-roofed photographic studio....Cocoa-palms nodded their fronds over our roof, and Indian sweet-scented flowers rejoiced our sense of smell; after the dismal sea-voyage it seemed like Paradise. The ladies of our friends' families called on H.P.B....and a number of Hindu and Parsi gentlemen on our whole party; but the rush of visitors began the next morning....

We had formed one acquaintanceship on the "Speke Hall" that turned into a lasting friendship, that of Mr. Ross Scott, B.C.S., a noble fellow and an Irishman of the better sort. His long conversations with us about Eastern Philosophy had resulted in his joining our Society. He called on the evening of our first day ashore, and provoked H.P.B. to doing a phenomenon that was quite new to me. They were sitting together on a sofa and I was standing with Hurrychund at the centre table, when Scott reproached H.P.B. for her evident intention of letting him go North to his official post, without giving him the least proof of the existence of the psychical powers in men, of which she had so much spoken. She liked him very much, and so consented to comply with his request. "What shall I do for you?" she asked. He snatched the handkerchief she was holding in her hand, and, pointing to her name "Heliona" embroidered across one corner, said: "Well, make that name disappear and another to take its place." "What name do you want?" she rejoined. Looking towards us, where we stood at a distance of a few paces, he pointed to our host and said: "Let it be Hurrychund's." We came over to them on hearing this, and saw what was done. She...[told] Scott to hold tight in his hand the embroidered corner of her handkerchief, retaining the opposite corner herself. After a minute or so she told him to look. He did so, found the substitution of names had been made, Hurrychund's being there in the same kind of embroidery, and in the first impulse of excitement, cried out: "Where is your physical science now? This beats all the professors in the world!...."

...On the evening of 17th February, a reception was held at the photographic studio, at which over 300 invited guests were present. The usual welcome address, with garlands, limes and rose-water as accompaniments, was given us....

We changed quarters, bought furniture and other necessaries, and on 7th March settled ourselves down in the little house, 108, Girgaum Back Road, for the next two years....Every evening we held an impromptu durbar, when the knottiest problems of philosophy, metaphysics, and science were discussed....Visitors kept

102

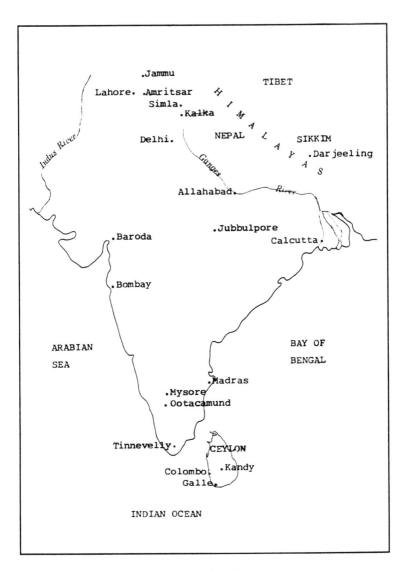

India in the 1880s

on crowding our bungalow, and stopping until late every evening to discuss religious questions....We were completely happy in our retired cottage under the cocoa-palms....And, under those umbrageous palms, we were visited in person by Mahatmas; and their inspiring presence made us strong to proceed in the path we were treading....

...[On July 15, Mahatma Morya] visited me in the flesh at Bombay, coming in full day light, and on horseback. He had me called by a servant into the front room of H.P.B.'s bungalow (she being at the time in the other bungalow talking with those who were there). He came to scold me roundly for something I had done in T.S. matters, and as H.P.B. was also to blame, he *telegraphed* to her to come, that is to say he turned his face and extended his finger in the direction of the place she was in. She came over at once with a rush, and seeing him dropped on her knees and paid him reverence. My voice and his had been heard by those in the other bungalow, but only H.P.B. and I, and the servant *saw* him.[*]

A.P. Sinnett[32]
Dec., 1879, Allahabad, India

...Col. Olcott['s] and Mme. Blavatsky['s]...arrival in India had been heralded with a few newspaper paragraphs dimly indicating that Mme. Blavatsky was a marvellous person, associated with a modern development of "magic," and I had seen her great book, "Isis Unveiled," which naturally provoked interest on my part in the authoress. From some remarks published in the *Pioneer*, of which I was at that time the editor, the first communications

---

[*] [In Colonel Olcott's diary for July 15. 1879. the following entry is written: "Had visit in body of the Sahib!! [He] sent Babula to my room to call me to H.P.B.'s bungalow. and there we had a most important private interview. Alas! how puerile and vain these men make one feel by contrast with them."---Editor.]

between us arose. In accordance with arrangements made by letter during the summer, she came to Allahabad to visit my wife and myself at our cold weather home at that station in December 1879.

I well remember the morning of her arrival, when I went down to the railway station to meet her. The trains from Bombay used to come into Allahabad in those days at an early hour in the morning, and it was still but just time for *chota hozree*, or early breakfast, when I brought our guests home. She had evidently been apprehensive, to judge from her latest letters, lest we might have formed some ideal conception of her that the reality would shatter, and had recklessly painted herself as a rough, old "hippopotamus" of a woman, unfit for civilised society; but she did this with so lively a humour that the betrayal of her bright intelligence this involved, more than undid the effect of her warnings. Her rough manners, of which we had been told so much, did not prove very alarming, though I remember going into fits of laughter at the time when Col. Olcott, after the visit had lasted a week or two, gravely informed that Madame was under "great self-restraint" so far. This had not been the impression my wife and I had formed about her, though we had learned already to find her conversation more than interesting....

I want to give my readers an idea of Mme. Blavatsky, as I have known her, that shall be as nearly complete as I can make it, and I shall not hesitate to put in the shadows of the picture. The first visit she paid us was not an unqualified success in all respects. Her excitability, sometimes amusing, would sometimes take an irritating shape, and she would vent her impatience, if anything annoyed her, by vehement tirades in a loud voice directed against Col. Olcott, at that time in an early stage of his apprenticeship to what she would sometimes irreverently speak of as the "occult business". No one with the least discernment could ever fail to see that her rugged manners and disregard of all conventionalities were the result of a deliberate rebellion against, not of ignorance or unfamiliarity with, the customs of refined society. Still the rebellion was often very determined, and she would sometimes colour her language with expletives of all sorts, some witty and amusing, some unnecessarily violent, that we should all have preferred her not to make use of. She certainly had none of the superficial attributes one might have expected in a spiritual teacher....

Recollection of this time supplies me with a very varied assortment of memory portraits of Madame, taken during different conditions of her nerves and temper. Some recall her flushed and voluble, too loudly declaiming against some person or other who had misjudged her or her Society; some show her quiet and companionable, pouring out a flood of interesting talk about Mexican antiquities, or Egypt, or Peru, showing a knowledge of the most varied and far-reaching kind, and a memory for names and places and archaeological theories she would be dealing with, that was fairly fascinating to her hearers. Then, again, I remember her telling anecdotes of her own earlier life, mysterious bits of adventure, or stories of Russian society, with so much point, vivacity, and finish, that she would simply be the delight for the time being of everyone present....

I have said a good deal of her impetuosity and indiscretions of speech and manner and of the way in which she will rage for hours, if allowed, over trifles which a more phlegmatic, not to speak of a more philosophical, temperament would barely care to notice. But it must be understood that, almost at any time, an appeal to her philosophical intellect will turn her right off into another channel of thinking, and then, equally for hours, may any appreciative companion draw forth the stores of her information concerning Eastern religions and mythology, the subtle metaphysics of Hindoo and Buddhist symbolism, or the esoteric doctrine itself....

The record of Mme. Blavatsky's residence in India is, of course, intimately blended with the history of the Theosophical Society, on which all her energies are spent, directly or indirectly, and indirectly in so far only as she was obliged during this period to do what literary work she could for Russian magazines to earn her livelihood, and supplement the narrow resources on which the headquarters of the Society were kept up.

The *Theosophist*, the monthly magazine devoted to occult research, which she set on foot in the autumn of her first year in India, paid its way from the beginning, and gradually came to earn a small profit, subject to the fact that its management was altogether gratuitous, and all its work in all departments,

The Theosophist, October, 1879

performed by the little band of Theosophists at head-quarters; but all the while the sneering critics of the movement in the papers would be suggesting, from time to time, that the founders of the Society were doing a very good business with "initiation fees", and living on the tribute of the faithful, Mme. Blavatsky was really at her desk from morning till night, slaving at Russian articles, which she wrote solely for the sake of the little income she was able to make in this way, and on which, in a far greater degree than on the proper resources of the Society, the head-quarters was supported, and the movement kept on foot....

It has been through...my acquaintance with Madame Blavatsky that I have obtained experiences in connection with occultism....The first problem I had to solve was whether Madame Blavatsky really did, as I heard, possess the power of producing abnormal phenomena....

...During her first visit to my house, Madame Blavatsky...was allowed to show that "raps" like those which spiritualists attribute to spirit agency, could be produced at will....

Spiritualists are aware that when groups of people sit round a table and put their hands upon it, they will, if a "medium" be present, generally hear little knocks which respond to questions and spell out messages. The large outer circle of persons who do not believe in spiritualism...imagine that all the millions who do are duped as regards this impression. It must sometimes be troublesome for them to account for the wide development of the delusion, but any theory, they think, is preferable to admitting the possibility that the spirits of deceased persons can communicate in this way; or, if they take the scientific view of the matter, that a physical effect, however slight, can be produced without a physical cause. Such persons ought to welcome the explanations I am now giving, tending as these do to show that the theory of universal self-deception as regards spirit-rapping...is not the only one by means of which the asserted facts of spiritualism...can be reconciled with a reluctance to accept the spiritual hypothesis as the explanation.

Now, I soon found out not only that raps would always come at a table at which Madame Blavatsky sat with the view of obtaining such results, but that all conceivable hypotheses of fraud in the matter were rapidly disposed of by a comparison of the various experiments we were able to make. To begin with, there was no necessity for other people to sit at the table at all. We could work with any table under any circumstances, or without a table at all. A window-pane would do equally well, or the wall, or any door, or anything whatever which could give out a sound if hit. A half glass door put ajar was at once seen to be a very good instrument to choose, because it was easy to stand opposite Madame Blavatsky in this case, to see her bare hands or hand (without any rings) resting motionless on the pane, and to hear the little ticks come plainly, as if made with the point of a pencil or with the sound of electric sparks passing from one knob of an electrical apparatus to another. Another very satisfactory way of obtaining the raps---one frequently employed in the evening---was to set down a large glass clockshade on the hearthrug, and get Madame Blavatsky, after removing all rings from her hands, and sitting well clear of the shade so that no part of her dress touched it, to lay her hands on it. Putting a lamp on the ground opposite, and sitting down on the hearthrug, one could see the under surfaces of the hands resting on the glass, and still under these perfectly satisfactory conditions the raps would come, clear and distinct, on the sonorous surface of the shade.

It was out of Madame Blavatsky's power to give an exact explanation as to how these raps were produced....But the fact that the raps were obedient to the will was readily put beyond dispute, in this way amongst others: working with the window-pane or the clockshade, I would ask to have a name spelled out, mentioning one at random. Then I would call over the alphabet, and at the right letters the raps would come. Or I would ask for a definite number of raps, and they would come. Or for a series of raps in some defined rhythmical progression, and they would come. Nor was this all. Madame Blavatsky would sometimes put her hands, or one only, on some one else's head, and make the raps come, audibly to an attentive listener, and perceptibly to the person touched, who would feel each little shock exactly as if he were taking sparks off the conductor of an electrical machine.

At a later stage of my inquiries I obtained raps under better circumstances again than these---namely, without contact between the object on which they were produced and Madame Blavatsky's hands at all....Madame Blavatsky used to produce the raps on a little table set in the midst of an attentive group, with no one touching it at all. After starting it, or charging it with some influence by resting her hands on it for a few moments, she would hold one about a foot above it and make mesmeric passes at it, at each of which the table would yield the familiar sound. Nor was this done only at our own house with our own tables. The same thing would be done at friends' houses, to which Madame Blavatsky accompanied us. And a further development of the head experiment was this: It was found to be possible for several persons to feel the same rap simultaneously. Four or five persons used sometimes to put their hands in a pile, one on another on a table; then Madame Blavatsky would put hers on the top of the pile and cause a current, or whatever it is which produces the sound, to pass through the whole series of hands, felt by each simultaneously, and record itself in a rap on the table beneath. Any one who has ever taken part in forming such a pile of hands must feel as to some of the hypotheses...put forward...by determined sceptics.... to the effect that the raps are produced by Madame Blavatsky's thumb-nails or by the cracking of some joint ---that such hypotheses are rather idiotic....

The raps...gave me a complete assurance that she was in possession of some faculties of an abnormal character....

Anonymous[33]
May, 1880, on board a ship travelling from Bombay, India to Colombo, Ceylon

Early in May, 1880, I took passage from Bombay for Colombo in Ceylon, on one of the comfortable little coasting steamships of the British India Navigation Company.

The fun of the trip consisted in the delight that the old woman [Madame Blavatsky] took in making life miserable for the first officer of the vessel, a huge, raw-boned, awkward Scotchman, with fiery red hair and whiskers, and an inborn hatred of anything in the way of religious belief that deviated an iota from the faith of his own Presbyterian church.

From the very first hour after sailing from Bombay harbour the first officer had wrangled with Mme. Blavatsky in argument until at last he openly declared he believed she was the only daughter of the Father of Lies, and added that he prayed to heaven that the ship bearing such an unholy person might reach port in safety. For his part he doubted it, but he prayed it might be so. This expression of the sturdy maritimer's opinion only caused the old woman to shake with laughter. Finally, one evening...after dinner she told him that she was weary of his pig-headed disbelief in her powers to force natural laws to assist her in performing what he was pleased to call showmen's tricks, and that she meant to teach him then and there to hold his tongue.

"Vera well, madame, do it if ye can. I'm sure y're truly welcome to try," he replied with a sneer.

"Have you a handkerchief in your pocket?" she asked.

110

He unbuttoned his coat and handed her his handkerchief, a plain cotton one with a narrow blue border.

Mme. Blavatsky tossed it on the table in front of her, pushed away her plate, coffee cup and glasses and pulled her chair in as close to the table as she could. I was sitting directly beside her, and watched her with the greatest interest, as, indeed, did all the rest, the first officer looking on from his place at the foot of the table, only a few feet away, with a very plain sneer on his rugged face.

Having cleared the space in front of her she placed both elbows on the edge of the table, picked up the handkerchief and began to roll it into as small a compass as she could. Then having done so, she squeezed it in her two fists until she turned scarlet in the face and then almost purple. The perspiration started out on her forehead and ran down her face and neck, but still she squeezed harder and harder, with her eyes tightly shut, and as we watched her an expression of pain came on her face, and the color rapidly faded away until she was as livid as a corpse.

I suppose all this occupied two minutes, certainly not more, and then she opened her hands and gasped as if her throat were parched from thirst. Col. Olcott motioned us to be silent, and in a few moments she opened her eyes and a faint color came back to her face. She made an effort to speak, but could only whisper, "Give it to him," at the same time pointing to the handkerchief. It was handed to the Scotchman, who looked somewhat anxious as he opened it and utterly astounded when he found his monogram most exquisitely embroidered in the centre, the letters being in white silk, and enclosed in a circle of light blue of the same color as the printed border of the handkerchief. The diameter of the circle was about two inches.

For a moment the first officer looked intently at the monogram, then at the pale but triumphant old woman who was gazing at him with blazing eyes, and then he uttered a mighty oath and walked away to his cabin on the forward deck. During the rest of the voyage he would not come near her, speak to her, nor sit at the table while she was there, and the only thing he would say about the affair was to repeat the hope that the vessel would be permitted by Providence to reach Ceylon in safety.

Henry S. Olcott[34]
May---July, 1880, Ceylon

A visit...to Ceylon, long urgently requested by the leading priests and laity of the Buddhist community, had been determined upon, and the preparations occupied us....

Everything being ready, we embarked on 7th May in a British India coasting steamer for Ceylon. The party consisted of the two Founders, Mr. [Edward] Wimbridge, Damodar K. Mavalankar [and others]....

We dropped anchor in Colombo harbor on the morning of 16th May, and after a while a large boat came alongside bringing Mohottiwatte Gunananda, the Buddhist orator-priest, John Robert de Silva, and some junior priests....We found the famed ...Mohottiwatte a middle-aged, shaven monk, of full medium stature, with a very intellectual head, a bright eye, very large mouth, and an air of perfect self-confidence and alertness...the most brilliant polemic [Buddhist] orator of the Island, the terror of the [Christian] Missionaries....H.P.B. had sent him from New York a presentation copy of *Isis Unveiled*, and he had translated portions where she describes some of the phenomena she had personally witnessed in the course of her travels. His greetings to us was especially cordial. He requested us to proceed with the steamer to Galle, where arrangements had been made for our reception; he himself would go that evening by train....

Before dawn on the 17th we were off Galle....The monsoon burst, and there was tremendous wind and rain, but the view was so lovely that we stopped on deck to enjoy it. A beautiful bay; a verdant promontory to the north, against which the surf dashed and in foamy jets ran high up against the rocky shore; a long, curved sandy beach bordered with tile-roofed bungalows almost hidden in an ocean of green palms; the old fort, custom house, lighthouse, jetty, and coaling sheds to the south, and to the east the tossing sea with a line of rocks and reefs walling it out from the harbor. Far away inland rose Adam's Peak and his sister mountains.

After breakfast, in a lull of the storm, we embarked in a large boat decorated with plantain trees and lines of bright-colored flowers, on which were the leading Buddhists of the place....On the jetty and along the beach a huge crowd awaited us....A white cloth was spread for us from the jetty steps to the road where carriages were ready, and a thousand flags were frantically waved in welcome. The multitude hemmed in our carriages, and the procession set out for our appointed residence, the house of Mrs. Wijeratne....The roads were blocked with people the whole distance, and our progress was very slow. At the house three Chief Priests received and blessed us at the threshold....Then we had a levee and innumerable introductions; the common people crowding every approach, filling every door and gazing through every window. This went on all day....Our hostess and her son, the Deputy Coroner of Galle, lavished every hospitality upon us....

The monks, who had read..[Mohottiwatte's] excerpts from H.P.B.'s book, pressed her to exhibit her powers, and young Wijeratne, on hearing about the handkerchief phenomenon on board ship, asked her to repeat it for him. So she did, and again for a Mr. Dias; each time obliterating her own embroidered name and causing theirs to replace it....The excitement, of course, rose to fever heat, and culminated when she made some fairy bells ring out sharp in the air, near the ceiling and out on the verandah. I had to satisfy the crowd with two impromptu addresses during the day....

Our rooms were packed with visitors all day. There were no end of metaphysical discussions with the aged High Priest Bulatgama Sumanatissa....Old Bulatgama was a particularly persistent disputant, very voluble and very kind. Among other topics of discussion was that of the psychical powers, and H.P.B., who thoroughly liked him, rang bells in the air (one a booming explosion like the striking of a large steel-bar), made "spirit" raps, caused the great dining-table to tremble and move, etc., to the amazement of her select audience....

This was the Prologue to such a drama of excitement as we had not dreamt we should ever pass through. In a land of flowers, and ideal tropical vegetation, under smiling skies, along roads shaded by clustering palm trees..the people could not do enough for us, nothing seemed to them good enough for us: we were the first white champions of their [Buddhist] religion, speaking of its excellence and its blessed comfort from the platform, in the face of the [Christian] Missionaries, its enemies and slanderers....

On 25th May, H.P.B. and I "took *pansil*" from the venerable Bulatgama, at a temple of the Ramanya Nikaya...and were formally acknowledged as Buddhists....We had previously declared ourselves Buddhists long before, in America, both privately and publicly, so that this was but a formal confirmation of our previous professions. H.P.B. knelt before the huge statue of the Buddha, and I kept her company. We had a good deal of trouble in catching the Pali words that we were to repeat after the old monk....A great crowd was present and made the responses just after us, a dead silence being preserved while we were struggling through the unfamiliar sentences. When we had finished the last of the *Silas*, and offered flowers in the customary way, there came a mighty shout to make one's nerves tingle, and the people could not settle themselves down to silence for some minutes, to hear the brief discourse which, at the Chief Priest's request, I delivered....

The next morning we began our journey northward in carriages supplied by the fishermen of Galle....Almost the entire Buddhist population of Galle massed together to see us leave town, and rent the air with friendly shouts....

...At...Panadure...we were lodged....[in a] building...comprising small bedrooms opening on a verandah which extended on all sides, and one small hall through the middle. There were no bathrooms....The windows were furnished only with wooden shutters, and when they were shut in the daytime, the rooms were dark. H.P.B. had one of the rooms in the south end. She wanted to bathe, and, as there was no other place, I arranged for a tub in her own room. As she would be in pitch darkness if the shutters were closed, I tied a large soft mat across the end of the shutters, left standing open, and she began her toilet. The rest of us were sitting around the corner, on the other verandah, chatting, when I heard my name shouted, and ran around to see what was the matter. At that moment three Sinhalese women were in the act of creeping out beneath the edge of the mat, and the old lady was abusing them in grand style. On hearing my voice, she said that these impertinent creatures, to gratify their curiosity, had actually crept under the mat and, when she happened to turn her head, she saw them standing close against the window still, calmly watching her ablutions. Her indignation was so tragic that, while hustling the intruders away, I could not help laughing heartily. Poor things! they meant no harm....

We left for Kandy by train on the 9th [of June], and after the run of one and a half hours through one of the most picturesque tracts of country in the world, arrived at about 7 p.m. Along with the usual crowd, a deputation of Kandyan Chiefs....received us at the station and accompanied us to our quarters in a great procession, bright with torches and ear-splitting with tom-toms and native trumpets. Two addresses were made to us, by the Chiefs' Committee and by a society of Buddhists...connected with the Temple of the Sacred Tooth of Buddha, the Dalada Maligawa...We went to the temple at 2 p.m. for my lecture..[On the] morning [of June 14th], the unusual honor was conferred upon us of admitting us to a special exhibition of the Buddha Tooth Relic. This is kept in a separate tower, protected by a thick door of entrance studded with iron and fastened with four great locks....The relic is of the size of an alligator tooth, is supported by a gold wire stem rising from a lotus flower of the same metal, and is much discolored by age. If genuine it would, of course, be twenty-five centuries old....On our return to our lodgings, the educated Sinhalese about us were eager to know H.P.B.'s opinion as to the genuineness of the relic, whether it is or is not a real tooth of the Buddha. This was a nice, not to say ticklish, question....H.P.B.'s jovial answer to her interrogators [was]: "Of course, it is his tooth: one he had when he was born as a tiger!"...

...At 2 p.m. [we] took train for Colombo....[Then] we proceeded on to Bentota....The trip was delightful, both by rail along the sea-beach, where the track skirts almost the wash of the surf, and by road through the continuous groves of palms....Our reception at Bentota was princely indeed. There was a procession a mile long; at least ten miles of...decorations along the roads and lanes....I lectured from a large decorated pavilion or platform...We passed the night at the rest-house, or travellers' bungalow, a Government affair....We were all agreed that we had never seen so delightful a house in the Tropics. The lofty ceilings, the floors of red tiles, the walls of laterite, thick and cool, a wide verandah at the back just over the rocky shore of the sea, the rooms at least thirty feet square, the sea-breeze sweeping through them night and day, a bathing-place on the beach, abundance of flowers....H.P.B. declared she should like to pass a whole year there....

[Finally returning to Galle]...the 12th [of July] was our last day in the Island [of Ceylon]; on the 13th our steamer arrived, and at two we embarked; leaving many weeping friends behind, and taking away with us many recollections of gracious kindnesses, cheerful help, lovely journeys, enthusiastic multitudes, and strange experiences....

Anagarika Dharmapala[35]
June, 1880, Colombo, Ceylon

When I was ten years old, I attended a great debate in a temple pavilion sixteen miles from [Colombo] Ceylon where the Christians on one side and [the Buddhist Mohottiwatte] Gunananda on the other argued out the truths of their respective religions....Thousands came from the most distant parts of the island to hear this famous debate. Mohottiwatte Gunananda supplied the oratory; and the Venerable Sumangala furnished him with the scholarly material and references. The debate lasted three days.

Dr. J.M Peebles, an American Spiritualist, who was visiting Colombo at the time, obtained an English report of the controversy between the Buddhists and Christians and, upon his return to the U.S., showed it to Colonel Henry S. Olcott and Madame H.P. Blavatsky, who had organized the Theosophical Society in New York in 1875. Deeply impressed, they wrote to Gunananda and Sumangala that, in the interest of universal brotherhood, they had just founded a society inspired by oriental philosophies and that they would come to Ceylon to help the Buddhists. The letters from Colonel Olcott and Madame Blavatsky were translated into Sinhalese and widely distributed. My heart warmed toward these two strangers, so far away and yet so sympathetic, and I made up my mind that, when they came to Ceylon, I would join them.

They did come to Colombo a few years later, when I was sixteen. The Buddhists entertained them royally. I remember going up to greet them. The moment I touched their hands, I felt overjoyed. The desire for universal brotherhood, for all the things they wanted for humanity, struck a responsive chord in me. I began to read their magazine....As I walked in the gardens overgrown with fragrant plants or along the shore shaded by teak and coco-palms, I pondered on the conversations I had had with the two Theosophists....I made up my mind not to entangle myself in the net of worldly desires. I would endeavor from then on to devote my life to the welfare of others. Exactly how I was to carry out my resolve, I was not certain, but I felt that somehow the way would be found in the writings of Madame Blavatsky....

Damodar K. Mavalankar[36]

June 23---July, 1880, Ceylon and then on ship back to Bombay

...In Ceylon...[in a] particular village, H.P.B., Col. Olcott and myself were the only three persons that stopped one night, the rest of our party having gone to a further place. We were all busy there initiating people and forming a branch of our [Theosophical] Society till about 12 in the night. H.P.B. and Col. Olcott went to bed at about one. As we had to stay in the village only one night we had got down in the Rest House where comfortable accommodation can be had only for two travellers. I had therefore to lie down in an arm-chair in the dining room. I had scarcely locked the door of the room from the inside and laid myself in the chair when I heard a faint knock at the door. It was repeated twice before I had time enough to reach the door. I opened it and what a great joy I felt when I saw...[Mahatma Morya] again! In a very low whisper he ordered me to dress myself and to follow him. At the back door of the Rest House is the Sea. I followed him as he commanded me to do....We walked about three quarters of an hour by the seashore. Then we turned in the direction of the sea. All around there was water *except the place we were walking upon which was quite dry*!! He was walking in front and I was following him. We thus walked for about seven minutes when we came to a spot that looked like a small island. On the top of the building was a triangular light. From a distance, a person, standing on the sea-shore would think it to be an isolated spot which is covered all over by green bushes. There is only one entrance to go inside....After we reached the Island...we came in front of the actual building. There in a little garden in front we found one of the Brothers sitting. I had seen him before...and it is to him that this place belongs....[Mahatma Morya] seated himself near him and I stood before them. We were there for about half an hour. I was shown a part of the place. How very pleasant it is! And inside this place he has...a small room where the body remains when the *Spirit* moves about. What a charming, delightful spot that is! What a nice smell of roses and various sorts of flowers!...The half hour was finished and the time for our leaving the place was near. The master of the place whose name I do not know, placed his blessing hand over my head and...[Mahatma Morya] and I marched off again. We came back near the door of the room wherein I was to sleep and he suddenly disappeared there on the spot....

...I omitted to mention to you the two other places where I was taken...One of them is near Colombo, a private house of...[Mahatma Morya] and the other one near Kandy, a library....

One evening...on the Steamer on our way back to Bombay [in July, 1880],...we finished our dinner [and] I went in [my cabin] and put on...[my] coat. Without thinking I put my hands into my pockets as I usually do and lo! in the right hand one I felt some paper...I took it out and to my surprise I found a letter addressed to Mme. Blavatsky. I took it nearer to the light....The cover was open and on it were written in red the words: "For Damodar to read." I then read the letter....Thinking all the time of this matter I lay down in my bed. Absorbed in deep thought I was startled on the sound of footsteps *in the* cabin which I had locked from inside. I looked behind and there was...[Mahatma Morya] again and two others! What a pleasant evening that was! Speaking of various things in regard to knowledge and philosophy for about half an hour!...

Henry S. Olcott[37]
July---Aug., 1880, Bombay

By way of contrast to the pleasant experiences of the Ceylon tour, we had a terribly rough sea-passage from Galle to Colombo, and all of us were miserably sea-sick....It rained cats and dogs on the last day of our return voyage---as it had nearly every day; the decks were wet....H.P.B. made absurd efforts to write at a table placed for her by the accommodating Captain on a couple of gratings, in a comparatively dry spot, but used more strong words than ink, her papers were so blown about by the gusts that swept the ship....At last we entered Bombay harbor and in due course had...solid ground under our feet....

On the evening of 4th August,...Mahatma [Morya] visited H.P.B., and I was called in to see him before he left. He dictated

119

a long and important letter to an influential friend of ours at Paris, and gave me important hints about the management of current [Theosophical] Society affairs. I was sent away before his visit terminated, and...left him sitting in H.P.B.'s room....

...[Then] we received from Mr. Sinnett an invitation to visit them at Simla....We---H.P.B. and I, with our servant Babula---left Bombay for the North by the evening mail train of 27th August....We came in sight of Simla just before sunset [on September 8th]....A servant of Mr. Sinnett's met us as we entered the town, with *jampans*---chairs carried by porters by long poles ---and we were soon under the hospitable roof of our good friends the Sinnetts, where a hearty welcome awaited us....

Simla, India

Damodar K. Mavalankar[38]
Sept., 1880, Bombay, India

[On]...Aug. 27---1880...H.P.B. and Col. O. left Bombay for Simla and other places in the North [of India]....I worked all alone in H.P.B.'s compartments....[One day in September] at about 2 in the morning after finishing my work I locked the door of the room and lay in my bed. Within about 2 or 3 minutes I heard H.P.B.'s voice in her room calling me. I got up with a start and went in. She said "some persons want to see you" and after a moment added "Now go out, do not look at me." Before however I had time to turn my face I saw her gradually disappear on the spot and from that very ground rose up the form of...[Mahatma Morya]. By the time I had turned back I saw two others dressed in what I afterwards learned to be Tibetan Clothes. One of them remained with...[Mahatma Morya] in H.P.B.'s room. The other one I found seated on my bed by the time I came out....Then he told me to stand still for some time and began to look at me fixedly. I felt a very pleasant sensation as if I was getting out of my body. I cannot say now what time passed between that and what I am now going to relate. But I saw I was in a peculiar place. It was the upper end of Cashmere at the foot of the Himalayas. I saw I was taken to a place where there were only two houses just opposite to each other and no other sign of habitation. From one of these came out the person [Koot Hoomi who]...ordered me to follow him. After going a short distance of about half a mile we came to a natural subterranean passage....After walking a considerable distance through this subterranean passage we came into an open plain....There is a large massive building thousands of years old....The entrance gate has a large triangular arch. Inside are various apartments....I went up with my *Guru* to the Great Hall. The grandeur and serenity of the place is enough to strike anyone with awe....While standing there I do not know what happened but suddenly I...found myself in my bed. It was about 8 in the morning. What was that I saw? Was it a dream or a reality?...Perplexed with these ideas I was sitting silent when down fell a note on my nose. I opened it and found inside that it was not a dream but that I was taken in some mysterious way in my astral body to the real place of Initiation....

A.P. Sinnett[39]
Oct. 3, 1880, Simla, India

We set out at the appointed time next morning. We were originally to have been a party of six, but a seventh person joined us just before we started. After going down the hill for some hours a place was chosen in the wood near the upper waterfall for our breakfast: the baskets that had been brought with us were unpacked, and...the servants at a little distance lighted a fire and set to work to make tea and coffee. Concerning this some joking arose over the fact that we had one cup and saucer too few, on account of the seventh person who joined us at starting, and some one laughingly asked Madame Blavatsky to create another cup and saucer....When Madame Blavatsky said it would be very difficult, but that if we liked she would try, attention was of course at once arrested. Madame Blavatsky, as usual, held mental conversation with one of the Brothers, and then wandered a little about in the immediate neighbourhood of where we were sitting ---that is to say, within a radius of half-a-dozen to a dozen yards from our picnic cloth---I closely following, waiting to see what would happen. Then she marked a spot on the ground, and called to one of the gentlemen of the party to bring a knife to dig with. The place chosen was the edge of a little slope covered with thick weeds and grass and shrubby undergrowth. The gentleman with the knife...[Major Philip Henderson] tore up these in the first place with some difficulty, as the roots were tough and closely interlaced. Cutting then into the matted roots and earth with the knife, and pulling away the *debris* with his hands, he came at last, on the edge of something white, which turned out, as it was completely excavated, to be the required cup. A corresponding saucer was also found after a little more digging. Both objects were in among the roots which spread everywhere through the ground, so that it seemed as if the roots were growing round them. The cup and saucer both corresponded exactly, as regards their pattern, with those that had been brought to the picnic, and constituted a seventh cup and saucer when brought back to where we were to have breakfast....Afterwards, when we got home, my wife questioned our principal khitmutgar as to how many cups and saucers of that particular kind we possessed. In the progress of years, as the set was an old set, some had been broken, but the man at once said that nine teacups were left. When collected and counted that number was found to be right, without reckoning the excavated cup. That made ten, and as regards the pattern, it was one of a somewhat peculiar kind, bought a good many years previously in London, and which assuredly could never have been matched in Simla.

...If the phenomenon was not what it appeared to be---a most wonderful display of a power of which the modern scientific world has no comprehension whatever---it was, of course, an elaborate fraud. That supposition...will only bear to be talked of vaguely....The cup and saucer were assuredly dug up in the way I describe. If they were not deposited there by occult agency, they must have been buried there beforehand. Now, I have described the character of the ground from which they were dug up; assuredly that had been undisturbed for years by the character of the vegetation upon it. But it may be urged that from some other part of the sloping ground a sort of tunnel may have been excavated in the first instance through which the cup and saucer could have been thrust into the place where they were found. ...If the tunnel had been big enough for the purpose it would have left traces which were not perceptible on the ground---which were not even discoverable when the ground was searched shortly afterwards with a view to that hypothesis. But the truth is that the theory of previous burial is...untenable in view of the fact that the demand for the cup and saucer---of all the myriad things that might have been asked for---could never have been foreseen. It arose out of circumstances themselves the sport of the moment. If no extra person had joined us at the last moment the number of cups and saucers packed up by the servants would have been sufficient for our needs, and no attention would have been drawn to them. It was by the servants, without the knowledge of any guest, that the cups taken were chosen from others that might just as easily have been taken. Had the burial fraud been really perpetrated it would have been necessary to constrain us to choose the exact spot we did actually choose for the picnic with a view to the previous preparations, but the *exact* spot on which the ladies' jampans were deposited was chosen by myself in concert with...[Mr. Henderson], and it was within a few yards of this spot that the cup was found. Thus...who could be the agents employed to deposit the cup and saucer in the ground, and when did they perform the operation? Madame Blavatsky was under our roof the whole time from the previous evening when the picnic was determined on to the moment of starting. The one personal servant she had with her, a Bombay boy and a perfect stranger to Simla, was constantly about the house the previous evening, and from the first awakening of the household in the morning. ...Colonel Olcott...also a guest of ours at the time...was certainly with us all evening...and was also present at the start. To imagine that he spent the night in going four or five miles...through forest paths difficult to find, to bury a cup and saucer of a kind that we were not likely to take, in a place we were not likely to go to, in order that in the exceedingly remote contingency of its being required for the perpetration of a hoax it might be there, would certainly be a somewhat extravagant conjecture. Another consideration---the destination for which we were making can be approached by two roads from opposite ends of the upper horseshoe of hills on which Simla stands. It was open to us to select either path, and certainly neither Madame Blavatsky nor Colonel Olcott had any share in the selection of that actually taken. Had we taken the other, we should never have come to the spot where we actually picniced.

...[Mr. Henderson] had been a good deal with us during the week or two that had already elapsed since Madame Blavatsky's arrival. Like many of our friends, he had been greatly impressed with much he had seen in her presence. He had especially come to the conclusion that the Theosophical Society...was exerting a good influence with the natives...He had declared his intention of joining this Society as I had done myself. Now, when the cup and saucer were found most of us who were present,...[Mr. Henderson] among the number, were greatly impressed, and in the conversation that ensued the idea arose that...[Mr. Henderson] might formally become a member of the Society then and there....

The proposal that...[Mr. Henderson] should then and there formally join the Society was one with which he was quite ready to fall in. But some documents were required---a formal diploma, the gift of which to a new member should follow his initiation into certain little masonic forms of recognition adopted in the

Society. How could we get a diploma? Of course for the group then present a difficulty of this sort was merely another opportunity for the exercise of Madame's powers. Could she get a diploma brought to us by "magic"? After an occult conversation with the Brother who had then interested himself in our proceedings, Madame told us that the diploma would be forthcoming. She described the appearance it would present---a roll of paper wound round with an immense quantity of string, and then bound up in the leaves of a creeping plant. We should find it about in the wood where we were, and we could all look for it, but it would be...[Mr. Henderson], for whom it was intended, who would find it. Thus it fell out. We all searched about in the undergrowth or in the trees, wherever fancy prompted us to look, and it was ...[Henderson] who found the roll, done up as described.

We had had our breakfast by this time...[Mr. Henderson] was formally "initiated" a member of the society by Colonel Olcott, and after a time we shifted our quarters to a lower place in the wood where there was the little Thibetan temple, or rest-house....We amused ourselves by examining the little building inside and out, "bathing in the good magnetism," as Madame Blavatsky expressed it, and then, lying on the grass outside, it occurred to someone that we wanted more coffee. The servants were told to prepare some, but...they had used up all our water. The water to be found in the streams near Simla is not of a kind to be used for purposes of this sort, and for a picnic, clean filtered water is always taken out in bottles. It appears that all the bottles in our baskets had been exhausted. This report was promptly verified by the servants by the exhibition of the empty bottles. The only thing to be done was to send to a brewery, the nearest building, about a mile off, and ask for water. I wrote a pencil note and a coolie went off with the empty bottles. Time passed, and the coolie returned, to our great disgust, without the water. There had been no European left at the brewery that day (it was a Sunday) to receive the note, and the coolie had stupidly plodded back with the empty bottles under his arm, instead of asking about and finding someone able to supply the required water. At this time our party was a little dispersed....[Mr. Henderson] and one of the other gentlemen had wandered off. No one of the remainder of the party was expecting fresh phenomena, when Madame suddenly got up, went

125

over to the baskets, a dozen or twenty yards off, picked out a bottle---one of those, I believe, which had been brought back by the coolie empty---and came back to us holding it under the fold of her dress. Laughingly producing it it was found to be full of water. Just like a conjuring trick, will some one say? Just like, except for the conditions. For such a conjuring trick, the conjurer defines the thing to be done. In our case the want of water was as unforeseeable in the first instance as the want of the cup and saucer. The accident that left the brewery deserted by its Europeans, and the further accident that the coolie sent up for water should have been so...stupid...to come back without, because there happened to be no European to take my note, were accidents but for which the opportunity for obtaining the water by occult agency could not have arisen. And those accidents supervened on the fundamental accident, improbable in itself, that our servants should have sent us out insufficiently supplied. That any bottle of water could have been left unnoticed at the bottom of the baskets is a suggestion that I can hardly imagine any one present putting forward, for the servants had been found at fault with for not bringing enough; they had just before had the baskets completely emptied out, and we had not submitted to the situation till we had been fully satisfied that there really was no more water left. Furthermore, I tasted the water in the bottle Madame Blavatsky produced, and it was not water of the same kind as that which came from our own filters. It was an earthy-tasting water, unlike that of the modern Simla supply, but equally unlike, I may add, though in a different way, the offensive and discoloured water of the only stream flowing through those woods.

How was it brought?...The fact is there whether we can explain it or not. The rough, popular saying that you cannot argue the hind leg off a cow, embodies a sound reflection which our prudent sceptics in matters of the kind with which I am now dealing are too apt to overlook. You cannot argue away a fact by contending that by the light in your mind it ought to be something different from what it is. Still less can you argue away a mass of facts like those I am now recording by a series of extravagant and contradictory hypotheses about each in turn. What the determined disbeliever so often overlooks is that the scepticism which may show an acuteness of mind up to a certain point, reveals a deficient intelligence when adhered to in face of certain kinds of evidence....

...[Mr. Henderson], I should add here, afterwards changed his mind about the satisfactory character of the cup phenomenon, and said he thought it vitiated as a scientific proof by the interposition of the theory that the cup and saucer might have been thrust up into their places by means of a tunnel cut from a lower part of the bank. I have discussed that hypothesis already, and mention the fact of...[Mr. Henderson's] change of opinion, which, does not affect any of the circumstances I have narrated, merely to avoid the chance that readers...might think I was treating the change of opinion in question as something which it was worth while to disguise....

It was on the evening of the day of the cup phenomenon that there occurred an incident destined to become the subject of very wide discussion in all the Anglo-Indian papers. This was the celebrated "brooch incident." The facts were related at the time in a little statement drawn up for publication, and signed by the nine persons who witnessed it. This statement will be laid before the reader directly, but as the comments to which it gave rise showed that it was too meagre to convey a full and accurate idea of what occurred, I will describe the course of events a little more fully....

We, that is, my wife and myself with out guests, had gone up the hill to dine, in accordance with previous engagements, with Mr. and Mrs. Hume. We dined, a party of eleven, at a round table, and Madame Blavatsky, sitting next [to] our host, tired and out of spirits as it happened, was unusually silent. During the beginning of dinner she scarcely said a word, Mr. Hume conversing chiefly with the lady on his other hand....At Indian dinner-tables...[there are] little metal platewarmers with hot water before each guest, on which each plate served remains while in use. Such platewarmers were used on the evening I am describing, and over hers---in an interval during which plates had been removed---Madame Blavatsky was absently warming her hands. Now, the production of Madame Blavatsky's raps and bell-sounds we had noticed sometimes seemed easier and the effects better when her hands had been warmed in this way; so some one, seeing her engaged in warming them, asked her some question, hinting in an indirect way at phenomena....So, merely in mockery, when asked why she was warming her hands, she enjoined us all to warm our hands too and see what would happen. Some of the people present actually did so, a few joking words passing among them. Then Mrs. Hume raised a little laugh by holding up her hands and saying, "But I have warmed my hands, what next?"...It appears from what I learned afterwards that just at this moment, or immediately before,...[H.P.B.] suddenly perceived by those occult faculties of which mankind at large have no knowledge, that one of the Brothers was present "in astral body" invisible to the rest of us in the room. It was following his indications, therefore, that she acted in what followed; of course no one knew at the time that she had received any impulse in the matter external to herself. What took place as regards the surface of things was simply this: When Mrs. Hume said what I have set down above, and when the little laugh ensued, Madame Blavatsky put out her hand across the one person sitting between herself and Mrs. Hume and took one of that lady's hands, saying, "Well then, do you wish for anything in particular?"...I cannot repeat the precise sentences spoken, nor can I say now exactly what Mrs. Hume first replied before she quite understood the situation; but this was made clear in a very few minutes. Some of the other people present catching this first, explained, "Think of something you would like to have brought to you; anything you like not wanted for any mere worldly motives; is there anything you can think of that will be very difficult to get?" Remarks of this sort were the only kind that were made in the short interval that elapsed between the remark by Mrs. Hume about having warmed her hands and the indication by her of the thing she had thought of. She said then that she had thought of something that would do. What was it? An old brooch that her mother had given her long ago and that she had lost.

Now, when this brooch, which was ultimately recovered by occult agency, as the rest of my story will show, came to be talked about, people said:---"Of course Madame Blavatsky led up the conversation to the particular thing she had arranged beforehand to produce." I have described *all* the conversation which took place on this subject, before the brooch was named. There was no conversation about the brooch or any other thing of the kind whatever. Five minutes before the brooch was named, there had been no idea in the mind of any person present that any phenomenon in the nature of finding any lost article, or of any other kind, indeed, was going to be performed. Nor while Mrs. Hume was going over in her mind the things she might ask for, did she speak any word indicating the direction her thoughts were taking.

From the point of the story now reached the narrative published at the time tells it almost as fully as it need be told...so I reprint it here....

"On Sunday, the 3rd of October, at Mr. Hume's house at Simla, there were present at dinner Mr. and Mrs. Hume, Mr. and Mrs. Sinnett, Mrs. Gordon, Mr. F. Hogg, Captain P.J. Maitland, Mr. Beatson, Mr. Davidson, Colonel Olcott, and Madame Blavatsky. Most of the persons present having recently seen many remarkable occurrences in Madame Blavatsky's presence, conversation turned on occult phenomena, and in the course of this Madame Blavatsky asked Mrs. Hume if there was anything she particularly wished for. Mrs. Hume at first hesitated, but in a short time said there was something she would particularly like to have brought her, namely, a small article of jewellery that she formerly possessed, but had given away to a person who had allowed it to pass out of her possession. Madame Blavatsky then said if she would fix the image of the article in question very definitely on her mind, she, Madame Blavatsky, would endeavour to procure it. Mrs. Hume then said that she vividly remembered the article, and described it as an old-fashioned breast-brooch set round with pearls, with glass at the front, and the back made to contain hair. She then, on being asked, drew a rough sketch of the brooch. Madame Blavatsky then wrapped up a coin attached to her watch-chain in two cigarette papers, and put it in her dress, and said that she hoped the brooch might be obtained in the course of the evening. At the close of dinner she said to Mr. Hume that the paper in which the coin had been wrapped was gone. A little later, in the drawing-room, she said that the brooch would not be brought into the house, but that it must be looked for in the garden, and then as the party went out accompanying her, she said she had clairvoyantly seen the brooch fall into a star-shaped bed of flowers. Mr. Hume led the way to such a bed in a distant part of

129

the garden. A prolonged and careful search was made with lanterns, and eventually a small paper packet, consisting of two cigarette papers, was found amongst the leaves by Mrs. Sinnett. This being opened on the spot was found to contain a brooch exactly corresponding to the previous description, and which Mrs. Hume identified as that which she had originally lost. None of the party, except Mr. and Mrs. Hume, had ever seen or heard of the brooch. Mr. Hume had not thought of it for years. Mrs. Hume had never spoken of it to any one since she parted with it, nor had she, for long, even thought of it. She herself stated, after it was found, that it was only when Madame asked her whether there was anything she would like to have, that the remembrance of this brooch, the gift of her mother, flashed across her mind."

"Mrs. Hume is not a spiritualist, and up to the time of the occurrence described was no believer either in occult phenomena or in Madame Blavatsky's powers....The brooch is unquestionably the one which Mrs. Hume lost. Even supposing, which is practically impossible, that the article, lost months before Mrs. Hume ever heard of Madame Blavatsky, and bearing no letter or other indication of original ownership, could have passed in a natural way into Madame Blavatsky's possession, even then she could not possibly have foreseen that it would be asked for, and Mrs. Hume herself had not given it a thought for months."

"This narrative, read over to the party, is signed by:

A.O. Hume	Alice Gordon
M.A. Hume	P.J Maitland
Fred R. Hogg	Wm. Davidson
A.P. Sinnett	Stuart Beatson"
Patience Sinnett	

...When this narrative was published the nine persons above mentioned were assailed with torrents of ridicule....Floods of more or less imbecile criticism have been directed to show that the whole performance must have been a trick; and for many persons...it is now, no doubt, an established explanation that Mrs. Hume was adroitly led up to ask for the particular article produced, by a quantity of preliminary talk about a feat which Madame Blavatsky specially went to the house to perform. A further established opinion...is that the brooch which...Mrs. Hume gave to her daughter, and which her daughter lost, must have been got from that young lady about a year previously, when she passed through Bombay, where Madame Blavatsky was living, on her way to England. The young lady's testimony to the effect that she lost the brooch before she went to Bombay, or ever saw Madame Blavatsky, is a little feature of this hypothesis which its contented framers do not care to inquire into....

P.J. Maitland[40]
Oct. 13, 1880, Simla, India

On the evening of...[October 13th] I was sitting alone with Madame Blavatsky and Colonel Olcott in the drawing-room of Mr. Sinnett's house in Simla. After some conversation on various matters, Madame Blavatsky said she would like to try an experiment in a manner which had been suggested to her by Mr. Sinnett. She, therefore, took two cigarette papers from her pocket and marked on each of them a number of parallel lines in pencil. She then tore a piece off the end of each paper across the lines, and gave them to me. At that time Madame Blavatsky was sitting close to me, and I intently watched her proceedings, my eyes being not more than two feet from her hands. She declined to let me mark or tear the papers, alleging that if handled by others they would become imbued with their personal magnetism, which would counteract her own. However, the torn pieces were handed directly to me, and I could not observe any opportunity for the substitution of other papers by sleight of hand. The genuineness or otherwise of the phenomena afterwards presented appears to rest on this point. The torn-off pieces of the paper remained in my closed left hand until the conclusion of the experiment. Of the larger pieces Madame Blavatsky made two cigarettes, giving the first to me to hold while the other was being made up. I scrutinized this cigarette very attentively, in order to be able to recognize it afterwards. The cigarettes being finished, Madame Blavatsky stood up, and took them between her hands, which she rubbed together. After about twenty or thirty seconds, the grating noise of the paper, at first distinctly audible, ceased. She then said: "The current is passing round this end of the room, and I can only send them somewhere near here."...The theory is that a current of what can only be called magnetism, can be made to convey objects, previously dissipated by the same force, to any distance, and in spite of the intervention of any amount of matter....A moment afterwards she said one had fallen on the piano, the other near that bracket. As I sat on a sofa with my back to the wall the piano was opposite, and the bracket, supporting a few pieces of china, was to the right, between it and the door. Both were in full view across the rather narrow room. The top of the piano was covered with piles of music books and it was among these Madame Blavatsky thought a cigarette would be found. The books were removed, one by one, by myself, but without seeing anything. I then opened the piano, and found a cigarette on a narrow shelf inside it. This cigarette I took out and recognized as the one I had held in my hand. The other was found in a covered cup on the bracket. Both cigarettes were still damp where they had been moistened at the edges in the process of manufacture. I took the cigarettes to a table, without permitting them to be touched or even seen by Madame Blavatsky and Colonel Olcott. On being unrolled and smoothed out, the torn, jagged edges were found to fit exactly to the pieces that I had all this time retained in my hand. The pencil marks also corresponded. It would therefore appear that the papers were actually the same as those I had seen torn. Both the papers are still in my possession. It may be added that Colonel Olcott sat near me with his back to Madame Blavatsky during the experiment, and did not move till it was concluded.

A.P. Sinnett[41]
Oct. 15, 1880, Simla, India

One day...I asked Madame Blavatsky whether if I wrote a letter to one of the Brothers...she could get it delivered for me. I hardly thought this was probable, as I knew how very unapproachable the Brothers generally are; but as she said that at any rate she would try, I wrote a letter, addressing it "to the Unknown Brother," and gave it her to see if any result would ensue. It was a happy inspiration that induced me to do this, for out of that small beginning has arisen the most interesting correspondence in which I have ever been privileged to engage....

The idea I had specially in mind when I wrote the letter above referred to, was that of all test phenomena one could wish for, the best would be the production in our presence in India of a copy of the London *Times* of that day's date. With such a piece of evidence in my hand, I argued, I would undertake to convert everybody in Simla who was capable of linking two ideas together, to a belief in the possibility of obtaining by occult agency physical results which were beyond the control of ordinary science....

A day or two elapsed before I heard anything of the fate of my letter, but Madame Blavatsky then informed me that I was to have an answer....She had not been able at first to find a Brother willing to receive the communication. Those whom she first applied to declined to be troubled with the matter. At last her psychological telegraph brought her a favourable answer from one of the Brothers with whom she had not for some time been in communication. He would take the letter and reply to it.

...A day or two after I found one evening on my writing-table the first letter sent me by my new correspondent....He was a native of the Punjab who was attracted to occult studies from his earliest boyhood. He was sent to Europe whilst still a youth at the intervention of a relative---himself an occultist----to be educated in Western knowledge, and since then has been fully initiated in the greater knowledge of the East....

My correspondent is known to me as Koot Hoomi Lal Sing. This is his "Thibetan Mystic name"--occultists ...taking new names on initiation....*

The letter I received began...about the phenomenon I had

_____

*[The correspondence between Mr. Sinnett and the Master Koot Hoomi extended from October. 1880 to March-April. 1885. In 1923. Master K.H.'s letters (as well as the letters of Master Morya) were published in London under the title **The Mahatma Letters to A.P. Sinnett**.---Editor.]

proposed. "Precisely," Koot Hoomi wrote, "because the test of the London newspaper would close the mouths of the sceptics," it was inadmissible. "See it in what light you will, the world is yet in its first stage of disenthralment....hence unprepared. Very true we work by natural, not supernatural, means and laws. But, as on the one hand science would find itself unable, in its present state, to account for the wonders given in its name, and on the other the ignorant masses would still be left to view the phenomenon in the light of a miracle, every one who would thus be made a witness to the occurrence would be thrown off his balance, and the results would be deplorable. Believe me it would be so especially for yourself, who originated the idea, and for the devoted woman [H.P.B.] who so foolishly rushes into the wide, open door leading to notoriety. This door, though opened by so friendly a hand as yours, would prove very soon a trap---and a fatal one, indeed, for her. And such is not surely your object...."

A.P. Sinnett[42]
Oct. 20, 1880, Simla, India

Accompanied by our guests [Madame Blavatsky, Colonel Olcott, and Alice Gordon], we went to have lunch one day on the top of a neighbouring hill. The night before, I had had reason to think that my correspondent, Koot Hoomi, had been in what...I may call subjective communication with me* ....After discussing the subject in the morning, I found on the hall-table a note from Koot Hoomi, in which he promised to give me something on the hill which should be a token of his (astral) presence near me the previous night.

---

*[A.P. Sinnett writes: "I saw K.H. in astral form on the night of 19th of October, 1880---waking up for a moment but immediately afterwards being rendered unconscious again (in the body) and conscious out of the body in the adjacent dressing-room where I saw another of the Brothers afterwards identified with one called 'Serapis' by Olcott...." **The Mahatma Letters**, p. 10.---Editor.]

So long as one has not developed a perfect sense of justice, he should prefer to err rather on the side of mercy than commit the slightest act of injustice. lead. Couloumb is a medium & as such irresponsible for many things she may say or do. At the same time she is kind and charitable. One must know how to act towards her to make of her a very good friend. She has her own weaknesses but their bad effects can be minimised by exercising on her mind a moral influence by a friendly & kindly feeling. Her mediumistic nature is a help in this direction, if proper advantage be taken of the same. It is desirable therefore that she shall continue in charge of the household business, the Board of Control of course exercising a proper supervisory control & seeing in consultation with her, that no unnecessary expenditure is incurred. A good deal of reform is necessary and can be made rather with their help than the antagonism of them. Couloumb, Damodar would have told you this but his mind was purposely obscured, without his knowledge, to test your intuitions. Show this to lead. C. so that she may co-operate with you.

K. H

A Letter from Master Koot Hoomi

135

We went to our destination, camped down on the top of the hill, and were engaged on our lunch, when Madame Blavatsky said Koot Hoomi was asking where we would like to find the object he was going to send me....Up to this moment there had been no conversation in regard to the phenomenon I was expecting. The usual suggestion will, perhaps, be made that Madame Blavatsky "led up" to the choice I actually made. The fact of the matter was simply that in the midst of altogether other talk Madame Blavatsky pricked up her ears on hearing her occult voice---at once told me what was the question asked, and did not contribute to the selection made by one single remark on the subject. In fact, there was no general discussion, and it was by an absolutely spontaneous choice on my own that I said, after a little reflection, "inside that cushion," pointing to one against which one of the ladies present was leaning. I had no sooner uttered the words than my wife cried out, "Oh no, let it be inside mine," or words to that effect. I said, "Very well, inside my wife's cushion"; Madame Blavatsky asked the Mahatma by her own methods if that would do, and received an affirmative reply. My liberty of choice as regards the place where the object should be found was thus absolute and unfettered by conditions. The most natural choice for me to have made under the circumstances, and having regard to our previous experiences, would have been up some particular tree, or buried in a particular spot of the ground; but the inside of a sewn-up cushion, fortuitously chosen on the spur of a moment, struck me, as my eye happened to fall upon the cushion I mentioned first, as a particularly good place; and when I had started the idea of *a* cushion, my wife's amendment to the original proposal was really an improvement, for the particular cushion then selected had never been for a moment out of her own possession all the morning. It was her usual jampan cushion; she had been leaning against it all the way from home, and leaning against it still, as her jampan had been carried right up to the top of the hill, and she had continued to occupy it. The cushion itself was very firmly made of worsted work and velvet, and had been in our possession for years. It always remained, when we were at home, in the drawing-room, in a conspicuous corner of a certain sofa, whence, when my wife went out, it would be taken to her jampan and again brought in on her return.

When the cushion was agreed to, my wife was told to put it under her rug, and she did this with her own hands, inside her jampan. It may have been there about a minute, when Madame Blavatsky said we could set to work to cut it open. I did this with a penknife, and it was a work of some time, as the cushion was very securely sewn all round, and very strongly, so that it had to be cut open almost stitch by stitch, and no tearing was possible. When one side of the cover was completely ripped up, we found that the feathers of the cushion were enclosed in a separate inner case, also sewn round all the edges. There was nothing to be found between the inner cushion and the outer case; so we proceeded to rip up the inner cushion; and this done, my wife searched among the feathers.

The first thing she found was a little three-cornered note, addressed to me in the now familiar handwriting of my occult correspondent. It ran as follows:

"My 'Dear Brother,'

"This brooch No. 2---is placed in this very strange place simply to show to you how very easily a real phenomenon is produced and how still easier it is to suspect its genuineness....

"The difficulty you spoke of last night with respect to the interchange of our letters I will try to remove....An address will be sent to you which you can always use; unless, indeed, you really would prefer corresponding through---pillows....

Koot' Hoomi Lal Sing."

While I was reading this note, my wife discovered, by further search among the feathers, the brooch referred to, one of her own, a very old and very familiar brooch which she generally left on her dressing-table when it was not in use....The whole force and significance to us of the brooch thus returned, hinged on to my subjective impressions of the previous night. The reason for selecting the brooch as a thing to give us, dated no earlier than then. On the hypothesis, therefore,...that the cushion must have been got at by Madame Blavatsky, it must have been got at since I spoke of my impressions that morning, shortly after breakfast; but from the time of getting up that morning, Madame Blavatsky had hardly been out of our sight, and had been sitting with my wife in the drawing-room. She had been doing this, by the by, against the grain, for she had writing which she wanted to do in her own room, but she had been told by her voices to go and sit in the drawing-room with my wife that morning, and had done so, grumbling at the interruption of her work, and wholly unable to discern any motive for the order. The motive was afterwards clear enough, and had reference to the intended phenomenon. It was desirable that we should have no *arriere pensee* [mental suspicion] in our minds as to what Madame Blavatsky might possibly have been doing during the morning, in the event of the incident taking such a turn as to make that a factor in determining its genuineness. Of course, if the selection of the pillow could have been foreseen, it would have been unnecessary to victimize our "old Lady", as we generally called her. The presence of the famous pillow itself, with my wife all the morning in the drawing-room, would have been enough. But perfect liberty of choice was to be left to me in selecting a *cache* for the brooch; and the pillow can have been in nobody's mind, any more than in my own, beforehand....

Martandrao Babaji Nagnath[43]
April, 1881, Bombay, India

...I have had constant occasions to visit [Theosophical] headquarters at Breach Candy, Bombay. My connection with the Founders of the Society has been close, and my opportunity good for studying Theosophy. I am therefore inclined, for my satisfaction and for the information of students of Nature, to record here my experiences of certain phenomena, which came under my observation on several occasions in the presence of brother Theosophists and strangers. I have also had the rare privilege to see the so-called and generally unseen Brothers [Mahatmas] of the 1st section of the Theosophical Society....

In the month of April 1881, on one dark night, while talking in company with other Theosophists with Madame Blavatsky about 10 P.M. in the open verandah of the upper bungalow, a man, six feet in height, clad in a white robe, with a white...[turban] on the head, made his appearance on a sudden, walking towards us through the garden adjacent to the bungalow from a point---a precipice---where there is no path for any one to tread. Madame then rose up and told us to go inside the bungalow. So we went in, but we heard Madame and he talking for a minute with each other in an Eastern language unknown to us. Immediately after, we again went out into the verandah, as we were called, but the Brother had disappeared.

On the next occasion, when we were chatting in the above verandah as usual, another Brother, clothed in a white dress, was suddenly seen as if standing on a branch of a tree. We saw him then descending as though through the air, and standing on a corner edge of a thin wall. Madame then rose up from her seat and stood looking at him for about two minutes, and as if it seemed---talking inaudibly with him. Immediately after, in our presence, the figure of the man disappeared, but was afterwards seen again walking in the air through space, then right through the tree, and again disappearing....

Sorab J. Padshah[44]
July 15 and 16, 1881, Bombay, India

I have received two letters in all from the revered Mahatma [Koot Hoomi]....The first [letter] I received...on the evening of the 15th July, 1881. I copy the endorsement which I immediately made on the back of the envelope which contained the letter:--- "Received about ten minutes to ten---a little while after Madame [Blavatsky] had retired and Babula had left the lamp on the table. I had just written the first two lines of a poem I was composing on the Brothers, and was thinking how to finish the third, when I heard a sound as if a large butterfly had fallen on the table. It was this letter. It fell from some height. The doors of the room and shutters were closed. My gratitude and thanks. 15-7-81., S.J.P." After I had examined the room to see that there was no trickery in the affair, and satisfying myself that none was possible, I fell on my knees and uttered some words to myself mentally. The following morning I saw Madame Blavatsky in her study. After some conversation she told me she was satisfied that I was devoted to the [Theosophical] cause, for the Master had watched me and she proceeded to relate all that had happened in my room *after* I had received the letter, startling me at the same time *by reciting word for word my unspoken thought*....

A.P. Sinnett[45]
July---Aug., 1881, Bombay and then later on the road to Simla

During [July]...1881 I returned to India from a visit to England, and on landing at Bombay spent a few days with Mme. Blavatsky at the headquarters of the Theosophical Society, then established at Breach Candy, in a bungalow called the Crow's Nest, perched up on a little eminence above the road. It had been unoccupied for some time I heard, discredited by a reputation for snakes and ghosts, neither of which encumbrances greatly alarmed the new tenants. The building was divided into two portions,--- the lower given over to the Society's service and to Colonel Olcott's Spartan accommodation; the upper part, reached by a covered stairway, corresponding to the slope of the hill, to Mme. Blavatsky and the office work of the *Theosophist*. There was also a spare room in this upper portion, all the rooms of which were on one level, and opening on to a broad covered-in verandah, which constituted Mme. Blavatsky's sitting, eating, and reception room all in one. Opening out of it at the further end she had a small writing-room....The covered verandah was all day long and up to late hours in the evening visited by an ebb and flow of native guests, admiring Theosophists who came to pay their respects to Madame....She would generally be up at an early hour writing at her Russian articles or translations, or at her endless letters she sent off in all directions in the interest of the Society, or at articles for the *Theosophist*; then during the day she would spend a large part of her time talking with native visitors in her verandah room, or...getting back to her work with wild protests against the constant interruption she was subject to, and in the same breath calling for her faithful "Babula", her servant, in a voice that rang all over the house, and sending for some one or another of the visitors she knew to be waiting about below and wanting to see her. Then in the midst of some fiery argument with a pundit about a point of modern Hindoo belief that she might protest against as inconsistent with the real meaning of the Vedas, or a passionate remonstrance with one of her aides of the *Theosophist* about something done amiss that would for the time overspread the whole sky of her imagination with a thundercloud, she would perhaps suddenly "hear the voice they did not hear," ---the astral call of her distant Master or of one of the other "Brothers"...and forgetting everything else in an instant she would hurry off to the seclusion of any room where she could be alone for a few moments, and hear whatever message or orders she had to receive.

She never wanted to go to bed when night came. She would sit on smoking cigarettes and talking---talking with a tireless energy that was wonderful to watch---on Eastern philosophy of any sort, on the mistakes of theological writers, on questions raised (but not settled) in "Isis", or, with just as much intensity and excitement, on some wretched matter connected with the administration of the Society, or some foolish sarcasm levelled against herself and the attributes imputed to her in one of the local newspapers....

She joined me at Allahabad a few [weeks] after my return to India in 1881, and went up to Simla with me to be the guest for the remainder of that season of Mr. A.O. Hume. She was far from well at the time, and the latter part of the journey---a trying one for the most robust passenger---was an ordeal that brought out the peculiar characteristics of her excitable temper in an amusing way...;for the "tongas" in which the eight hours' drive up the mountain roads from Kalka at the foot of the hills to the elevated sanatorium [Simla] is accomplished, are not luxurious conveyances. They are low two-wheeled carts hung on a crank axle, so that the foot-boards are only about a foot above the road, with seats for four persons, including the driver, two and two back to back--- just accommodation enough in each for one passenger with his portmanteau (equivalent, if he has one with him, to a passenger), and a servant. We had two tongas between us, putting our servants with some of the luggage in one, while Mme. Blavatsky

141

and I occupied the back seat of the other with a portmanteau on the seat beside the driver....A tonga...gets over the ground rapidly, and the ponies, frequently changed, trot or canter up all but the steepest gradients. The traveller is jolted frightfully, but he is not likely to be capsized, though even that happens sometimes, for the mountain roads are very rough, and the ponies apt to be troublesome....The animals are attached to the vehicle by a strong crossbar resting in sockets on saddles they carry for the purpose, and though on this system ponies and cart are as firmly united as a bunch of keys by its steel ring, still they are no less loosely linked together, and a nervous passenger is liable to be disturbed by the extraordinary positions into which they get during any little disagreement between the team and the driver. One such disagreement arose soon after our start on the journey..., and Madame's impassioned anathemas directed against the whole service of the tonga dak and the civilisation of which it formed a part, ought not, I remember thinking at the time, to have had their comicality wasted upon an audience of one. Then as the day and the weary drive wore on, Madame's indignation at the annoyance of the situation only waxed more vehemently. ...Especially...incensed whenever the driver sounded his ear-piercing horn close behind us...she would break off whatever she was talking about to launch invectives at this unfortunate "trumpet"....

John Smith[46]
Jan. 31, 1882, Bombay, India

On the evening of 31st January, when the daily batch of letters was being opened, one was found to contain some red writing different from the body of the letter. Col. Olcott then took two unopened letters and asked Madame Blavatsky if she could perceive similar writing in them. Putting them to her forehead, she said one contained the word "carelessly" and the other something about Col. Olcott and a branch at Cawnpore. I then examined these letters and found the envelopes sound. I

142

opened them and saw the words mentioned. One letter was from Meerut, one from Cawnpore, and one from Hyderabad. Next day...Col. Olcott remarked that if I were to get any letters while here, there might be some of the same writing in them. I replied that there would be *"no chance* of that, as no one would write to me." Madame Blavatsky then, looking fixedly for a little, said: "I see a Brother here. He asks if you would like some such token as that we have been speaking of"....I replied that I would be much gratified. She rose from the table and told us to follow her. Taking my hand, she led me along the verandah, stopping and looking about at some points till we reached the door of my bedroom. She then desired me to enter alone and look round the room to see if there was anything unusual, and to close the other doors. I did so, and was satisfied the room was in its usual condition. She then desired us to sit down, and in doing so took my hands in both of hers. In a few seconds a letter fell at my feet. It seemed to me to appear first a little above the level of my head. On opening the envelope I found a sheet of note-paper, headed with a Government stamp of the North-Western Provinces and Oudh, and the following words written with red pencil, *in exactly the same handwriting as that in the letters of the previous evening:* "NO CHANCE of writing to you inside your letters, but I can write *direct*. Work for us in Australia, and we will not prove ungrateful, but will prove to you our actual existence, and thank you." A fair review of the circumstances excludes, in my opinion, any theory of fraud.

William Eglinton[47]
March 22---24, 1882, "S.S. Vega," Indian Ocean, west of Ceylon

...It was not until the last week of my stay in India that I began to receive evidence of the existence of the beings designated the "Himalayan Brothers." One night I was sitting with Colonel and Mrs. Gordon at their house in Howrah [a suburb of Calcutta] when my [spirit] guide, "Ernest," came and informed us that he had been in communication with certain of the

143

Brotherhood. This aroused my curiosity, because I knew I could depend upon a statement so made, but nothing more happened to convince me until I was homeward bound on board the S.S. Vega....

On the 22nd March, 1882, I was at sea, having left [Colombo,] Ceylon about 6 p.m. the same day. I occupied a deck cabin forward under the bridge....About ten o'clock I was in this cabin undressing preparatory to sleeping on deck, my back being to the open door. On turning round to make my exit, I found the entrance barred by what I took, at first sight, to be a khitmaghur or native butler. Thinking he had come on some message, I waited for him to speak, but as he did not do so, and deeming his manner insolent from his not having demanded entrance, and not paying the deference usual to Europeans, I angrily told him, in Hindustani, to go away; whereupon he stepped into the cabin, grasped me by the right hand, and gave me the grip of a Master Mason before I had sufficiently recovered from my astonishment. I requested him to tell me why he had intruded upon me and to state his business. Speaking in perfect English he deliberately informed me he was "Koot Hoomi Lal Singh," and I was at the moment so profoundly impressed with his general appearance, his knowledge of Freemasonry, and the statement that he really was the person, mystic, or Adept of whom I had heard so much during my residence in India, that without hesitation I accepted him as such. We then entered into conversation of some length, of no particular importance to anyone but myself, but it proved to me that he was intimately acquainted with both the Spiritualistic and Theosophical movements, as well as with friends of mine in India. He was in every respect an intelligent man, perfectly formed, and in nowise differing, in outward semblance at any rate, from the thousands of natives one sees in the East. Nor was it hallucination, for I was in full possession of all my faculties; and that it was not a subjective vision is proved by the grasp of the hand, and the very evident materiality of the figure. Some little thing...attracted my attention from him for a moment, for I was criticising him keenly, and when I turned my head again---he was gone! Two steps took me to the open door, where I had the advantage of scanning both the fore and aft decks, but I could observe no one in the act of retreating, although no living being could have in the time escaped from the range of my vision. The next day I searched the ship, even going down into the shaft-tunnel to find a person in appearance like the man I had seen on the previous night, but without obtaining the slightest clue to his identity, although my mind was then dwelling upon the possibility of a man having been commissioned to come on board at Ceylon on purpose to deceive me. But the more I reflected the more difficult I found it to accept such a theory, and two days after I penned the hasty and enthusiastic letter which appears in "The Occult World"...."Koot Hoomi" had promised to take a letter to Mrs. Gordon, at Howrah, if I would write one when on board....I thought my having seen the "figure" a good opportunity to convey the news in the manner suggested, and I accordingly wrote, asserting my complete belief that the person I had seen was none other than the Great Master....After I had written the letter..., I went on to the deck, and knowing a certain lady to be on board who was much interested in psychical matters, I read her the letter, and invited her to mark the envelope as a little test between ourselves and those at the "other end of the line." This she did. On my return to the smoking-room I told some of my fellow-passengers what I had done, whereupon a gentleman who claimed to be a Theosophist and acquainted with Madame Blavatsky, asked why, if I could send a letter, could he not do the same? I saw no objection to his doing so, and he at once wrote a short note....I opened the envelope and enclosed both letters in another, and again sought the lady to re-mark it. She was not on the deck at the time, so I returned to the smoking-room, and on mentioning the matter to those assembled, one said "Put a cross upon it"; another remarked "Add a second"; and a third person wished that three crosses should be put. As each one spoke I added the cross, until there were three in all, and I then took the envelope, placed it in my...locked writing-case, and put it (the case) upon a shelf in my cabin. I opened it at intervals to see whether the envelope was still there, and I last saw it, to the best of my recollection, about four p.m., for when I looked again just before dinner it was gone. ...The same night, in the presence of Colonel Olcott and Colonel and Mrs. Gordon, an envelope marked with three crosses and stated to contain my letter, was dropped from the ceiling of the bedroom I had occupied when at Howrah....I have not been able to verify whether the letter was in my writing, but I imagine it to be mine as the letter was similar in terms to the one written by me---in addition to which Mrs. Gordon was intimately acquainted with my writing.

Mrs. Alice Gordon[48]
March 24, 1882, Howrah, a suburb of Calcutta, India

...Colonel Olcott...told me that he had had an intimation in the night from his *Chohan* (teacher) that K.H. had been to the *Vega* and seen Eglinton. This was at about eight o'clock on Thursday morning, the 23rd [of March]. A few hours later a telegram, dated at Bombay...9 minutes past 9 P.M. on Wednesday evening, came to me from Madame Blavatsky, to this effect: "K.H. just gone to *Vega*."...It corroborated, as will be seen, the message of the previous night to Colonel Olcott. We then felt hopeful of getting the letter by occult means from Mr. Eglinton. A telegram [from Mme. Blavatsky] later on Thursday asked us to fix a time for a sitting, so we named 9 o'clock Madras time, on Friday 24th. At this hour we three---Colonel Olcott, Colonel Gordon, and myself---sat in the room which had been occupied by Mr. Eglinton. We had a good light, and sat with our chairs placed to form a triangle, of which the apex was to the north. In a few minutes Colonel Olcott saw outside the open window the two "Brothers"...and told us so; he saw them pass to another window, the glass doors of which were closed. He saw one of them point his hand towards the air over my head, and I felt something at the same moment fall straight down from above on to my shoulder, and saw it fall at my feet in the direction *towards* the two gentlemen. I knew it would be the letter, but for the moment I was so anxious to see the "Brothers" that I did not pick up what had fallen. Colonel Gordon and Colonel Olcott both saw and heard the letter fall. Colonel Olcott had turned his head from the window for a moment to see what the "Brother" was pointing at, and so noticed the letter falling from a point about two feet from the ceiling. When he

146

looked again the two "Brothers" had vanished.*

There is no verandah outside, and the window is several feet from the ground.

I now turned and picked up what had fallen on me, and found a letter in Mr. Eglinton's handwriting, dated on the *Vega* the 24th....We opened the letter carefully, by slitting up one side, as we saw that someone had made on the flap in pencil three Latin crosses, and so we kept them intact for identification. The letter is as follows:

"My Dear Mrs. Gordon,---At last your hour of triumph has come! After the many battles we have had at the breakfast-table regarding K.H.'s existence, and my stubborn scepticism as to the wonderful powers possessed by the 'Brothers,' I have been forced to a *complete belief* in their being living distinct persons....I am not allowed to tell you all I know, but K.H. *appeared* to me in person two days ago, and what he told me dumbfounded me...."

Henry S. Olcott[49]
June 19, 1882, Baroda, India

In June, 1882, H.P.B. and I accepted an invitation to visit Baroda, the flourishing capital of H.H. the Gaikwar. Judge Gadgil...and other high officials...met us at the station, and took us to a bungalow adjoining the new and splendid palace....We had... many visitors...[and] our reception-room...[was] crowded with inquirers day and evening....

I had been out to see the Gaikwar, and on my return found [Mr.] Kirtane and [Judge] Gadgil standing at the threshold of

------

*[Colonel Olcott in his diary for March 24, 1882 pens the following: "At 9 the Gordons and I sat together. Morya and K.H. appeared at the windows. and notes from Eglinton (from on board the **Vega**). Morya. K.H. and H.P.B.. tied together. dropped through the air on Mrs. Gordon's shoulder. A stupendous phenomenon all round. E. says in his note that he is sending it off by the Brothers to H.P.B. after showing it to a fellow passenger. Mrs. Boughton. and having her mark the envelope."---Editor.]

H.P.B.'s open door, while she was in the middle of the room with her back towards us. Our two friends told me not to step inside, as Madame B. was doing a phenomenon and had just turned them out on the verandah where I found them. The next minute she came towards us, and, taking a sheet of paper from the table, told the gentleman to mark it for identification. Receiving it back, she said: "Now turn me in the direction of his residence." They did so. She then laid the paper between her palms (held horizontally), remained quiet a moment, then held it towards us and went and sat down. Cries of amazement broke from the two...on seeing on the just before clean sheet of paper, a letter addressed to me in the handwriting and bearing the signature of the then British Resident at that Court. It was a most peculiar, small caligraphy, and the signature more like a tiny tangle of twine than a man's name. They then told me the story. It seems that they were asking H.P.B. to explain the scientific rationale of the process of precipitating upon paper, cloth, or any other surface, a picture or writing, then invisible to the onlooker, and without the help of ink, paints, pencils, or other mechanical agents. She told them...that inasmuch as the images of all objects and incidents are stored in the Astral Light, it did not require that she should have seen the person or known the writing, the image of which she wished to precipitate; she had only to be put on the trace and could find and see them for herself and then objectivate them. They urgently begged her to do the thing for them. "Well, then," she finally said, "tell me the name of some man or woman most unfriendly to the Theosophical Society, one whom neither Olcott nor I could have ever known." At once, they mentioned Mr....the British Resident, who held us and our Society in especial hatred, who never missed the chance of saying unkind things of us, and who had prevented the Gaikwar from inviting H.P.B. and myself to his enthronement, as he had otherwise intended, on the suggestion of Judge Gadgil. They thought this a poser. That it was not, the sequel proved. I thought they would explode with laughter when they read the contents of the note. It was addressed to "My dear Colonel Olcott," begged my pardon for the malicious things he had said against us...and said he wished to become a member of the Theosophical Society: it was signed "Yours sincerely" and with his name. She had never seen a line of the gentleman's writing nor his signature, never met him in the flesh, and the note was precipitated on that sheet of paper, held between her hands, as she stood in the middle of the room, in broad daylight, with us three witnesses looking on....

R. Casava Pillay[50]

Sept., 1882, Bombay, India and then later on a train near Allahabad, India

...[On the night of September 13th] while retiring to bed in Colonel Olcott's room [at Theosophical Headquarters, Bombay], with all doors closed, and in a good lamp light, I was startled to see, coming as it were out of the solid wall, the form of my most revered Guru Deva [Koot Hoomi] and I prostrated myself before him and he blessed me and, in good Telugu, desired me to come and see him beyond the Himalayas. A conversation of a private character then followed in the Telugu language. He disappeared in the same way as he had appeared....

...[Later] while I was travelling by Railway between the Allahabad and Mogal Sarai stations, a letter fell in the compartment of the Railway carriage in which I was sitting. I was alone in the compartment and the carriage was in motion. I had wished that Mahatma K.H. should give me instructions regarding a certain matter about which I was then thinking, and when I opened the letter I found that my thoughts had been answered, and that the letter was in the handwriting of Mahatma K.H., whose writing I know so well....[*]

---

[*][Later on this journey to Darjeeling when near Sikkim. Mr. Pillay reported that he saw the Mahatmas Koot Hoomi and Morya in their physical bodies. See **Report of the Result of an Investigation into the Charges Against Madame Blavatsky**. etc.. Madras. 1885. p. 89.---Editor.]

149

S. Ramaswamier[51]

Sept.---Oct., 1882, Darjeeling, India and later in Sikkim

My health having been disturbed by official work and worry, I applied for leave on medical certificate and it was duly granted. One day in September last, while I was reading in my room [in the town of Tinnevelly, southern India], I was ordered by the audible voice of my blessed Guru, [Morya]..., to leave all and proceed immediately to Bombay, whence I had to go in search of Madame Blavatsky wherever I could find her and follow her wherever she went. Without losing a moment, I closed up all my affairs and left the station. Arrived at Bombay, I found Madame Blavatsky gone....Really not knowing whither I had best go, I took a through ticket to Calcutta; but, on reaching Allahabad, I heard the same well-known voice directing me to go to Berhampore....

On the 23rd [of September]..., I was brought by Nobin Babu from Calcutta to Chandernagore where I found Madame Blavatsky, ready to start...with the train....When the train arrived, she got into the carriage....I myself had barely the time to jump...into the last carriage...

The first days of her arrival [at Darjeeling] Madame Blavatsky was living at the house of a Bengalee gentleman, a Theosophist; was refusing to see any one....To all our importunities we could get only this answer from her: that we had no business, *to stick to and follow her*, that she did not want us, and that she had no right to disturb the Mahatmas with all sorts of questions....

In despair, *I determined, come what might*, to cross the frontier which is about a dozen miles from here, and find the Mahatmas, or---DIE. Without breathing a word of my intentions to anyone, one morning, namely, October 5, I set out in search of the Mahatma....The same afternoon I reached the banks of the Rungit River, which forms the boundary between the British and Sikkim territories....

That whole afternoon I travelled on foot, penetrating further and further into the heart of the Sikkim Territory, along a narrow foot-path....I travelled before dusk...not less than twenty or twenty-five miles. Throughout, I saw nothing but impenetrable jungles and forests on all sides of me, relieved at very long intervals by solitary huts belonging to the mountain population.

At dusk I began to search around me for a place to rest in at night....After a sound sleep, undisturbed by any dream, I woke and found it was just dawning....

I lost no time....When it became quite light, I wended my way on through hills and dales....

It was, I think, between eight and nine A.M. and I was following the road to the town of Sikkim whence, I was assured by the people I met on the road, I could cross over to Tibet easily in my pilgrim's garb....when I suddenly saw a solitary horseman galloping towards me from the opposite direction. From his tall stature and the expert way he managed the animal, I thought he was some military officer of the Sikkim Raja. Now, I thought, am I caught....But as he approached me, he reined the steed. I looked at and recognized him instantly....I was in the...presence of...my own revered *Guru*....The very same instant saw me prostrated on the ground at his feet. I arose at his command and, leisurely looking into his face, I forgot myself entirely....I knew not what to say: joy and reverence tied my tongue....I was at last face to face with "the Mahatma of the Himavat" and he was no myth....It was no night dream; it is between nine and ten o'clock of the forenoon. There is the sun shining and silently witnessing the scene from above....He speaks to me in accents of kindness and gentleness....Nor was it until a few moments later that I was drawn to utter a few words, encouraged by his gentle tone and speech. ...Never have I seen a countenance so handsome, a stature so tall and so majestic....He wears a short black beard, and long black hair hanging down to his breast....He wore a yellow mantle lined with fur, and, on his head...a yellow Tibetan felt cap....

When the first moments of rapture and surprise were over and I calmly comprehended the situation, I had a long talk with him. He told me to go no further, for I would come to grief. He said I should wait patiently if I wanted to become an accepted *Chela*....

The Mahatma, I found, speaks very little English---or at least it so seemed to me----and *spoke to me in my mother-tongue---Tamil*....I asked the blessed Mahatma whether I could tell what I saw and heard to others. He replied in the affirmative....He was pleased to say when I offered my farewell *namaskarams* (prostration) that he approached the British Territory to see...[H.P.B.].

151

Before he left me, two more men came on horseback, his attendants I suppose, probably *Chelas*, for they were dressed...like himself, with long hair streaming down their backs. They followed the Mahatma, as he left, at a gentle trot.

For over an hour I stood gazing at the place that he had just quitted, and then, I slowly retraced my steps....I had eaten nothing since the day before, and...I was too weak to walk further. My whole body was aching in every limb. At a little distance I saw petty traders with country ponies, taking burden. I hired one of these animals. In the afternoon I came to the Rungit River and crossed it. A bath in its cool waters renovated me. I purchased some fruit in the only bazaar there and ate them heartily. I took another horse immediately and reached Darjeeling late in the evening.

I could neither eat, nor sit, nor stand. Every part of my body was aching. My absence had seemingly alarmed Madame Blavatsky. She scolded me for my rash and mad attempt to try to go to Tibet, after this fashion....I recounted all that had happened to me....

A.P. Sinnett[52]
Dec., 1882---March, 1883, Adyar, Madras, India

On the 16th of December 1882, a farewell entertainment was given by native friends to the founders of the Theosophical Society, just before their departure from Bombay to take up their residence at Adyar, Madras, where a house had been purchased for the Society by subscription....

The house at Madras...was a great improvement on the cramped and comfortless bungalow at Bombay....Madras is a station of enormous extent, straggling along seven or eight miles of the sea-shore. Adyar is a suburb at the southern extremity, through which a small stream finds its way to the sea, and just before it reaches the beach spreads out into a broad shallow expanse of water, beside which the Theosophical house stands in extensive grounds. Here we found Mme. Blavatsky and her heterogeneous household comfortably installed when my wife and I visited her on our way home [to England] from India in March 1883....The upper rooms of the house were her own private domain....[One of these rooms] just built...was destined by Madame to be her "occult room," her own specially private sanctum....She had especially devoted herself to decorating a certain hanging cupboard to be kept exclusively sacred to the communications passing between...[the] Masters and herself, and...bestowed upon it the designation...the Shrine. Here she had established some simple occult treasures,...two small portraits she possessed of the Mahatmas, and some other trifles....The purpose of this special receptacle was of course perfectly intelligible to everyone familiar with the theory of occult phenomena....A place kept pure of all "magnetism" but that connected with the work of integrating and disintegrating letters, would facilitate the process, and the "shrine" was used....for the transaction of business between the Masters and the chelas....

William Q. Judge[53]
Dec., 1882, Adyar, Madras, India

...The Headquarters of the [Theosophical] Society in India... are...in a suburb of Madras called Adyar, so named from the Adyar river...[that] runs past the building, washes, indeed, the base of the wide piazza at the back. The building is made of brick and plaster, painted white, except some rooms erected upon the roof....The grounds comprise about twenty-one acres, bounded in front of the house, by a large grove of trees, on the back by the river, and on one side by the main road leading out of Madras....There are numerous mango trees in the compound between the house and the main road, and these afford a grateful shade, their spreading branches covering great distances around their trunks....

...[The picture on the next page gives] the point of view...as you come up the drive from the entrance gate. It shows the front of the building as it faces the compound....The *porte cochere*...is seen

153

in perspective. It gave a grand air to the front. The whole building was…of a white color, appearing at a distance like a marble structure, but in reality is constructed of brick plastered white, as is very usual in India.…

Just appearing over the ornamental balustrade which encloses the roof is the front of H.P.B.'s own room, which led into the shrine-room shown in the second picture [on the next page]. Her room was an addition to the building, and in a way served to join the two towers which rise at the back corners at either end. The stairs of the tower illustrated [on the next page] were the means of communication with her apartment, although the other tower had also a stairway.…

That part of the compound extending from the entrance gate on the highway was full of mango trees, and through them the driveway brought you up to the house and under the *port cochere.* Alighting there, a short flight of steps took you up to the entrance hall, where the floor was of black and white marble. Here there were two tables, sofas, and some chairs, and on the floor many a night slept Damodar K. Mavalankar..., together with several others....

Part of the end of the building on the side near the main road is given [in the second illustration above]. It is a continuation of the corner seen in the first cut. The tower finished the river end of the building, and the river itself can be just seen at the back. On the top is the occult room with the extension or verandah. The roof of the "occult room" was slanting and tiled in red, the plaster being tinted yellow. In this was the shrine. It was entered from the other side, and, being a few feet lower than the rooms used by H.P.B., a short flight of steps ran down into it. In the tower is a winding brick stairway....

Damodar's room was in this tower at the top as you came up the narrow stairs....A corridor, as you might call it, ran across the back of H.P.B.'s rooms from tower to tower, open to the river and giving a view of the little island opposite and the long...bridge which carries the highway across the river....

155

This [third illustration] is reproduced from a photograph of the back of the building taken from the little island....It shows the other tower, companion to that in which was Damodar's room. The lower floor under the roof was the back part of the middle of the building, and was occupied by *The Theosophist* magazine. Trees and shrubs almost hid the view. A plastered embankment ran for a short distance along this side so as to protect the foundations.

These pictures give a very correct idea of the house when H.P.B. lived in it....

Damodar K. Mavalankar[54]
April, 1883, Adyar, Madras, India

Last night was a memorable one....Narasimhulu Chetty and myself were seated on a chair quite close to Mme. Blavatsky's bed, fanning her and talking together, so as gradually to induce sleep in her....Suddenly Mme. B. gave a start and exclaimed, "I feel HIM [Mahatma Morya]." She enjoined on us strictly not to leave our places, nor to get excited, but remain where we were…and be perfectly calm and quiet. Suddenly she asked for our hands and the right hand of each of us was held by her. Hardly two minutes had elapsed…and we saw HIM coming from the screen-door of Mme. B.'s bed-room and approaching her…His manner of walking was so gentle that not a footstep, not the slightest sound, was audible; nor did HE *appear* to move, by His gestures. It was only the change of position that made us see HE had come nearer and nearer. HE stood exactly opposite Mme. B.---*not quite an arm's length from us.* We were on this side of the bed; HE on the other. You know I have seen HIM often enough to enable me to recognize HIM at once…HIS usual long white coat, the peculiar Pagri [turban]…, long black hair flowing over the broad shoulders, and long beard---were as usual striking and picturesque. HE was standing near a door the shutters of which were open. Through these the lamp-light, and through the windows which were all open, the moonlight, were full upon HIM. And we being in the dark, *i.e.,* having no light on our eyes---we being turned against the windows through which the moonlight came---we could see distinctly and clearly. HE held out and put HIS hands twice over Mme. B.'s head. She then stretched out her hand *which passed through* HIS---a fact proving that what we saw was a *Mayavi Rupa* [apparitional body], although so vivid and clear as to give one the impression of a material physical body. She immediately took the letter from HIS hands. It crumpled, as it were, and made a sound. He then waved HIS hands toward us, walked a few steps, *inaudibly and imperceptibly as before,* and disappeared!… Mme. B. then handed the letter to me, as it was intended for me.…Never shall I forget last night's experience; so clear, so vivid and tangible it was!

Henry S. Olcott[55]
Aug.---Sept., 1883, Ootacamund, India

...I went...to Ootacamund to rejoin my dear colleague H.P.B., at the hospitable home of Major-General and Mrs. Morgan. The railway ends...at the foot of the Nilgiri Hills, and the traveller proceeds up the well-metalled mountain road in a horse tonga, or two-wheeled mail cart drawn by a pair of galloping ponies. The ride up is simply charming, and passing through forests, by banks of flowers, and past swarms of lovely painted butterflies, the air grows cooler and cooler, until midway one is obliged to stop at the rest-house and change one's light tropical costume for heavy woollens and even put on a topcoat. At almost every turn in the winding road splendid panoramas of scenery present themselves to view, while one finds Ootacamund a lovely village of picturesque houses, spreading over the foot-slopes of the grassy and forest-covered adjacent hills, the roads lined with roses, the enclosures joyous with lilies, verbenas, heliotropes....At the toll-gate on the Coonoor Road, H.P.B. met me in company with our dear Mrs. Morgan, Mrs. Batchelor and others of the family, the General being absent from home temporarily. My old "chum" seemed really overjoyed to see me and rattled on in her affectionate way like one who greets a long-absent relative. She was looking well; the champagne-like mountain air set her blood to leaping through her body, and she was in the highest spirits about the civilities that were being shown her by some of the high officials and their families. She worked off some of her excitement that same night by keeping me up until 2 a.m. to read proofs and correct her MS! What an amusing creature she was when in the mood; how she would make a roomful of people hang on her lips as she would tell stories of her travels and adventures in search of the wonder-workers in Magic and Sorcery; and their eyes open in amazement when she would, now and again, ring some astral bell, or make some raps, or do some other minor phenomenon!....

...Our joint desk work went on and the hard labor was diversified with her bright talk and frequent grumblings at the cold. Certainly with cause, for the mercury marked forty degrees more of cold than we feel on the plains, the houses are heated with wood fires in open fire-places, the winds blow in gusts down

158

the open throated chimneys, filling the rooms with smoke and dusting one's paper and books with fine ashes. H.P.B. wrote in a fur coat, with a woollen shawl on her head and her feet wrapped in a travelling rug---a funny sight. Part of her work was the taking from dictation, from her invisible teacher, of the "Replies to an English F.T.S."....That she was taking down from dictation was fully apparent to one who was familiar with her ways....

...[On September 16th] we two left beautiful Ooty in tongas for Coimbatore [and then on to Pondicherry]....We left Pondicherry for Madras, September 23rd, and got home that afternoon, rejoiced to see the dear place again....

William T. Brown[56]
Sept.---Dec., 1883, India

I...sailed [from England] for India upon the 25th of August.... [On September 29th] I reached the Head Quarters of the Theosophical Society at Adyar, Madras, and was welcomed by Madame Blavatsky, the learned Author, Editor, and Corresponding Secretary. I was established in a bungalow, situated beautifully by the river side, and felt at home in a very short time.

In regard to Madame Blavatsky...never before have I met anyone who evidences such vast and varied learning, nor one who is more large hearted....

One evening, shortly after my arrival at Adyar, some letters were being sent by Chelas to their Masters, and I was permitted to enter the "Occult Room" and see the process going on. The letters were put into an almirah, in a richly ornamented recess called by some "the Shrine." There were some seven of us then present, four of whom were Chelas. These gentlemen, after placing their letters as aforesaid, offered up incense and prostrated themselves according to the Hindu manner of evincing devotion and respect. In about two minutes Madame, who was standing by my side in an attentive attitude, received a psychic telegram, and indicated that the answers had come to hand. The almirah was accordingly opened, and, in place of the letters "posted," others were there, enclosed in Tibetan envelopes and written on Tibetan paper. D[amodar] K. M[avalankar] (a Chela of the Master Koot Hoomi) discovered something more than was expected, and exclaimed, "Here is a letter from my Master to Mr. Brown." I then received from his hands a memorandum, written with blue pencil....

I need scarcely say how honoured and grateful I felt at being noticed by the Mahatma, whose teachings had so strongly impressed me....I rose, and going forward, reverently said, "Mahatma Koot Hoomi! I sincerely thank you." Immediately all those present in the room said, "There's a bell---did you hear it?" I said that I had *not*....Madame B. then expressed regret that I had not observed the Master's acknowledgement of having heard my words, and said "Oh Master! let us hear the bell, once more, if it be possible." We stood silently for about a minute and then there was distinctly heard by all of us (myself included) the sound of a bell....

After a railway journey [from Madras] of six and twenty hours, I joined Colonel Olcott at the town of Sholapur....I shall confine myself to speaking of a few of the places on our journey [to Northern India] which call for special mention....

...We arrived at Jubbulpore...[and] on the evening of the lecture, Colonel Olcott, Damodar, several fellows of the Society and I drove together to the place of the public meeting. There the Colonel delivered an impressive address to a large audience....During the lecture some three or four majestic figures had attracted my particular attention. They did not seem to hang upon the lips of the speaker, as did the rest of the audience, but remained calmly dignified, occasionally only exchanging pleasant glances....I was not surprised to learn afterwards that some Mahatmas had been present at the meeting in astral form....

And now let us proceed to Allahabad....At this ancient city a most stirring lecture was delivered....Here I saw and *recognised* the Mahatma [Koot Hoomi].

Although I was enabled to look at him but for a minute, I knew that it was he and recognised him by his portrait, which I had scrutinized some weeks before. On our return to the bungalow at which we were being entertained my impression was corroborated by Damodar, who volunteered the remark that his

160

master had been there. Damodar, I may remark, had not been at the lecture....

...The place to which our narrative really next pertains is the City of Lahore. Here, as elsewhere, Colonel Olcott delivered stirring addresses to large audiences; but Lahore has a special interest, because there we saw, in his own physical body, Mahatma Koot Hoomi himself.

On the afternoon of the 19th November, I saw the Master in broad daylight, and recognised him, and on the morning of the 20th he came to my tent, and said "Now you see me before you in the flesh; look and assure yourself that it is I," and left a letter of instructions and silk handkerchief....

This letter is as usual written seemingly with blue pencil, is in the same handwriting as that in which is written communications received at Madras, and has been identified by about a dozen persons as bearing the caligraphy of Mahatma Koot Hoomi. The letter was to the effect that I had first seen him in visions, then in his astral form, then in body at a distance, and that finally I now saw him in his own physical body, so close to me as to enable me to give to my countrymen the assurance that I was from personal knowledge as sure of the existence of the Mahatmas as I was of my own....

On the evening of the 21st, after the lecture was over, Colonel Olcott, Damodar and I were sitting outside the *shamiana*, (pavilion or pandal), when we were visited by Djual Khool, the Master's head Chela,...who informed us that the Master was about to come. The Master then came near to us, gave instructions to Damodar, and walked away.

On leaving Lahore the next place visited was Jammu, the winter residence of His Highness the Maharajah of Cashmere....

...We enjoyed a most inspiring holiday in full view of the Himalayan Mountains.

At Jammu I had another opportunity of seeing Mahatma Koot Hoomi in *propria persona*. One evening I went to the end of the "compound," (private enclosure) and there I found the Master awaiting my approach. I saluted in European fashion, and came, hat in hand, to within a few yards of the place on which he was standing....After a minute or so he marched away, the noise of his foot-steps on the gravel being markedly audible....

Henry S. Olcott[57]
Nov. 20, 1883, Lahore, India

My camp was thronged with visitors during the three days of our stay, and I gave two lectures under the largest *shamiana* to multitudes, with great pots of fire standing along the sides to modify the biting November cold....

I was sleeping in my tent, the night of the 19th, when I rushed back towards external consciousness on feeling a hand laid on me. The camp being on the open plain, and beyond the protection of the Lahore Police, my first...instinct was to protect myself from some possible religious fanatical assassin, so I clutched the stranger by the upper arms, and asked him in Hindustani who he was and what he wanted. It was all done in an instant, and I held the man tight, as would one who might be attacked the next moment and have to defend his life. But the next instant a kind, sweet voice said: "Do you not know me? Do you not remember me?" It was the voice of the Master K.H. A swift revulsion of feeling came over me, I relaxed my hold on his arms, joined my palms in reverential salutation, and wanted to jump out of bed to show him respect. But his hand and voice stayed me, and after a few sentences had been exchanged, he took my left hand in his, gathered the fingers of his right into the palm, and stood quiet beside my cot, from which I could see his divinely benignant face by the light of the lamp that burned on a packing-case at his back. Presently I felt some soft substance forming in my hand, and the next minute the Master laid his kind hand on my forehead, uttered a blessing, and left my half of the large tent to visit Mr. W.T. Brown, who slept in the other half behind a canvas screen that divided the tent into two rooms. When I had time to pay attention to myself, I found myself holding in my left hand a folded paper enwrapped in a silken cloth. To go to the lamp, open and read it, was naturally my first impulse. I found it to be a letter of private counsel....On hearing an exclamation from...[Brown's] side of the screen, I went in there and he showed me a silk-wrapped letter of like appearance to mine though of different contents, which he said had been given him much as mine had been to me, and which we read together....[*]

The next evening, after the visits to Mr. Brown and myself, we two and Damodar sat in my tent, at 10 o'clock, waiting for an expected visit from Master K.H. The camp was quiet, the rest of our party dispersed through the city of Lahore. We sat on chairs at the back of the tent so as not to be observed from the camp: the moon was in its last quarter and had not risen. After some waiting we heard and saw a tall Hindu approaching from the side of the open plain. He came to within a few yards of us and beckoned Damodar to come to him, which he did. He told him

---

[*][In Colonel Olcott's diary for Tuesday, November 20. 1883. the entry reads: "1.55 a.m. Koot Hoomi came in body to my tent. Woke me suddenly out of sleep, pressed a note (wrapped in silk) into my left hand, and laid his hand upon my head. He then passed into Brown's compartment and integrated another note in his hand (Brown's). He spoke to me...."---Editor.]

that the Master would appear within a few minutes, and that he had some business with Damodar. It was a pupil of Master K.H. Presently we saw the latter coming from the same direction, pass his pupil---who had withdrawn to a little distance---and stop in front of our group, now standing and saluting in the Indian fashion, some yards away. Brown and I kept our places, and Damodar went and conversed for a few minutes with the Teacher, after which he returned to us and the king-like visitor walked away. I heard his footsteps on the ground....Before retiring, when I was writing my Diary, the pupil lifted the *portiere*, beckoned to me, and pointed to the figure of his Master, waiting for me out on the plain in the starlight. I went to him, we walked off to a safe place at some distance where intruders need not be expected, and then for about a half-hour he told me what I had to know....There were no miracles done at the interview...just two men talking together, a meeting, and a parting when the talk was over....

Damodar K. Mavalankar[58]
Nov.---Dec., 1883, Lahore, India and later at Jammu, Kashmir

While on my tour [of northern India] with Col. Olcott,...we reached Lahore, where we expected to meet in body my... MASTER [Koot Hoomi]. *There I was visited by him in body, for three nights consecutively*...and, in one case, even went...outside the house...meeting...[the Master] in the compound...re-entering the house with him, offering him a seat and then holding a long converse...Moreover, HIM whom I saw in person at Lahore was the same I had seen in astral form at the Headquarters of the Theosophical Society, and the same again whom I, in my visions and trances, had seen at His house, thousands of miles off, to reach which in my astral Ego, I was permitted, owing, of course, to His direct help and protection. In those instances with my psychic powers hardly developed yet, I had always seen Him as a rather hazy form, although His features were perfectly distinct and their remembrance was profoundly graven on my soul's eye and memory; while now at Lahore, Jammu, and elsewhere, the impression was utterly different. In former cases, when making *Pranam* (salutation) my hands passed through his form, while on the latter occasions they met solid garments and flesh....I shall not here dwell upon the fact of His having been corporeally seen by both Col. Olcott and Mr. Brown separately, for two nights at Lahore....[Later at] Jammu...I had the good fortune of being sent for, and permitted to visit a Sacred *Ashram* where I remained for a few days in the blessed company of several of the much doubted MAHATMAS of Himavat and Their disciples. There I met not only my beloved Gurudeva [Koot Hoomi] and Col. Olcott's Master [Morya], but several others of the Fraternity, including One of the Highest....Thus, I saw my beloved Guru not only as a *living* man, but actually as a young one in comparison with some other Sadhus of the blessed company, only far kinder, and not above a merry remark and conversation at times. Thus on the second day of my arrival, after the meal hour I was permitted to hold an intercourse for over an hour with my Master. Asked by Him smilingly, what it was that made me look at Him so perplexedly, I asked in my turn:---"How is it, MASTER, that some of the members of our Society have taken into their heads a notion that you were 'an elderly man,' and that they have even seen you clairvoyantly looking an old man passed sixty?" To which he pleasantly smiled and said, that this latest misconception was due to the reports of a certain...pupil of a Vedantic Swami....As to his being perceived clairvoyantly as an "elderly man," that could never be, he added, as *real* clairvoyance could lead no one into such mistaken notions; and then he kindly reprimanded me for giving any importance to the age of a Guru, adding that appearances were often false, etc., and explaining other points....

Bhavani Shankar[59]
Jan., 1884, Jubbulpore, India

In the month of January 1884, I was at Jubbulpore...with Brother Nivaran Chandra Mookerjee, who was then the Secretary of the...[local] Theosophical Society [branch]. One night, while I was with him, I was...[talking] to some twenty-seven members of that Branch...and they were listening to me with great attention. On a sudden, there was deathlike silence for some time. I then felt the influence of Madame Blavatsky's Venerated Master [Morya], and it was so strong that I could not bear it. The current of electricity generated by an electro-magnetic battery is nothing when compared with that current generated by the trained Will of an Adept. When a Mahatma means to show himself to a Chela, he sends off a current of electricity to the Chela indicating his approach. It was this influence which I felt at that time. A few minutes after, the Mahatma [Morya]...was actually present in the room where the meeting of the members was held and was seen by me and Bro. Nivaran while some of the members only felt the influence. All the members would have seen him much more vividly, had it not been for the fact that he did not materialize himself much more objectively. I have seen the same Mahatma...several times in his [astral] double during my travels in the North [of India]. Not only have I seen Madame B.'s Master in his double but also my Venerated Guru Deva "K.H." I have also seen...Master [K.H.] in HIS PHYSICAL BODY....

Franz Hartmann[60]
Dec., 1883----Feb., 1884, Adyar, Madras, India, and then later at Bombay, India

On the evening of December 4, 1883, I arrived at Madras...and was kindly received by Mr. G. Muttuswami Chettyar, who conducted me to his carriage and away we went towards Adyar ...situated in a suburb of the city of Madras, about six miles from the landing place of the steamer....

166

It was dark when we arrived, and the object of my dreams, who was said to possess the key that was to open before me the sanctuary of Occultism, was sitting in the lighted entrance hall, surrounded by a few friends. Poor and yet envied Madame Blavatsky, the sphinx of the nineteenth century; at once a sage and a woman. She upon whose brow shines the serene tranquility of a god, and who a minute afterwards will fly into a stew because the coffee is too hot....Her appearance neither surprised nor disappointed me. A stately figure, dressed in a loose flowing robe, she might as well have sat for the picture of one of the saints, and her kind and cordial manner at once gained my confidence.

Before retiring to rest I expressed a desire to see the pictures of the Mahatmas, these mysterious beings, superior to man, of whom I had heard so much, and I was taken upstairs, to see the "shrine" in which those pictures were kept. The pictures represented two men with oriental features and in corresponding dress. The expression of their faces was mild and yet serene....

A week or two after my arrival at Adyar, seeing that several others, strangers as well as members of our Society, occasionally received letters from the Masters either by having them dropped from the air, thrust at them through solid walls or sent to them through the "Shrine;" I concluded to try whether I might not be equally fortunate.

Accordingly I wrote the following lines:---

"*Revered Master*! The undersigned offers you his services. He desires that you would kindly examine his mental capacity and if desirable give him further instructions.

Respectfully yours, etc."

I copy this letter verbatim, so that the reader may not think me so silly as to trouble the "Adepts" of the Himalayas with my little private affairs. I am in the habit of keeping my own counsel, and there was not one in India or outside of San Francisco that knew anything about..[my] affairs. I gave my letter to Col. Olcott and he put it into the Shrine.

A couple of days afterwards, I reasoned with myself about this matter, and thought that, if the Masters should find it worth the while to say anything to me, they would undoubtedly do so without my asking, and I therefore begged Colonel Olcott to return me my letter. Colonel Olcott would have done so, but my letter had disappeared in a mysterious manner. In its place I received another, the contents of which showed not only a complete knowledge of some of the events of my past life, but it also went into details about...very private business....It will be perceived, that this letter was not given as a "test,"---although it was a "test" to me,---but to give me some information and advise (which afterwards proved very useful to me).

...[Later] I [saw]...Mahatma [Morya] in his astral form....He appeared to me, accompanied by the astral forms of two Chelas....His presence left an exhilarating and elevating influence, which did not fade away until several days after....

The impaired health of Madame Blavatsky had rendered it desirable that she should have a change of air, and the physicians which were consulted, advised her to go to Europe, where Col. Olcott was called on account of some official business....Madame Blavatsky therefore resolved to accompany Col. Olcott, and having received an urgent invitation to visit the Thakore Sahib of Wadhwan and our friend Hurrisinghjee, she made up her mind to visit them before embarking at Bombay....

Two days before Madame Blavatsky left, February 5th, 1884,...I went unasked up to her room to speak with her in regard to Society matters....

After this conversation the thought came in my mind to ask her opinion in regard to a certain subject of which I had been thinking. Madame Blavatsky advised me to apply to the Master [Morya] himself, to ask him mentally, and that the Master himself would answer my question. A few seconds later she said she felt his presence, and that she saw him writing. I must say that I too felt his influence and seemed to see his face, but of course this circumstance will carry conviction to no one but myself.

Just then another lady came in, to my great annoyance, and expressed her wish to have a pair of pincers, which was needed for some purpose, and remembering that I had such a pair of pincers in the drawer of my writing desk, I went downstairs into my room to get them. I opened the drawer, saw the pincers and a few other things in there, but no vestige of any letter, as I had removed my papers the day before to another place. I took the pincers and was about to close the drawer, when---there lay *in the drawer* a great envelope, addressed to me in the well-known handwriting of the Master and...with the seal bearing his initials in Thibetan characters. On opening it, I found a long, very kind letter treating of the identical questions, about which I had just been talking with Madame Blavatsky, besides giving a detailed and satisfactory answer to the very question which had so perplexed my mind, and a satisfactory explanation of certain matters, which for some time had been foremost in my mind, but of which I had said nothing at all.

Moreover, there was in the same envelope a photograph, cabinet-size, of the Master's face, with a dedication to me at the back.

Now, if I know anything at all, I know that my drawer contained no such letter, when I opened it, and that there was nobody visible in my room at that time. The letter, giving a detailed answer to my question, must have been written, sealed and put into the drawer in less than four minutes, while it took exactly forty minutes to copy it the next day; and finally, it treated a very difficult problem in such an elaborate and yet concise manner, that only an intelligence of the highest order could have done the same....

On the seventh of February, Madame Blavatsky,... Mohini Chatterji and myself in company of Madame Coulomb left Adyar [for Bombay]...On the way we...stopped at the residence of the Thakore Sahib of Wadhwan....

I left Wadhwan on the 15th of February in company with Madame Blavatsky and...Mohini....We were on our way to Bombay. ...A few hours before we started, Madame Blavatsky had read...[an] article [of mine], corrected a few words and returned it to me. I read it carefully to see what corrections she had made, and whether I might not myself make some changes. I only found a few words corrected, folded the paper, put it in my pocket-book, deposited the pocket-book in my satchel, locked the same, entered the car [of the train] and put the satchel on my seat, where it never left me and never was out of my sight, until the event which I am about to describe occurred. We travelled on, Madame Blavatsky being in the same car. Towards evening Madame Blavatsky requested me to let her see the article again. I took it out of my satchel, unfolding the paper before handing it to her, and as I did so, imagine my surprise to find on it four long lines written on a space which was blank before, in the well-known handwriting of our Master, and in a different kind of ink than that used by Madame Blavatsky. How that writing could have been done in my satchel and during the shaking of the car, I do not pretend to explain.

Another incident occurred [at Bombay] when I was alone by myself. On the morning of the 20th of February, I received a curious Tibetan medal from our Master through Madame Blavatsky. I then accompanied her on board the steamer on which she was to sail for Europe. On my return to the shore I went into a native jewellery shop and bought a locket to deposit my medal, but could not find a chain long enough for my purpose. I then returned to my room, and paced the floor, studying what to do in regard to the chain. I finally came to the conclusion that I would buy a rose-coloured silk ribbon. But where to get it, being a stranger in Bombay; that was the question. My pacing the floor brought me again in front of the open window, and there right before me on the floor lay exactly the very silk ribbon, brand new, and just the one I wanted....

———————————

Chapter 5

A VISIT TO EUROPE

RETURN TO INDIA

1884-1885

William Q. Judge[61]
March---April, 1884, Paris

I have been here now since the 25th [of March], and H.P.B.
arrived on the 28th. Crowds of people have been here constantly,
and, therefore, I have not been able to have any long private
conversations with her. I have had some talks with her....

...I am ordered by the Masters to stop here and help Madame
in writing the *Secret Doctrine*....

After the first hurry was over here, I said I had to go to India
at once. Olcott thought I had better stay with H.P.B., and so did
she. But I said that all the orders I had were to go to India, and
without further ones I was going, and so she said I was probably
right; and then it was decided that I would wait here until
...[Olcott] could get me a steamer in London....All was thus arranged
definitely. But the next morning, as I was sitting in the bedroom
with Mohini, in which he and I slept, and after we had been there
about an hour after coffee, Olcott came from his room, which was
at the other end of the hall, and called me out, and told me
privately that the Master [Morya] had been then to his room and
had told him that I was not to go yet to India, but to stay and
help H.P.B. on the *Secret Doctrine*....

So then, here I am for how long or short I do not know, and I am to make suggestions and write upon the work....

...[One day] for about an hour the Masters sent messages through H.P.B. in the parlor, questions to me to try her. Each message made a distinct effect upon my skin before she repeated it....

On the fifth [of April] Olcott and Mohini left for London, leaving Madame and me here, as she had been ordered not to go to London. We went through the day and in the evening were sitting together in the parlor alone, talking very seriously of old times.

As we sat there I felt the old signal of a message from the Master and saw that she was listening. She said: "Judge, the Master asks me to try and guess what would be the most extraordinary thing he could order now?" I said, "That Mrs....[Anna Kingsford]* should be made the President of the London Lodge." Try again. "That H.P.B. should be ordered to go to London." That was right and he ordered her to take the 7:45 express, giving the exact hours it would arrive at the different stations and in London---all of which was correct, and we had no time table in the house. She disliked the order awfully and I can tell you, knowing her ill health and present unwieldy size, it was an awful journey. But last night I took her to the station and saw her go off in the train with a little hand bag. There is some peculiar object in this, as she might have gone with Olcott....

All the time she confessed her inability to see why she was ordered, as the Londoners will think it done for effect after her refusal to go then, and Olcott, when he sees her, will certainly feel like swearing. But the London situation is serious, and maybe they intend to work some phenomena there for some good end. So I am left here alone in this house....

---

*
[Mrs. Anna Bonus Kingsford (1846-1888). English mystical writer and doctor of medicine, was the author (in collaboration with Edward Maitland) of **The Perfect Way, or The Finding of Christ** (1882), an esoteric interpretation of Christianity.---Editor.]

A.P. Sinnett[62]
April 7, 1884, London

In the beginning of April, 1884, Colonel Olcott arrived in London, Madame Blavatsky remaining behind at Nice and Paris. Colonel Olcott was accompanied by a young Indian Theosophist, Mohini...who became for a time a very conspicuous person in theosophical activities. He was introduced to us as a chela of the Master K.H. and was made cordially welcome.

The 7th [of April] was the occasion of the important meeting of the...[London Lodge of the Theosophical Society]....It was held at Mr. Finch's Chambers in Lincoln's Inn, and its purpose was the election of a new President...Many of the members wished me to become President but I...shrank from allowing...a personal rivalry between Mrs. [Anna] Kingsford and myself in regard to the Presidency. So I had arranged to nominate Mr. Finch for the office.

...I duly proposed Mr. Finch and I think that Mr. Maitland went through the form of proposing Mrs. Kingsford. Anyhow, when the show of hands was taken (Colonel Olcott being in the chair) the vote was practically unanimous in favour of Mr. Finch....

The excitements of the meeting on the 7th were by no means confined to the circumstances of the election. After this was over I was in the midst of an address to the meeting when a disturbance at the door interrupted me and in a moment the whole room was aware that Madame Blavatsky had arrived. I broke off and went to meet her. A little crowd collected round her...[and she] was formally introduced to the meeting.

The minutes relating to this meeting...go on as follows:

She "intimated that if any members would communicate to her any inquiries they might like to make in regard to the meaning of obscure passages in 'Isis Unveiled' such inquiries would receive attention and would be made the subject of explanations in the new version of that book which under the title 'The Secret Doctrine' she proposed to bring out."

173

"Mr. [F.W.H.] Myers[*] inquired whether documentary evidence could be obtained from India for the service of the Psychic Research Society in reference to cases in which the astral apparitions of the Mahatmas had been seen at various times and places."

"Madame Blavatsky called on Mr. Mohini to give some information on the subject and Mr. Mohini described the recent appearance of the astral figure of one of the Mahatmas at the Headquarters of the Society at Madras...."

After the meeting was over Madame Blavatsky returned with us to Ladbroke Gardens, where she stayed with us for a week....and then...returned to Paris.

Archibald Keightley[63]
April 7, 1884, London

The first time I ever saw Mme. Blavatsky was in 1884, shortly after I had joined the Theosophical Society. A meeting had been called and was being held in the chambers of a member in Lincoln's Inn. The reason for the meeting lay in differences of opinion between Mr. Sinnett on the one hand and Mrs. Kingsford and Mr. Maitland on the other. Colonel Olcott was in the chair and endeavored to adjust the differences of opinion, but without success. By him were seated the contending parties, Mohini M. Chatterji and one or two others, facing a long narrow room which was nearly filled with members of the Society. The dispute proceeded, waxing warm, and the room steadily filled, the seat next to me being occupied by a stout lady who had just arrived,

[*][Frederic W. H. Myers (1843-1901). English essayist. minor poet. and psychical researcher. He joined the Theosophical Society in 1883. He was on the S.P.R. Committee to investigate Madame Blavatsky's psychic phenomena and her claim to be in contact with the Mahatmas. He became convinced that she was a fraud and resigned his membership in the T.S. His major work was published in 2 volumes in 1903 under the title **Human Personality and Its Survival of Bodily Death**.---Editor.]

very much out of breath. At the moment some one at the head of the room alluded to some action of Mme. Blavatsky's, to which the stout lady gave confirmation in the words "That's so." At this point the meeting broke up in confusion, everybody ran...to the stout lady, while Mohini arrived at her feet on his knees. Finally she was taken up to the end of the room where the "high gods" had been enthroned, exclaiming and protesting in several tongues in the same sentence and the meeting tried to continue. However, it had to adjourn itself....Next day I was presented to Mme. Blavatsky, who was my stout neighbor of the meeting. Her arrival was totally unexpected and her departure from Paris was, she told me long afterwards, only arranged "under orders" half an hour before she left. She arrived at Charing Cross [Railway Station] without knowing the place of meeting, only knowing she had to attend it. "I followed my occult nose," she told me, and by this means got from the station to Lincoln's Inn and found her way to the rooms on foot. Her arrival was singularly opportune, for it broke up a meeting which declined to be peaceful, in spite of all the oil which Colonel Olcott was pouring on its troubled waters....

William Q. Judge[64]
May, 1884, Enghien, France

In the spring of 1884, H.P.B. was staying in Rue Notre Dame des Champs, Paris....She was...engaged daily with her writing, save for an occasional drive or visit. Many visitors from all classes were constantly calling, and among the rest came the Countess d'Adhemar, who at once professed a profound admiration for H.P.B. and invited her to come to the Chateau owned by the Count at Enghien, just outside the city, including in her invitation myself and Mohini Chatterji....The invitation was accepted and we all went out to Enghien, where H.P.B. was given two large rooms downstairs and the others slept in rooms on the upper floors. Every convenience was given to our beloved friend, and there she continued her writing....

175

A lake was at one side of the house and extensive grounds covered with fine timber hid the building from the road, part being a well kept fruit and flower garden....Wide stairs led up to the hall; on one side, which we may call the road front, was the billiard room, the high window of which opened upon the leaden roof of the porch; the dining room looked out at the back over the edge of the lake, and the drawing room opened from it on the other side at right angles to the side of the billiard room. This drawing room had windows opening on three sides, so that both garden and lake could be seen from it. In it was the grand piano at the end and side opposite the dining room door, and between the two side windows was a marble slab holding ornaments; between the windows, at the end near the piano, was the fireplace, and at that corner was one of the windows giving a view of the lake. Every evening it was the custom to spend some time in the drawing room in conversation, and there, as well as in the dining room, took place some phenomena which indeed were no more interesting than the words of H.P.B., whether those were witty, grave or gay. Very often Countess d'Adhemar's sister played the piano in a manner to delight even H.P.B., who was no mean judge. I remember well one melody, just then brought out in the world of Paris, which pleased her immensely, so that she often asked for its repetition. It was one suggestive of high aspiration and grandiose conceptions of nature. Many lively discussions with the Count on one side and H.P.B. on the other had taken place there, and often in the very midst of these she would suddenly turn to Mohini and myself, who were sitting listening, to repeat to us the very thoughts then passing in our brains.

...One day at dinner, when there were present the Count and Countess, their son Raoul, H.P.B., Mohini, the Countess' sister, myself, and one other, the strong and never-to-be-forgotten perfume which intimate friends of H.P.B. knew so well as often accompanying phenomena or coming of itself, floated round and round the table, plainly perceptible to several and not perceived either before or afterwards. Of course many sceptics will see nothing in this, but the writer and others well know that this of itself is a phenomenon, and that the perfume has been sent for many miles through the air as a message from H.P.B. or from those hidden persons who often aided in phenomena or in teachings. At this dinner, or at some other during the visit, we had all just come in from the flower garden. I had plucked a small rosebud and placed it upon the edge of the tumbler between myself and the Countess' sister who was on my left, H.P.B. being seated on my right. This lady began to talk of phenomena, wondering if H.P.B. could do as related of the Indian yogis. I replied that she could if she would, but did not ask her, and added that she could make even that small rosebud bloom at once. Just then H.P.B. stretched her hand out towards the rose, not touching it, and said nothing, continuing at once her conversation and the dinner. We watched the bud until the end of the meal and saw that it grew in that space of time much larger and bloomed out into a rose nearly full grown.

On another evening after we had been in the drawing room for some time, sitting without lights, the moon shining over the lake and all nature being hushed, H.P.B. fell into a thoughtful state. Shortly she rose and stood at the corner window looking over the water, and in a moment a flash of soft light shot into the room and she quietly smiled....

[Concerning this evening] the Countess d'Adhemar writes...:

"H.P.B. seemed wrapped in thought, when suddenly she rose from her chair, advanced to the open window, and raising her arm with a commanding gesture, faint music was heard in the distance, which advancing nearer and nearer broke into lovely strains and filled the drawing room where we were all sitting...."

This astral music was very plain to us all, and the Count especially remarked upon its beauty and the faintness of it as it sank away into the unknown distance. The whole house was full of these bell sounds at night when I was awake very late and others had retired. They were like signals going and coming to H.P.B.'s room downstairs. And on more than one occasion as we walked in the grounds under the magnificent trees, have they shot past us, sometimes audible to all and again only heard by one or two....

...I took away with me a book which could not be finished there, and just before leaving France went out to Enghien to return it. There I met the Countess d'Adhemar, who said that the peculiar and unmistakable perfume of which I spoke above had come in the house after we had left. It was one evening about two days after H.P.B.'s departure and the d'Adhemars had some friends for dinner. After dinner they all went into the drawing room and soon noticed the perfume. It came, as they said to me, in rushes, and at once they began to hunt it out in the room, coming at last to the marble slab described, where, from one spot in the stone, they found the perfume rushing out in volumes. Such was the quantity of it that, as the Countess said to me, they were compelled to open the windows, since the odour was overpowering in large masses. In returning to Paris I told H.P.B. of this and she only said: "It sometimes happens."

Vera P. de Zhelihovsky[65]
May, 1884, Paris

We were four of us at *Rue Notre Dame des Champs*, 46,---Mme. N.A. de Fadeyev, Mme. Blavatsky, the eminent Russian author, M. Solovyov, and I,---having tea at the same table of the little drawing-room, about 11 P.M.....Mme. B. was asked to narrate something of her "Master," and how she had acquired from him her occult talents. While telling us many things....she offered us to see a portrait of his in a gold medallion she wore on a chain round her neck, and opened it. It is a perfectly flat locket, *made to contain but one miniature, and no more.* It passed from hand to hand, and we all saw the handsome Hindoo face in it, painted in India.

Suddenly our little party felt disturbed by something *very strange*, a sensation which it is hardly possible to describe. It was as though the air had suddenly changed, was rarefied---the atmosphere became positively oppressive, and we three could hardly breathe.....H.P.B. covered her eyes with her hand, and whispered:---

"...I feel that something is going to happen.....Some phenomenon...He is preparing to do it...."

She meant by "He," her *guru-master*, whom she considers so powerful....

178

At that moment Mr. Solovyov fixed his eyes on a corner of the room, saying that he saw something like a ball of fire, of oval form, looking like a radiant golden and bluish egg....He had hardly pronounced these words when we heard, coming from the farthest end of the corridor, a long melodious harp---a melody far fuller and more definite than any of the musical sounds we had previously heard.

Once more the clear notes were repeated, and then died away. Silence reigned again in the rooms.

I left my seat and went into the passage hall, brightly lighted with a lamp. Useless to say that all was quiet, and that it was empty. When I returned to the drawing-room I found H.P. Blavatsky sitting quietly as before at the table between Mme. de Fadeyev and Mr. Solovyov. At the same time, I saw as distinctly as can be, the figure of a man, grayish, yet quite clear form, standing near my sister, and who, upon my looking at him, receded from her, paled, and disappeared in the opposite wall. This man---or, perhaps, his astral form---was of a slight build, and of middle size, wrapped in a kind of mantle, and with a white turban on his head. The vision did not last more than a few seconds, but I had all the time to examine it, and to tell every one what I distinctly saw, though, as soon as it had disappeared, I felt terribly frightened and nervous....Hardly come back to our senses, we were startled with another wonder, this one palpable and objective. H.P.B. suddenly opened her locket, and instead of one portrait of a Master, there were two---her own facing his!

Firmly set inside the other half of the *medallion*, under its oval glass, there was her own miniature likeness, which she had just casually mentioned.

The locket was once more carefully examined by the three witnesses, and passed from hand to hand.

This was not the *finale*. A quarter of an hour later the magical locket, *from which we three literally never took off our eyes for one second*, was opened at the desire of one of us---*her portrait was no more to be found in it*....It had disappeared.

179

Francesca Arundale[66]
June 30---Aug. 16, 1884, London

H.P.B. returned to London...June [30th]...taking up her abode with us at No. 77 Elgin Crescent, Notting Hill....

The few months of the summer of 1884 which she passed in our house in Elgin Crescent were marked by events of a curious and exceptional character, all alike bearing witness to the fact that the personality called Madame Blavatsky was different in most characteristics from those around, and crowds of visitors of all classes testified to the interest she invoked.

It was her custom while with us to devote the earlier part of the day to writing; she usually began at seven o'clock, but often earlier, and it was very rarely indeed that when I went into her room at about eight o'clock in the morning I did not find her already at her desk, at which she continued with a slight interval for lunch till about three or four o'clock in the afternoon. Then...the reception time began, and from early afternoon to late evening, one constant succession of visitors arrived. The old lady sitting in her armchair in the same drawing-room, which was barely large enough for the influx of guests, would be the centre of an enquiring circle. Many, of course, drawn by the fame of her great powers, merely came from curiosity....

Mohini M. Chatterji accompanied Madame Blavatsky, and Colonel Olcott was with us from time to time as his tours allowed. There was also a very important member of the Indian contingent, namely Babula, H.P.B.'s servant; in his picturesque turban and white dress, he created quite a little sensation...; and on the afternoons when tea was served and H.P.B.'s Russian samovar glistened and shone on the table, and Babula bore cups of tea and sweet cakes to the visitors, we were certainly a unique house in suburban London. The house was always full of visitors, and as H.P.B. often liked to invite friends to stay, I never knew whether I should have one person or twenty to lunch or dinner as the case might be. The house was not large, but there were two good rooms with folding doors between, and it was a sight to see H.P.B. seated in a big armchair surrounded by learned as well as fashionable people. A brilliant conversationalist, she kept young and old entranced, and at the same time her graceful fingers were constantly diving into the Nubian basket of tobacco that was ever by her side, and twisting the little cigarettes that she was constantly smoking. That was her social aspect....Then very often Mohini Chatterji would answer questions on Indian philosophy. ...His lectures were much sought after, and we rarely closed our doors till one or two o'clock in the morning.

During this time the little George Arundale was sent to a day school quite near, but he was not entirely out of it all, and I remember one afternoon a party was made up to go to the Zoological Gardens....We all went there in carriages and the child with us. Then a bath-chair was procured for H.P.B. and we proceeded to visit the animals. There were no occult phenomena on that visit, but there was the manifestation of a trait that showed forth the kindly nature of H.P.B. The child was running about as children will, and running near H.P.B.'s chair suddenly missed his footing and fell to the ground. H.P.B., in spite of the fact that she moved with difficulty, almost sprang out of the chair, throwing her umbrella on one side, and tried to help the child up. It was but a little thing, it is true, but it showed the...kindly disregard of self....

A curious happening which has never been effaced from my memory took place in the early part of H.P.B.'s stay with us. Many people at that time wished to get into communication with the Masters through H.P.B., and would sometimes bring letters asking that they should be forwarded to the Masters. H.P.B. always said: "It is not for me to forward the letters; the Masters will take them if They wish," and the letters were put into a certain drawer in her room. Sometimes the writers received a message through H.P.B., very often they did not; but the drawer was kept open. One day Mr. Sinnett had something he wished to ask of Master K.H., and that letter also was placed in the drawer. More than a week passed and there was no answer, and I was grieved, for we all desired that the questions should be answered. Day after day I looked into the drawer, but the letter was still there. One morning at about 7.30 I went in to H.P.B. (I always went to her room the first thing); I found her at her table, writing as usual, and I said to her: "How much I wish that letter could be taken." She looked very straight at me and said: "Bring me the letter," in rather a severe tone. I gave the letter into her hand.

There was a candle on the table and: "Light the candle," she said; then giving me the letter she said: "Burn the letter." I felt rather sorry to burn Mr. Sinnett's letter but, of course, did as she said; "Now go to your room and meditate." I went up to my room, which I had only left a short time before. My room was at the top of the house, in what we call an attic, for all the lower rooms were being used by our visitors, and I and the little boy slept upstairs. I went to the window, which looked on to a beautiful garden with lovely trees. Before the window there was a box, covered with a pink cloth, and I stood there for a minute or two wondering what H.P.B. meant...[and] what I was to meditate on....In a few minutes I cast my eyes down on the pink cloth, and in the middle of the cloth there was a letter which either I had not noticed before or which had not been there. I took up the envelope and looked at it, and found there was no address on it; it was quite blank, but it contained a thickness of paper and I concluded it was a letter. I held it in my hand and looked at it once or twice, and still finding the envelope without name or address, I felt sure it must be something occult and wondered for whom it could be. At length I decided to take the letter to H.P.B., and looking at it once again saw, in the clear writing of the Master K.H., Mr. Sinnett's name. That the name had not been on it at the beginning I am sure, nor during the many times when I looked at it most carefully. The letter was an answer to the one I had burnt, and it gave me much joy to be the recipient in the curious way in which it was sent.

There were several instances of the same kind. Once, when the letter I wanted answered was very private to myself, instead of putting it in the usual drawer I carried it in my pocket unknown to H.P.B. or to anyone else. But one night when I was sitting with her just before going up to my room, she handed me a letter in the well-known handwriting [of Master K.H.]....

It was a time of continual excitement; many people of note came to see H.P.B. Among them I remember well Mr. Frederick W.H. Myers of Psychic Research fame. H.P.B. happened to be alone that afternoon, and she and her visitor began talking about the phenomena in which Mr. Myers was so interested. "I wish you would show me a proof of your occult power," said he, "will you not do something that will prove that there are these occult forces of which you speak?" "What would be the good?" said Madame Blavatsky. "Even if you saw and heard, you would not be convinced." "Try me," he said. She looked at him for a moment or so in that strange, penetrating manner she had, and turning to me said: "Bring me a finger-bowl and some water in it." They were sitting in the full light of a summer's afternoon; she was to the right of Mr. Myers who was seated in a small chair about three feet away. I brought the glass bowl of water and she told me to place it on a stool just in front of Mr. Myers and a fairly long distance from her, which I did. We sat for a few moments in quiet expectation, and then from the glass there seemed to come four or five notes, such as we have called the "astral bells". It was evident that Mr. Myers was astonished; he looked at H.P.B. and her folded hands in her lap, and then again at the glass bowl; there was no visible connection between the two. Again the notes of the astral bell sounded, clear and silvery, and no movement on the part of Madame Blavatsky. He turned to me, and one could see that he was quite confused as to how the sounds could have been produced. H.P.B. smiled, and said: "Nothing very wonderful, only a little knowledge of how to direct some of the forces of nature." As Mr. Myers left he turned to me and said: "Miss Arundale, I shall *never* doubt again." But alas for the fickle, doubting mind; before a fortnight had passed he wrote to say he was not convinced, and that the sounds might have been produced in this way or that. H.P.B. was not one whit disturbed, in fact she said: "I knew it, but I thought I would give him what he asked for." This incident goes to show that conviction is rarely gained through phenomena; they arouse the attention, and if the mind is receptive and willing to investigate and not declare that that which is not understood cannot be, then there is a possibility that new facts and laws may be discovered.

...I see her of an early morning in her room writing at her table, the floor strewn with burnt matches which were my despair, careful housekeeper as I was, for coverlets, tablecovers, and carpets might well get burned, and even the house itself might have received considerable damage, for H.P.B. was accustomed to throw her lighted match away without any consideration as to where it might fall. I have also lively remembrances of some of the difficult times involved by H.P.B.'s absolute disregard of all conventionality. People would come long distances to see her, and it was generally understood that visitors might come between four and six in the afternoon. Sometimes, however, for no reason that we could see, she would decline to come from her room. I remember well one afternoon there was quite a distinguished set waiting to meet her, and when I went up to inform her that visitors had come to see her, I found her in a state of undress incompatible with a visit to the drawing-room. When I told her who was there, a little strong language was used and she said that Mr. and Mrs. X might come up. I gently remonstrated that neither her room nor her person was quite in a suitable condition for visitors; she told me I might go somewhere, but if she came down she should come down as she was, and if she saw anyone she would see them as she was, and that I was to send her food as soon as possible for she was hungry. The visitors had to leave and I made what excuses I could.

The most pleasant time I had was always in the early morning; she always seemed more get-at-able then, her mouth settled in pleasant curves, her eyes kind and brilliant, and she always seemed to understand and sympathise not only with what one said but also with what one did not say. I never felt afraid of H.P.B. in spite of the very strong language she sometimes used. One always somehow felt it was *surface* strong language....

Laura C. Holloway[67]
July, 1884, London

...Mr. [Hermann] Schmiechen, a young German artist...[was] residing in London....[and] a number of Theosophists gathered at his studio. Chief among Mr. Schmiechen's guests...was H.P.B., who occupied a seat facing a platform on which was...[Schmiechen's] easel. Near him on the platform sat several persons, all of them women, with one exception. About the room were grouped a number of well-known people, all equally interested in the attempt to be made by Mr. Schmiechen. The most clearly defined memory of that gathering, always in the mind of the writer, is the picture of Madame Blavatsky placidly smoking cigarettes in her easy chair and two women on the platform who were smoking also. She had "ordered" one of these women [Laura Holloway herself] to make a cigarette and smoke it, and the order was obeyed though with great hesitation, for it was a first attempt and even the mild Egyptian tobacco used was expected to produce nausea. H.P.B. promised that no such result would follow, and encouraged by Mrs. Sinnett, who was also smoking, the cigarette was lighted. The result was a curious quieting of the nerves, and, soon all interest was lost in the group of people about the room, and only the easel and the hand of the artist absorbed her attention.

Strange to relate that though the amateur smoker considered herself an onlooker it was her voice which uttered the words "begin it," and the artist quickly began to outline a head. Soon the eyes of every one present were upon him as he worked with extreme rapidity. While quiet reigned in the studio and all were eagerly interested in Mr. Schmiechen's work, the amateur smoker on the platform saw the figure of a man outline itself beside the easel and, while the artist with head bent over his work continued his outlining, it stood by him without a sign or motion. She leaned over to her friend and whispered: "It is the Master K.H.; he is being sketched. He is standing near Mr. Schmiechen."

"Describe his looks and dress," called out H.P.B. And while those in the room were wondering over Madame Blavatsky's exclamation, the woman addressed said: "He is about Mohini's height; slight of build, wonderful face full of light and animation; flowing curly black hair, over which is worn a soft cap. He is a symphony in greys and blues. His dress is that of a Hindu--- though it is far finer and richer than any I have ever seen before ---and there is fur trimming about his costume. It is his picture that is being made...."

...H.P.B.'s heavy voice arose to admonish the artist, one of her remarks remaining distinctly in memory. It was this: "Be careful, Schmiechen; do not make the face too round; lengthen the outline, and take note of the long distance between the nose and the ears." She sat where *she could not see the easel, nor know what was on it.*

...How many of the number of those in the studio on that first occasion recognized the Master's presence was not known. There were psychics in the room, several of them, and the artist, Mr. Schmiechen, was a psychic, or he could not have worked out so successfully the picture that was outlined by him on that eventful day....

Henry Sidgwick[68]
Aug. 9 & 10, 1884, Cambridge, England

...[On August 8th] we went back to Cambridge....[The next day] after dinner we...[went] to a meeting of the Cambridge Branch of the S.P.R. [Society for Psychical Research], where Madame Blavatsky, Mohini, and other Theosophists are to show off. The meeting is in Oscar Browning's spacious rooms: which are crowded to overflowing---all the members of the Branch, and more than as many outsiders. There must have been over seventy; I should not have thought that such a crowd could have been got together in the Long [Summer] Vacation. [F.W.H.] Myers and I had the task of "drawing" Mme. B. by questions, Mohini taking a share of the answers. We kept it up better than I expected for a couple of hours; the interest of the miscellaneous throng---half of whom, I suppose, came with the very vaguest notions of Theosophy---being apparently fairly well sustained. On the whole I was favourably impressed with Mme. B. No doubt the *stuff* of her answers resembled [her book] *Isis Unveiled* in some of its worst characteristics; but her manner was certainly frank and straightforward---it was hard to imagine her the elaborate impostor that she must be if the whole thing is a trick....[On August 10] we all went to a Theosophical lunch with Myers....Our favourable impression of Mme. B. was sustained; if personal sensibilities can be trusted, she is a genuine being, with a vigorous nature intellectual as well as emotional, and a real desire for the good of mankind. This impression is all the more noteworthy as she is externally unattractive---with her flounces full of cigarette ashes---and not prepossessing in manner. Certainly we like her, both Nora [Mrs. Sidgwick] and I. If she is a humbug, she is a consummate one: as her remarks have the air not only of spontaneity and randomness but sometimes of an amusing indiscretion. Thus in the midst of an account of the Mahatmas in Tibet, intended to give us an elevated view of these personages, she blurted out her candid impression that the chief Mahatma of all was the most utter dried-up old mummy that she ever saw....[*]

Francesca Arundale[69]
Aug., 1884, Elberfeld, Germany

In the summer of 1884 we received an invitation from a kind friend at Elberfeld, Herr Gustav Gebhard, to come and spend a few weeks at his home. Not only did he invite Colonel Olcott and Madame Blavatsky and Mr. Mohini, but he invited a large party to accompany them---my mother, myself and my little George, Bertram Keightley, and some others....and many joined the party later....

....The drawing-room at Elberfeld was a large, high room with very high doors. We used to sit in this room before going down to dinner, which was on a lower floor. It often happened that H.P.B. did not go down and something was served to her upstairs. On the evening I am speaking of, she decided to remain upstairs and settled her bulky figure comfortably in a large armchair while all the rest of us went down, her host asking her what she would like sent up. After dinner the party returned to the drawing-room and found H.P.B. quietly ensconced in her chair, as if she had never left it. A party gathered round her as usual and talk was being carried on, when somebody said: "What is that white thing on the top of the portal of the door?" A high chair was brought, and the "white thing" proved to be an envelope [containing a letter from Mahatma K.H.] addressed to me as Treasurer of the London Lodge. I fully realised that there seemed

---

[*] [Henry Sidgwick, first president of the Society for Psychical Research, was on the special Committee that investigated Madame Blavatsky and her claims. In the end, Sidgwick came to believe that H.P.B. was a fraud and that her Mahatmas did not exist.---Editor.]

to be no special reason why the missive should have been given in that peculiar manner. It may have been intended to show that H.P.B. had no connection with it, for it would have been almost impossible for H.P.B. to have mounted on a chair and placed a letter at that height....

Rudolph Gebhard[70]
Aug. 25 & 26, 1884, Elberfeld, Germany

I have always taken a great interest in conjuring tricks. When in London, I had an opportunity of taking lessons from Professor Field, a most skilful sleight-of-hand conjuror, who very soon made me quite proficient in his art. From that time forward I have given performances wherever I went (as an *amateur*, of course), and made the acquaintance of nearly all our renowned "wizards," with whom I exchanged tricks. As every conjuror has some favourite sleight in which he excels, I was bound to be very careful in watching them, in order to make myself perfect in all the different lines of card or coin conjuring, or the famous mediumistic feats. This of course made me in good time a pretty close observer, as far as *tricks* are concerned; and I feel justified in giving here an opinion on the phenomena which came under my observation.

Two of them occurred in our house in Elberfeld, during the stay in it of Mme. Blavatsky, Colonel Olcott, and a small party of friends and Theosophists.

The first one was a letter from Mahatma K.H. to my father, and took place one evening in the presence of a number of witnesses....It was about nine P.M. We were sitting in the drawing-room discussing different topics, when Mme. Blavatsky's attention was suddenly attracted by something unusual taking place in the room. After a while she said that she felt the presence of the "Masters." That they had, perhaps, the intention of doing something for us, and so she asked us to think of what we should like to occur. Then a little discussion took place as to what would be the best thing, and finally it was unanimously resolved that a letter should be asked for, addressed to my father, Mr. G. Gebhard, on a subject on which he should mentally decide himself.

Now my father had, at the time being, great anxiety about a son in America, my elder brother, and was very eager to get advice from the Master concerning him.

Meanwhile, Mme. B., who, on account of her recent illness, was resting on a sofa, and had been looking around the room, suddenly exclaimed that there was something going on with a large oil painting hanging over the piano in the same room, she having seen like a ray of light shooting in the direction of the picture. This statement was immediately corroborated by Mrs. [Holloway]..., and then by my mother also; who, sitting opposite a looking-glass and turning her back to the picture, had also observed in the mirror, like a faint light going towards the painting. Mme. B. then required Mrs. [Holloway]...to see, and say what was going on, when Mrs. [Holloway]...said that she saw something forming over the picture, but could not distinctly make out what it was.

Everybody's attention was now fixed in the direction of the wall high above and under the ceiling, where so many saw bright lights. But, I must confess, that for my part, not being clairvoyant, I could neither see lights, nor any other thing except what I had always seen on that wall. And when Madame Blavatsky said she now felt absolutely sure that there was something going on, I got up (we had kept our seats all this while) and climbing on the piano lifted the picture right off the wall, but not off the hook, shook it well and looked behind it---nothing! The room was well lit up, and there was not an inch of the picture which I could not see. I dropped the frame, saying that I could see nothing; but Madame Blavatsky told me that she felt sure that there must be something, so on I climbed once more and tried again.

The picture in question was a large oil painting, suspended from the wall by a hook and a rope, which made it hang over at the top, so that when the lower part of the frame was lifted off the wall, there was a space of fully six inches between the wall and the back of the picture, the latter being virtually entirely off the wall. There being a wall gas-bracket fixed on each side of the painting, the space between the latter and the wall was well lit up. But the second time, no better than the first, was I able to detect anything, though I looked very close. It was in order to make perfectly sure that I got up on the piano, and passed my hand twice very carefully along the frame, which is about three inches thick, up and down---nothing. Letting the picture drop back, I then turned round to Madame Blavatsky to ask her what was to be done further, when she exclaimed: "I see the letter; there it is!" I turned quickly back to the picture, and saw at that moment a letter dropping from behind it on the piano. I picked it up. It was addressed to "Herr Consul G. Gebhard," and contained the information he had just asked for. I must have made rather a perplexed face, for the company laughed merrily at the "family juggler."

Now for me this is a most completely demonstrated phenomenon. Nobody had handled the picture but myself; I was careful to examine it very closely, and as I was searching for a letter, such a thing could not have escaped my attention, as perhaps would have been the case if I had been looking for some other object; as then I might not have paid any attention to a slip of paper. The letter was fully four by two inches, so by no means a small object.

Let us consider this phenomenon from a sleight-of-hand point of view.

Suppose several letters had been prepared beforehand, addressed to different persons, treating of different subjects. Is it possible to get a letter to an appointed place by a sleight-of-hand trick? Quite possible; it only depends what place it is, and if our attention is drawn beforehand to such a place or not. To get that letter behind that picture would have been very difficult, but might have been managed if our attention had for a moment been directed to another place, the letter being thrown behind the picture in the meantime. What is sleight-of-hand? Nothing else but the execution of a movement more or less swift, in a moment when you are not observed. I draw your attention for a short while to a certain spot, say for instance my left hand, my right is then free to make certain movements unobserved; as to "the quickness of the eye deceives the hand" theory, it is entirely erroneous. You cannot make a movement with your hand so quickly that the eye would not follow and detect it, the only thing you can do is either to conceal the necessary movement by another one which has nothing to do with what you are about, or to draw the attention of the looker-on to another point, and then quickly do what is required.

Now, in this instance all our attention had been drawn to the picture, before ever the question was put as to what we should like to have, and was kept there all the while; it would have been impossible for anyone to throw a letter without being observed. As for the letter having been concealed behind the picture beforehand, this is out of the question altogether, it could not have escaped my attention while I repeatedly searched for it. Suppose the letter had been placed on the top of the frame, and my hand had disturbed it passing along without my knowing it, this would have caused the letter to drop down instantly, whereas, about thirty seconds passed before it put in an appearance. Taking all circumstances together, it seems to me an impossibility to have worked this phenomenon by a trick.

The day after this had occurred, I went into Madame's room about noon; but seeing that she was engaged I retired to the drawing-room, where we had been sitting the night before, and just then the idea struck me to try that picture again, in order to make perfectly sure that the letter could not have been concealed somewhere behind it, without being detected. I was alone in the room, and during my examination of the painting, nobody entered it; I fully satisfied myself that a letter could not have escaped my attention, had it been concealed behind the picture. I then went back to Madame's room, where I found her still engaged with the same woman. In the evening we were again sitting together.

"The Masters watched you to-day, and were highly amused with your experiments. How you did try to find out if that letter could not have been concealed behind the picture."

Now I am positively certain, first, that nobody was in the room at the time I tried the picture; and secondly, that I had told no one in the house of my experiment. It is impossible for me to explain how Madame could have found out my movements, except through clairvoyance....

Vsevolod S. Solovyov[71]

Aug. 26 & 27, 1884, Brussels, Belgium and then later at Elberfeld, Germany

Having received a letter from my countrywoman, Madame Helena Blavatsky, in which she informed me of her bad health and begged me to go to see her at Elberfeld, I decided to take the journey. But as the state of my own health obliged me to be careful, I preferred to stop at Brussels, which town I had never seen, to rest, the heat being unbearable.

I left Paris on the 24th of August. Next morning, at the Grand Hotel in Brussels, where I was staying, I met Mlle. [Justine de Glinka]...(daughter of...[a] Russian ambassador...and maid of honour to the Empress of Russia). Hearing that I was going to Elberfeld to see Mme. Blavatsky, whom she knew and for whom she had much respect, she decided to come with me. We spent the day together expecting to leave in the morning by the nine o'clock train.

At eight o'clock, being quite ready to depart, I go to Miss...[de Glinka's] room and find her in a great state of perplexity. All her keys, which she always kept about her person in a little bag and that she had in this bag on going to bed, had disappeared during the night, although the door was locked. Thus, as all her baggage was locked, she could not put away the things she had just been using and wearing. We were obliged to postpone our departure to the one o'clock train and called a locksmith to open the largest trunk. When it was opened, all the keys were found in the bottom of the trunk, *including the key of this trunk itself, attached as usual to the rest.* Having all the morning to spare, we agreed to take a walk, but suddenly I was overcome by weakness and felt an irresistible desire to sleep. I begged Miss [de Glinka]...to excuse me and went to my room, and threw myself on the bed. But I could not sleep and lay with my eyes shut, but awake, when suddenly I saw before my closed eyes a series of views of unknown places that my memory took in to the finest detail. When this vision ceased, I felt no more weakness and went to Miss [de Glinka]..., to whom I related all that had happened to me and described to her in detail the views I had seen.

We left by the one o'clock train and lo! after about half an hour's journey, Miss [de Glinka]..., who was looking out of the window, said to me, "Look, here is one of your landscapes!" I recognized it at once, and all that day until evening, I saw, with open eyes, all that I had seen in the morning with closed eyes. I was pleased that I had described to Miss [de Glinka]...all my vision in detail ....The route between Brussels and Elberfeld is completely unknown to me, for it was the first time in my life that I had visited Belgium and this part of Germany.

On arriving at Elberfeld in the evening, we took rooms in a hotel and then hurried off to see Madame Blavatsky at Mr. Gebhard's house. The same evening, the members of the Theosophical Society who were there with Mme. Blavatsky showed us two superb oil-paintings of the Mahatmas...[Morya] and Koot Hoomi [painted by Mr. Schmiechen]. The portrait of M. especially produced on us an extraordinary impression, and it is not surprising that on the way back to the hotel, we talked on about him and had him before our eyes. Miss [de Glinka]...may be left to relate her own experience during that night.[*]

But this is what happened to me:

Tired by the journey, I lay peacefully sleeping when suddenly I was awakened by the sensation of a warm penetrating breath. I open my eyes and in this feeble light that entered the room through the three windows, I see before me a tall figure of a man, dressed in a long white floating garment. At the same time I heard or felt a voice that told me, in I know not what language, although I understood perfectly, to light the candle. I should explain that, far from being afraid, I remained quite tranquil, only I felt my heart beat rapidly. I lit the candle, and in lighting it, saw by my watch that it was two o'clock. The vision did not disappear. There was a living man in front of me. And I recognized instantly the beautiful original of the portrait we had seen during the evening before. He sat down near me on a chair and began to speak. He talked for a long time....Among other things, he told me that in order to be fit to see him *in his astral body* I had had to undergo much preparation, and that the last lesson had been given me that morning when I saw, with closed

---

[*][Miss de Glinka's experience was similar to Solovyov's.---Editor.]

eyes, the landscapes that I was to see in reality the same day. Then he said that I possess great magnetic power, now being developed. I asked him what I ought to do with this force. But without answering, he vanished.

I was alone, the door of my room locked. I thought I had had an hallucination and even told myself with fright that I was beginning to lose my mind. Hardly had this idea arisen when once again I saw the superb man in white robes. He shook his head and smiling, said to me: "Be sure that I am no hallucination and that your reason is not quitting you. Blavatsky will prove to you to-morrow before everyone that my visit is real." Then he disappeared. I saw by my watch that it was three o'clock. I put out the candle and immediately went into a deep sleep.

Next morning, on going with Miss [de Glinka]...to Madame Blavatsky, the first thing she said to us with an enigmatical smile was: "Well! How have you passed the night?" "Very well," I replied and I added, "Haven't you anything to tell me?" "No," she replied, "I only know that the Master was with you with one of his pupils."

That same evening, Mr. Olcott found in his pocket a little note, that all the theosophists said was in the handwriting of M.:

"Certainly I was there, but who can open the eyes of him who will not see."

This was the reply to my doubts, because all the day I had been trying to persuade myself that it was only an hallucination, and this made Madame Blavatsky angry.

I should say that on my return to Paris, where I am now, my hallucinations and the strange happenings that surrounded me, have completely stopped.

Laura C. Holloway[72]
Aug.---Oct., 1884, Elberfeld, Germany

Mme. Blavatsky could produce a sound like the chime of bells, low and sweet, but perfectly clear, and these were heard by us all under various conditions. She would know what was going on in other parts of the building, and one day reproached one of the party for something that was said in the park, fully a mile away from the castle. Her hostess said that Mme. B had not left her room all the afternoon. I remember an occasion when I excused myself to go to my room to write. In the evening when we all assembled in the drawing-room, I was astonished to have her say to me: "You have not written to-day. I saw you idling the time away." It was true that I had sat at the large window the entire afternoon, looking out upon the hills, watching the clouds and pondering over many things. Mme. Blavatsky had been much in my thoughts, as I considered the question----a grave one to me---of remaining longer with the party or of returning to England. She knew by some means what had been agitating my mind, and said to me as we passed down the stairs: "You will go back with me." I said to myself that I would not, but events so shaped themselves that I did travel back to London in her company.

She seemed to divine the future in many ways, and sometimes when she made prophecies, it was dreadful to hear her voice, she would be so excited and vehement. Curious study she was; curious things she did. Her powers were phenomenal and were exhibited without premeditation. With no ambition, no home, no home ties, no strong attachments, she seemed alone in the world, and was in many respects the most indifferent person I ever knew. Reckless in statement, defiant in action, she made enemies without thought and pained those who loved her with apparent indifference. Sometimes it would be my confidential opinion that she mesmerized those about her when she desired, but never could prove it. Her heart was not such a hard one, but she cared very little for manifestations of affection. She was alone in some sphere of her own, and none could know her intimately. I have been in the room with her when I felt her real self to be far away, and have seen her look at strangers once and talk of them as though their past lives were all before her.

She sat at the desk writing one day when I entered her room without invitation, and, putting on a bold front, walked directly to her with a sealed letter in my hand, which I had written to the guru, or teacher, who had sent me letters through her. "I want an answer to this letter, and I have come to ask you to send it, Madam." She railed at me, flew into a rage, demanded to know by what right I intruded upon her and ordered her to send letters

Madame Blavatsky in 1884-1885

to the Mahatmas. When she had concluded I quietly asked her to send it, adding that it was important. "Nothing that concerns the emotions of people is important," she retorted. "You all think that if you make a prayer it must have an immediate personal response from Jehovah. I am tired of nonsense." I coolly laid the letter on the table, sat down near to and facing her, and looked at my letter. She opened a drawer of the desk, which I saw was empty, and told me to put it there, I pushed the letter from the table into it and closed it myself. She leaned back in her chair, looked with some interest at me, and remarked that my will was developing. I told her that I had staked much in writing the letter, and its reply would influence my future course. Impelled by a sudden feeling I asked her if the letter had not gone, and not waiting for her to reply, I pulled open the drawer and it was not there. I looked for it carefully everywhere....Days after I met Mme. Blavatsky in the hall as she was going out to drive with one of the guests, and she put out her hand for me to assist her down the step. As I took her hand, I smilingly said, "Where's my letter?" She looked at me steadily for a moment, and it suddenly occurred to me, but why I do not know, that it was answered. I ran my hand into the pocket of my dress and there was a letter folded and sealed in a Chinese envelope....

The world has abused her more than almost any other woman of her day. She is an object of suspicion not only to individuals, but to governments, and she is defended by those who would count it a privilege to die for her. To a person who once asked her who she was, she said, with much simplicity of matter: "I am an old Buddhist pilgrim, wandering about the world to teach the only true religion, which is truth."

C.W. Leadbeater[73]
Oct. 31, 1884, London

...I had addressed [a letter] to the Master Kuthumi....I received a reply eventually...[But] I knew of no way to send...[another letter] to the Master but to take it to Madame Blavatsky, and as she was to leave England on the following day for India, I hastened up to London to see her.

It was with difficulty that I induced her to read the letter [from Master K.H.], as she said very decidedly that such communications were intended only for the recipient. I was obliged to insist, however, and at last she read it and asked me what I wished to say in reply. I answered...and asked her how this information could be conveyed to the Master. She replied that He knew it already, referring of course to the exceedingly close relation in which she stood with Him....

She then told me to wait by her, and not to leave her on any account. She adhered absolutely to this condition, even making me accompany her into her bedroom when she went to put on her hat and, when a cab was required, declining to allow me to leave the room and go to the door to whistle for it. I could not at all understand the purpose of this at the time, but afterwards I realized that she wished me to be able to say that she had never been out of my sight for a moment between the time when she read my letter from the Master and my receipt of the reply to it. I remember as vividly as if it were yesterday how I rode with her in that hansom cab, and the bashful embarrassment that I felt, caused partly by the honour of doing so, and partly by my fear that I must be inconveniencing her horribly, for I was crushed side ways into a tiny corner of the seat, while her huge bulk weighed down her side of the vehicle, so that the springs were grinding all through the journey. Mr. and Mrs. Cooper-Oakley were to accompany her on the voyage to India, and it was to their house that I went with her very late that night....

Even at that hour a number of devoted friends were gathered in Mrs. Oakley's drawing-room to say farewell to Madame Blavatsky, who seated herself in an easy-chair by the fireside. She was talking brilliantly to those who were present, and rolling one of her eternal cigarettes, when suddenly her right hand was jerked out towards the fire in a very peculiar fashion, and lay palm upwards. She looked down at it in surprise, as I did myself, for I was standing close to her, leaning with an elbow on the mantel-piece: and several of us saw quite clearly a sort of whitish mist form in the palm of her hand and then condense into a piece of folded paper, which she at once handed to me, saying: "There is your answer." Every one in the room crowded round, of course, but she sent me away outside to read it, saying that I must not let anyone see its contents. It was a very short note....

Isabel Cooper-Oakley[74]
Nov., 1884, Egypt

H.P.B....[joined] Mr. Oakley and myself [during the middle of October], and remained with us until we started for India with her. The house party [in London] consisted of H.P.B., my sister [Laura Cooper], Dr. [Archibald] Keightley, Mr. Oakley and myself. It was early in November, 1884, that we left Liverpool for Port Said *en route* for Madras. It had been arranged that we were to go first to Cairo in order to get some definite information about the antecedents of the Coulombs, who were well known there, as the news of their treachery [against H.P.B.] had already reached us some months before....We reached Port Said on the 17th of November, 1884, and there remained some few days for Mr. Leadbeater to join us; on his arrival we took the mail boat down the Suez Canal to Ismailia, and then went by train to Cairo....H.P.B. was a most interesting fellow-traveller, her varied information about every part of Egypt was both extensive and extraordinary. Would that I had space to go into the details of that time in Cairo, the drives through the quaint and picturesque bazaars, and her descriptions of the people and their ways. Especially interesting was one long afternoon spent at the Boulak Museum on the borders of the Nile, where H.P.B. astonished [Gaston] Maspero, the well-known Egyptologist, with her knowledge, and as we went through the museum she pointed out to him the grades of the Initiate kings and how they were to be known from the esoteric side....On leaving Cairo, H.P.B. and I went straight to Suez. Mr. Oakley remained at Cairo to get documents from the police about the Coulombs; Mr. Leadbeater joined us at Suez....

C.W. Leadbeater[75]
Nov., 1884, Egypt

In those days there was no railway running from Port Said, and the only way in which we could reach Cairo was by travelling down the Suez Canal as far as Ismailia, whence we could take train to the capital. The journey down the canal was performed in a tiny little steamer somewhat like a tug-boat....Every night it left Port Said at midnight and reached Ismailia in the early morning....

...In the pale gold of the Egyptian morning we moored beside the wharf at Ismailia. There was an interval of some hours before our train started, so it seemed reasonable to go to a hotel and have some breakfast....So in due course we took our places in the train.

As the journey continued Madame Blavatsky...favoured us with the most gloomy prognostications of our future fate:

"Ah! you Europeans," she said, "you think you are going to enter upon the path of occultism and pass triumphantly through all its troubles; you little know what is before you; you have not counted the wrecks by the wayside as I have. The Indians know what to expect, and they have already passed through tests and trails such as have never entered into your wildest dreams; but you, poor feeble things, what can you do?"

She continued these Cassandralike prophecies with a maddening monotony, but her audience was far too reverential to try to change the subject. We sat in the four corners of the compartment, Madame Blavatsky facing the engine, and Mr. Oakley sitting opposite to her with the resigned expression of an early Christian martyr; while Mrs. Oakley, weeping profusely, and with a face of ever-increasing horror, sat opposite to me....

In those...days trains were usually lit by smoky oil lamps, and in the centre of the roof of each compartment there was a large round hole into which porters inserted these lamps as they ran along the roofs of the carriages. This being a day train, however, there was no lamp, and one could see the blue sky through the hole. It happened that Mr. Oakley and I were both leaning back in our respective corners, so that we both saw...a kind of ball of whitish mist forming in that hole, and a moment later it had condensed into a piece of folded paper, which fell to the floor of our compartment. I started forward, picked it up, and handed it at once to Madame Blavatsky, taking it for granted that any communication of this nature must be intended for her. She at once unfolded it and read it, and I saw a red flush appear upon her face.

"Umph," she said, "that's what I get for trying to warn you people of the troubles that lie before you," and she threw the paper to me.

"May I read it?" I said, and her only reply was: "Why do you think I gave it to you?"

I read it and found it to be a note signed by the Master Kuthumi, suggesting very gently but quite decidedly that it was perhaps a pity, when she had with her some earnest and enthusiastic candidates, to give them so very gloomy a view of a path which, however difficult it might be, was destined eventually to lead them to joy unspeakable. And then the message concluded with a few words of kindly commendation addressed to each of us by name....

I need hardly say that we were all much comforted and uplifted and filled with gratitude; but, though no rebuke could possibly have been more gently worded, it was evident that Madame Blavatsky did not altogether appreciate it. Before our conversation began she had been reading some book which she wished to review for *The Theosophist*, and she was still sitting with the book open upon her knee and the paper-knife in her hand. She now resumed her reading, stroking the dust of the desert (which came pouring in at the open window) off the pages of the book with her paper-knife as she read. When an especially vicious puff came in Mr. Oakley started forward and made a motion as if to close the window; but Madame Blavatsky looked up at him balefully, and said with unmeasured scorn: "You don't mind a little dust, do you?" Poor Mr. Oakley shrank back into his corner like a snail into its shell, and not another word did our leader utter until we steamed into the station at Cairo. The dust certainly was rather trying, but after that one remark we thought it best to suffer it in silence....

Isabel Cooper-Oakley[76]
Dec., 1884---March, 1885, Adyar, Madras, India

On leaving Cairo, H.P.B. and I went straight to Suez....After waiting two days for the steamer we started for Madras....Col. Olcott and some members met us at Colombo [Ceylon], and we stayed there nearly two days, paying some deeply interesting visits to the old Buddhist Temples, and one especially charming visit to Sumangala, the High Priest, who evidently had a very high respect for H.P.B....We then proceeded to Madras. Never shall I forget the quaint picturesqueness of our arrival [at Madras on Dec. 21th]. A deputation, accompanied by a brass band, came off in boats to meet us; but the sound of the music was somewhat marred by the fact that the drop between the waves is so great that sometimes our band was on the top of a high roller, and sometimes almost engulfed between two big waves. On landing at the pier head there were hundreds to meet H.P.B., and we were literally towed by enthusiastic members down the pier in a truck, wildly decorated with paper roses, etc., and then surrounded by masses of smiling dark faces. She was driven off to Pachiappah Hall, where we had garlands of pink roses festooned round us, and were sprinkled somewhat copiously with rose water. Then H.P.B. and I were conducted by a Rajah to his carriage and driven off to Adyar. Here the warmest welcome awaited her. Members were assembling from all parts of India for the approaching [Theosophical Society] Convention; we went into the large hall and at once began discussing the all-absorbing Coulomb case.

Col. Olcott then informed us that the Society of Psychical Research [London] was sending out a member to investigate the matter, and accordingly a few days after, the notorious [Richard] Hodgson arrived fresh from Cambridge....Mr. Hodgson was an Australian by birth....I am quite confident that if an older man had come, one with more experience and a maturer judgment, the Coulomb affair would have been presented to the world in a very different way....Mr. Hodgson's investigations were not conducted with an unbiased mind, and from hearing everyone say Madame Blavatsky was an impostor he began to believe it: after a few interviews with Madame Coulomb and the Missionaries we saw that his views were turning against the minority. Now his report was not by any means accurate, for he omitted some very valuable evidence of phenomena given to him by Mr. Oakley and myself. Mr. Hodgson was treated with the greatest courtesy and friendliness by H.P.B. and Col. Olcott, and every opportunity was afforded him for investigating every hole and corner at Adyar; and yet he preferred, and gave more credence to, the testimony of a discharged servant, whose bad character was by that time universally known, than to that of H.P.B. and her friends, who had no monetary interest in giving their evidence. The trap doors and sliding panels had all been made by [Alexis] Coulomb, in H.P.B.'s absence, and his wife sold the character of...[H.P.B.] who had saved her from starvation to the Missionaries and forged the letters she showed to them. Any person of ordinary intellect and common sense could see that the trap doors and sliding panels were quite new, so new as to be immovable, *the grooves being quite fresh and unmarked by any* usage whatever, as Mr. Oakley and I found when we tried to move the largest sliding door. If we could not do so with our combined efforts, surely it is ridiculous to think Madame Blavatsky could have used them for conjuring tricks; the arrangements were so bad that any trick would have been inevitably discovered. However Mr. Hodgson was so bent on being a "success" that these simple common-sense facts were disregarded by him. Immediately after the convention was over he left [Adyar] Headquarters, and went to live in Madras, until his investigations were ended....

...The effect of all this worry was that...[H.P.B.] became seriously ill. Col. Olcott had started for Burma, Mr. Oakley and I were comparatively alone with her. Very anxious were the hours and days of nursing that I went through those three weeks, as she grew worse and worse and was finally given up in a state of coma by the doctors. It proves how wonderful was the protective influence of H.P.B., ill or well; for though I was completely isolated with her near the roof of the house, an open staircase leading up, hardly a soul within call, yet night after night have I wandered up and down the flat roof, to get a breath of fresh air between 3 and 4 a.m., and wondered as I watched the daylight break over the Bay of Bengal, why I felt so fearless even with her lying apparently at the point of death; I never could imagine a sense of fear coming near H.P.B. Finally came the anxious night when the doctors gave her up, and said that nothing could be done, it was impossible. She was then in a state of coma and had been so for some hours. The doctors said that she would pass away in that condition, and I know, humanly speaking, that night's watch must be the last. I cannot here go into what happened, an experience I can never forget; but towards 8 a.m. H.P.B. suddenly opened her eyes and asked for her breakfast, the first time she had spoken naturally for two days. I went to meet the doctor, whose amazement at the change was very great. H.P.B. said, "Ah! doctor, you do not believe in our great Masters." From that time she steadily improved. The doctor insisted on her being sent to Europe as soon as possible....

Richard Hodgson[77a]

Dec., 1884---Jan., 1885, Adyar, Madras, India

In November...[1884] I proceeded to India for the purpose of investigating on the spot the evidence of the phenomena connected with the Theosophical Society....

...We may first take the "raps"...which Mr. [A.P.] Sinnett seems to regard as constituting important test phenomena...The raps occurring when Madame Blavatsky places her hands upon the patient's head, I have...experienced,---though as Madame Blavatsky sat behind me and placed her hands upon the back of my head, I was unable to watch her fingers. She had not informed me what she intended doing, and I conjectured that she was attempting to "mesmerise" me; the so-called "shocks" which I felt impressed me simply as movements of impatience on the part of Madame Blavatsky. My attention being then drawn to them as "phenomena," they were repeated, but I found them not at all like the "shocks" experienced when taking off sparks from the conductor of an electrical machine, as Mr. Sinnett describes them. The sharp thrilling or tingling feeling was quite absent. Unfortunately, I am unable to gently crack any of the joints of my fingers, I can but clumsily and undisguisedly crack one of the joints of my thumbs, yet I find that the *quality* of the feeling produced when I thus crack my thumb-joint against my head exactly resembles that which I perceived under the supple hands of Madame Blavatsky....

...The problem of her motives, when I found myself being forced to the conclusion that her claims and her phenomena were fraudulent, caused me no little perplexity....At last a casual conversation opened my eyes. I had...put aside as unworthy of consideration the idea...that the objects of the Theosophical Society were political, and that Madame Blavatsky was a "Russian spy.' But a conversation with Madame Blavatsky, which arose out of her sudden and curious excitement at the news of the recent Russian movement upon the Afghan frontier, compelled me to ask myself seriously whether it was not possible that the task which she had set herself to perform in India was to foster and foment as widely as possible among the natives a disaffection towards British rule....I cannot profess myself, after my personal experiences of Madame Blavatsky, to feel much doubt that her real object has been the furtherance of Russian interests....

Henry S. Olcott[77b]
Feb. 7 & 8, 1885, Adyar, Madras, India

Again has our Master [Morya] snatched H.P.B. from the jaws of death. A few days ago she was dying and I was recalled from Burma by telegraph, with little or no prospect of seeing her again. But, when three physicians were expecting her to sink into coma and so pass senseless out of life, *He* came, laid his hand upon her, and the whole aspect of the case changed....

...The day before yesterday things looked so bad that Subba Row and Damodar lost heart and got quite panicky and said the T.S. would go to the dogs....Well, yesterday came here a certain Indian yogi, dressed in the usual saffron robes, and accompanied by a female ascetic---his supposed disciple. I was called, came and sat down, and we stared at each other in silence. Then he closed his eyes, concentrated himself, and---gave me psychically his message. He had been sent by the Mahatma [Narayana] at Tirivellum (the one who dictated to H.P.B. the "Replies to an English F.T.S.") to assure me that I should *not* be left alone. He recalled to me my conversation of the 7th with...[Damodar] and...[Subba Row]....And he asked me (mentally) if I could for a moment have believed that he, who had always been so true to me, would leave me to go on without help. Then he and his Maya of a she-chela went up to H.P.B.'s sick-chamber, and she---contrary to every Hindu usage for females of the sort---went straight at the...[Old Lady] and made passes over her, and at the Guru's command began to recite mantrams. Then the Guru took from beneath his robe a ball, the size of an orange, of the *Nirukti*, or sacred ashes used in Hindu temples for external application after the bath, and told the disciple to put it in a small cupboard that hangs over the head of H.P.B.'s bed. He told the latter that when she needed him she should simply think of him *in his present visible form* and mentally repeat his name thrice. Then there was some conversation all around, and they went away....

Chapter 6

ITALY, GERMANY AND BELGIUM

1885-1887

Charles Johnston[78]
June, 1885, London

During 1884, the..."Society for Psychical Research" had become deeply interested in the phenomena described in *The Occult World* and in Mme. Blavatsky's magazine, *The Theosophist*, and had appointed a Committee to investigate these phenomena. A very favorable preliminary report had been issued....It was decided to supplement this preliminary work by further investigation in India, and a young student of psychic phenomena, Mr. Richard Hodgson, was asked to go to India to carry this out.

During this period, events had been happening at Adyar, near Madras, the headquarters of the Theosophical Society. While Mme. Blavatsky and Colonel Olcott were absent in Europe, two members of the Society,...[Alexis] and...[Emma] Coulomb, who had for years been sheltered at the headquarters at Bombay and Madras, were asked to withdraw. There were charges of misappropriation of funds, evil speaking and trickery, which made it inexpedient for them to remain at the central office of the Society in a position of trust. These two persons presently retaliated by making an attack on Mme. Blavatsky, to which publicity was given by a Madras [Christian] missionary organ, and in which it was asserted that the phenomena described in *The Occult World* and elsewhere were tricks, and that many of them had been produced by these two members [the Coulombs], who now repented of their misdeeds. Letters were published by them, which they said had been written by Mme. Blavatsky, and which gave color to the charge of fraud; but the originals of these letters were never available for impartial examination, and the alleged copies were full of mistakes, vulgarity and puerility, and bore little resemblance to the genuine letters of the great Theosophical writer. Mr. Richard Hodgson arrived in India shortly after this attack was made. He found something congenial in the thought and methods of these two retired members who accused themselves of fraud, and he practically adopted their views and pretensions as to the whole of the phenomena he had been sent to investigate. He spent a short time in India, and returned to England early in 1885. Toward the end of June, 1885, he read a part of his Report on the phenomena before a meeting of the "Society for Psychical Research."

That meeting made an epoch in the attitude of public opinion toward the Theosophical Movement. Never sympathetic, public opinion thereafter became frankly hostile and incredulous. Mme. Blavatsky was treated as an imposter, and her friends as fools. The public accepted Mr. Hodgson's view without question or examination....

With others, I was present at that fateful meeting. After Mr. Hodgson had read his Report, members of the Committee went among the audience to discuss it. Mr. F.W.H. Myers was one of these. When he asked what impression the meeting had made on me, I remember replying that the whole thing was so scandalously unfair that, had I not been a member of the Theosophical Society, I should have joined it forthwith, on the strength of Mr. Hodgson's performance....

A.P. Sinnett[79]
Aug.---Oct., 1885, Wurzburg, Germany

...[Leaving India, Madame Blavatsky] arrived in Naples [Italy] some time in April, 1885, and went to a hotel at Torre del Greco, near by....Madame Blavatsky only stayed a few months at Torre Del Greco and then went on to Wurzburg [Germany]....My wife and I went to see her at Wurzburg in the course of our autumn tour in 1885. She was staying at 6, Ludwigstrasse....

The "Secret Doctrine" was still untouched in September, 1885 when my wife and I saw her....We found her settled in an economical way, but in comfort and quietude, cheered just then by the companionship of her aunt, Mme. de Fadeyev...She was naturally seething with indignation at the wrongs she had suffered at the hand of the S.P.R. committee....On the whole, however, she seemed in better health and spirits than we expected, and some premonitory symptoms indicated that the preparation of the "Secret Doctrine" might shortly be set on foot.

A month or so after our return to London in October I received a note from Mme. Blavatsky, in the course of which she wrote:---

"I am very busy on 'Secret D.' The thing at New York [meaning the circumstances under which 'Isis Unveiled' was written] is repeated---only far clearer and better. I begin to think it shall vindicate us. Such pictures, panoramas, scenes, antediluvian dramas, with all that! Never saw or heard better."

Countess Constance Wachtmeister[80]
Dec., 1885---May, 1886, Wurzburg, Germany

In the autumn of 1885, I was making preparations to leave my home in Sweden...to spend the winter with some friends in Italy, and incidentally, *en route* to pay Madame Gebhard a promised visit at her residence in Elberfeld [Germany].

It was while I was engaged in putting my affairs in order, in view of my long absence, that an incident occurred, not indeed singular in my experience, but out of the normal. I was arranging and laying aside the articles I intended to take with me to Italy, when I heard a voice saying, "Take that book, it will be useful to you on your journey." I may as well say at once that I have the faculties of clairvoyance and clairaudience rather strongly developed. I turned my eyes on a manuscript volume I had placed among the heap of things to be locked away until my return.

209

Countess Wachtmeister

Certainly it seemed a singular inappropriate *vade mecum* for a holiday, being a collection of notes on the "Tarot" and passages in the *Kabbalah* that had been compiled for me by a friend. However, I decided to take it with me, and laid the book in the bottom of one of my travelling trunks.

At last the day came for me to leave Sweden, in October, 1885, and I arrived at Elberfeld, where I met with a cordial and affectionate greeting from Madame Gebhard....However, the time was drawing near for me to pass on into Italy. My friends never ceased pressing me to join them there, and at last the date of my departure was fixed

When I told Madame Gebhard that I must leave her in a few days, she spoke to me of a letter she had received from H.P.B....She was ill in body and depressed in mind. Her sole companions were her servant and an Indian gentleman...."Go to her," said Madame

Gebhard, "she needs sympathy, and you can cheer her up...."

I thought the matter over....Madame Gebhard was genuinely pleased when I made known my decision to her and showed her a letter I had written to "the old lady" in Wurzburg suggesting that if she cared to receive me I would spend a few weeks with her....The letter was despatched, and we waited eagerly for the reply. When at last it lay upon the breakfast table, there was much excitement in regard to its contents, but anticipation soon turned into consternation on Madame Gebhard's part and disappointment on mine, when we found nothing more nor less than a polite refusal....Madame Blavatsky was sorry, but she had no room for me; besides, she was so occupied in writing her *Secret Doctrine* that she had no time to entertain visitors, but hoped we might meet on my return from Italy....After the first natural disappointment, I set my eyes hopefully southward.

My luggage was soon ready, and a cab was actually waiting for me at the door when a telegram was put into my hands containing these words, "Come to Wurzburg at once, wanted immediately---Blavatsky."

It may easily be imagined that this message took me by surprise....There was no resisting...and instead of taking my ticket to Rome I took one to Wurzburg....

It was evening when I reached Madame Blavatsky's lodgings, and as I mounted the stairs my pulse was a little hurried while I speculated upon the reception which awaited me....

Madame Blavatsky's welcome was a warm one, and after the first few words of greeting, she remarked, "I have to apologize to you for behaving so strangely. I will tell you the truth, which is, that I did not want you. I have only one bedroom here, and I thought that you might be a fine lady and not care to share it with me. My ways are probably not your ways. If you came to me I knew that you would have to put up with many things that might seem to you intolerable discomforts. That is why I decided to decline your offer, and I wrote to you in that sense; but after my letter was posted Master spoke to me and said that I was to tell you to come. I never disobey a word from Master, and I telegraphed at once. Since then I have been trying to make the bedroom more habitable. I have bought a large screen which will divide the room, so that you can have one side and I, the other, and I hope you will not be too uncomfortable."

I replied that whatever the surroundings to which I had been accustomed might have been, I would willingly relinquish them all for the pleasure of her companionship.

I remember very well that it was then, on going into the dining room together to take some tea, that she said to me abruptly, as of something that had been dwelling on her mind.

"Master says you have a book for me of which I am much in need."

"No, indeed," I replied, "I have no books with me."

"Think again," she said, "Master says you were told in Sweden to bring a book on the Tarot and the *Kabbalah*."

Then I recollected the circumstances that I have related before. From the time I had placed the volume in the bottom of my box it had been out of my sight and out of my mind. Now, when I hurried to the bedroom, unlocked the trunk, and dived to the bottom, I found it in the same corner I had left it when packing in Sweden, undisturbed from that moment to this. But this was not all. When I returned to the dining-room with it in my hand, Madame Blavatsky made a gesture and cried, "Stay, do not open it yet. Now turn to page ten and on the sixth line you will find the words..." And she quoted a passage.

I opened the book which, let it be remembered, was no printed volume of which there might be a copy in H.P.B.'s possession, but a manuscript album in which...had been written notes and excerpts by a friend of mine for my own use, yet, on the page and at the line she had indicated I found the very words she had uttered.

When I handed her the book I ventured to ask her why she wanted it.

"Oh," she replied, "for *The Secret Doctrine*. That is my new work that I am so busily engaged in writing. Master is collecting material for me. He knew you had the book and told you to bring it that it might be at hand for reference."

No work was done that first evening, but the next day I began to realize what the course of H.P.B.'s life was, and what mine was likely to be while I stayed with her.

The description of a single day will serve to give an idea of the routine of her life at this time.

At six o'clock I was awakened by the servant coming with a cup of coffee for Madame Blavatsky, who, after this slight refreshment, rose and dressed, and by seven o'clock was at her desk in the sitting room.

She told me that this was her invariable habit, and that breakfast would be served at eight. After breakfast she settled herself at her writing desk and the day's work began in earnest. At one o'clock dinner was served, whereupon I rang a small hand-bell to call H.P.B. Sometimes she would come in at once; at other times her door would remain closed hour after hour, until our Swiss maid would come to me, almost with tears in her eyes, to ask what was to be done with Madame's dinner, which was either getting cold, or dried up, burnt, and utterly spoiled. At last, H.P.B. would come in weary with so many hours of exhausting labor and fasting; then another dinner would be cooked, or I would send to the Hotel to get her some nourishing food.

At seven o'clock she laid aside her writing, and after tea we would spend a pleasant evening together.

Comfortably seated in her big armchair, H.P.B. used to arrange her cards for a game of Patience, as she said to rest her mind. It seems as if the mechanical process of laying her cards enabled her mind to free itself from the pressure of concentrated labour during the day's work. She never cared to talk of Theosophy in the evenings. The mental tension during the day was so severe that she needed above all things rest, and so I procured as many journals and magazines as I could, and from these I would read the articles and passages that I thought most likely to interest and amuse her. At nine o'clock she went to bed, where she would surround herself with her Russian newspapers and read them until a late hour.

It was thus our days passed in the same routine; the only change worth noticing being that sometimes she would leave the door open between her writing room and the dining room where I sat, and then from time to time we would converse together, or I would write letters for her, or discuss the contents of those we had received....

The quiet studious life...continued for some little time, and the work progressed steadily, until, one morning, a thunderbolt descended upon us....Without a word of warning, H.P.B. received a copy of the well-known *Report of the Society for Psychical Research*....I shall never forget that day nor the look of blank and stony despair that she cast on me when I entered her sitting-room and found her with the book open in her hands.

"This," she cried, "is the Karma of the Theosophical Society, and it falls upon me. I am the scapegoat. I am made to bear all the sins of the Society, and now that I am dubbed the greatest impostor of the age, and a Russian spy into the bargain, who will listen to me or read *The Secret Doctrine*? How can I carry on Master's work? O cursed phenomena, which I only produced to please private friends and instruct those around me. What an awful Karma to bear! How shall I live through it? If I die Master's work will be wasted, and the Society will be ruined!"

In the intensity of her passion at first she would not listen to reason, but turned against me, saying, "Why don't you go? Why don't you leave me? You are a Countess, you cannot stop here with a ruined woman, with one held up to scorn before the whole world, one who will be pointed at everywhere as a trickster and an impostor. Go before you are defiled by my shame."

"H.P.B.," I said, as my eyes met hers with a steady gaze, "you know that Master lives and that He is your Master, and that the Theosophical Society was founded by Him. How, then, can it perish? And since I know this as well as you, since for me, now, the truth has been placed beyond the possibility of doubt, how can you for one moment suppose that I could desert you and the Cause we both are pledged to serve? Why, if every member of the Theosophical Society should prove traitor to that Cause you and I would remain, and would wait and work until the good times come again."

...It is little to be wondered at that the progress of *The Secret Doctrine* was brought to a standstill during these stormy days, and that when, at last, the work was resumed, the necessary detachment and tranquillity of mind were found hard of attainment....

One day at this time, when I walked into H.P.B.'s writing room, I found the floor strewn with sheets of discarded manuscript. I asked the meaning of this scene of confusion, and she replied, "Yes, I have tried twelve times to write this one page correctly, and each time Master says it is wrong. I think I shall go mad, writing it so often; but leave me alone, I will not pause until I have conquered it, even if I have to go on all night."

I brought a cup of coffee to refresh and sustain her, and then left her to prosecute her weary task. An hour later I heard her voice calling me, and on entering found that, at last, the passage was completed to satisfaction, but the labor had been terrible, and the results were often at this time small and uncertain.

As she leant back enjoying her cigarette and the sense of relief from arduous effort, I rested on the arm of her great chair and asked her how it was she could make mistakes in setting down what was given to her. She said: "Well, you see, what I do is this. I make what I can only describe as a sort of vacuum in the air before me, and fix my sight and my will upon it, and soon scene after scene passes before me like the successive pictures of a diorama, or, if I need a reference or information from some book, I fix my mind intently, and the astral counterpart of the book appears, and from it I take what I need. The more perfectly my mind is freed from distractions and mortifications, the more energy and intentness it possesses, the more easily I can do this; but to-day, after all the vexations I have undergone..., I could not concentrate properly, and each time I tried I got the quotations all wrong. Master says it is right now, so let us go in and have some tea...."

...Living in such close and familiar intercourse with H.P.B. as I did at this time, it naturally happened that I was a witness of many of the "phenomena" which took place in her vicinity.

There was one occurrence, continuously repeated over a long period, which impressed me very strongly with the conviction that she was watched and cared for by unseen guardians. From the first night that I passed in her room, until the last that preceded our departure from Wurzburg, I heard a regularly intermittent series of raps on the table by her bedside. They would begin at ten o'clock each evening, and would continue, at intervals of ten minutes, until six o'clock in the morning. They were sharp, clear raps, such as I never heard at any other time. Sometimes I held my watch in my hand for an hour at a stretch, and always as the ten minute interval ticked itself out, the rap would come with the utmost regularity. Whether H.P.B. was awake or asleep mattered nothing to the occurrence of the phenomenon, nor to its uniformity.

When I asked her for an explanation of these raps I was told that it was an effect of what might be called a sort of psychic telegraph which placed her in communication with her Teachers, and that the chelas might watch her body while her astral left it.

...Another incident...proved to me that there were agencies at work in her neighbourhood whose nature and action were inexplicable on generally accepted theories of the constitution and laws of matter.

As I have already remarked, H.P.B. was accustomed to read her Russian newspapers at night after retiring, and it was rarely that she extinguished her lamp before midnight. There was a screen between my bed and this lamp, but, nevertheless, its powerful rays, reflected from the ceiling and the walls, often disturbed my sleep. One night this lamp was burning after the clock had struck one. I could not sleep, and, as I heard by H.P.B.'s regular breathing that she slept, I rose, gently walked round to the lamp, and turned it out. There was always a dim light pervading the bedroom, which came from a night-light burning in the study, the door between that room and the bedroom being kept open. I had extinguished the lamp, and was going back, when it flamed up again, and the room was brightly illuminated. I thought to myself---what a strange lamp, I suppose the spring does not act, so I put my hand again on the spring, and watched until every vestige of flame was extinct, and, even then, held down the spring for a minute. Then I released it and stood for a moment longer watching, when, to my surprise, the flame reappeared and the lamp was burning as brightly as ever. This puzzled me considerably, and I determined to stand there by that lamp and put it out all through the night, if necessary, until I discovered the why and wherefore of its eccentricities. For the third time I pressed the spring and turned it down until the lamp was quite out, and then released it, watching eagerly to see what would take place. For the third time the lamp burned up, and this time I saw a brown hand slowly and gently turning the knob of the lamp. Familiar as I was with the action of astral forces and astral entities on the physical plane, I had no difficulty in coming to the conclusion that it was the hand of a chela, and, surmising that there was some reason why the lamp should remain alight, I returned to my couch. But a spirit of perversity and curiosity dwelt within me that night. I wanted to know more, so I called out, "Madame Blavatsky!" then, louder, "Madame Blavatsky!" and again "Madame Blavatsky!" Suddenly I heard an answering cry ---"Oh, my heart! my heart! Countess, you have nearly killed me;" and then again, "My heart! my heart!" I flew to H.P.B.'s bedside. "I was with Master," she murmured, "why did you call me back?" I was thoroughly alarmed, for her heart fluttered under my hand with wild palpitation.

I gave her a dose of digitalis, and sat beside her until the symptoms had abated and she had become calmer. Then she told me how Colonel Olcott had once nearly killed her in the same way, by calling her back suddenly when her astral form was absent from her body. She made me promise that I would never try experiments with her again, and this promise I readily gave, out of the fulness of my grief and contrition for having caused her such suffering....

We had a small, but very comfortable, apartment in Wurzburg; the rooms were of a good size, lofty, and on the ground floor so as to enable H.P.B. to move in and out in comfort. But during all the time that I was with her I could only persuade her to take fresh air three times. She seemed to enjoy these drives, but the trouble and exertion of preparing for them wearied her, and she esteemed them mere loss of time. I was in the habit...of going out daily for half an hour, as I felt that both air and exercise were necessary for my health, and I recall a curious incident which happened to me in connection with one of these walks....As I passed a perfumer's shop, I saw some soap in a glass bowl in the display window. Remembering that I required some, I walked into the shop and chose a piece from the bowl. I saw the shopman wrap paper around it, took the parcel from his hand, put it in my pocket, and continued my walk. When I returned to my apartment I went straight to my room, without first going to see H.P.B., and took off my hat and cloak. Taking the parcel out of my pocket, I began to unfasten the string and pull off the wrappings, and, as I did so, I perceived a small sheet of folded paper inside. I could not help thinking, how fond people are of advertisements, they even stick them on a cake of soap! but then I suddenly remembered that I had seen the man fasten up the parcel, and that he assuredly had not inserted any. This struck me as strange, and, as the paper had fallen to the ground, I stooped down and picked it up, opened it, and there found a few remarks addressed to me from H.P.B.'s Master in His handwriting, which I had often seen before. They were an explanation of events which had been puzzling me for some days past, and gave me some directions as to my future course of action. This phenomenon was peculiarly interesting to me as having taken place without H.P.B.'s knowledge, and independently of her, for she was writing quite unconcernedly at her table in her writing room at the time....

I have been lingering on many points which have nothing directly to do with the writing of *The Secret Doctrine*; but it seems to me that by showing some of the details of H.P.B.'s life at that time, one gains a better comprehension of the woman who wrote that stupendous work. Day after day she would sit there writing through all the long hours, and nothing could be more monotonous and wearisome than her life regarded from an outside point of view. But, I suppose, at that time she lived much in the inner world, and there saw sights and visions which compensated for the dreariness of her daily life. She had, however, a distraction of rather a peculiar nature. In front of her writing table, attached to the wall, was a cuckoo clock, and this used to behave in a very extraordinary manner. Sometimes it would strike like a loud gong, then sigh and groan as if possessed, cuckooing in the most unexpected way. Our maid, Louise...was very much afraid of it, and told us solemnly one day that she thought the devil was in it. "Not that I believe in the devil," she said, "but this cuckoo almost speaks to me at times." And so it did. One evening I went into the room and saw what appeared to me like streams of electric light coming out of the clock in all directions. On telling H.P.B. she replied, "Oh, it is only the spiritual telegraph, they are laying it on stronger to-night on account of to-morrow's work." Living in this atmosphere and coming into contact so continually with these, usually unseen, forces, this all seemed the true reality to me, and the outer world was that which appeared vague and unsatisfactory....

But the winter sped by, and the spring came on, and one morning H.P.B. received a letter from a friend of several years' standing,...Miss [Emily] Kislingbury, who wrote that she would come and pay us a visit....At this time, too, we received a visit from Mr. and Madame Gebhard....As we were now in full spring it was time to think of our summer plans and H.P.B. decided to spend the ensuing summer months at Ostend with her sister and niece.

Madame Gebhard was anxious to make a short visit to Austria and persuaded me to accompany her to Kempten....We made our plans, and began the arduous task of packing. In a few days all H.P.B.'s boxes were corded and locked and the eventful journey was about to begin. Miss Kislingbury was returning to London, and kindly promised to accompany H.P.B. as far as Ostend....

It was always a formidable thing for H.P.B. to travel, and I looked in dismay at the nine packages which were to be placed inside her railway carriage. We started very early to go to the station, and there we seated H.P.B., surrounded by her numerous belongings, while we tried to make arrangements with the conductor to let her be alone in the compartment with Miss Kislingbury and her maid, Louise....Then began the serious task of piling up all the baggage, consisting of pillows, coverlets, handbags, and the precious box containing the manuscript of *The Secret Doctrine*....Well, poor H.P.B. who had not been out of her room for weeks, had to walk all along the platform, and this was performed with difficulty. We got her comfortably settled, and were just rejoicing to think that the onerous task was satisfactorily completed, when one of the officials came to the door and began to remonstrate violently against the carriage being crowded with packages. He talked in German, H.P.B. answered in French, and I began to wonder how it would all end, when, fortunately, the whistle was heard and the train began to move out of the station....

219

Julia W. Keightley[81]
(the wife of Archibald Keightley)
1886-1891, Pennsylvania

Living some thousand miles from England, I never met
Madame Blavatsky in person....Like others of my acquaintance, I
first heard of...[H.P.B.] by coming across the S.P.R. pamphlet
denouncing her as an impostor and asserting the Hodgson-
Coulomb slander as a true fact....

Soon, however, I began to realise, through my own experience,
that she was not what she seemed to be....The evidence I had,
caused me to ask H.P.B. to teach me; and that fact that I fully
trusted in and believed her, is precisely what gained for me the
fulfillment of my wish. The mental attitude of belief sets up, in
our aura and in our inner bodies, magnetic and attractive
conditions, very different to those of contraction and
densification, which exist where doubt or criticism fill the mind.
A literal quickening of my aura and inner body took place....The
contraction in which men and women enfold themselves is too
little understood. To be known, faith and devotion must first be
had....

After H.P.B. accepted me as a pupil, no rules were laid down,
no plans formulated. I continued my daily routine, and at night,
after I fell into a deep sleep, the new life began. On waking in
the morning from a sleep so profound that the attitude of the
previous night was still retained, I would vividly remember that
I had gone, as it were, to H.P.B. I had been received in rooms
which I could and did describe to those who lived with her---
described, even to the worn places or holes in the carpet. On the
first occasion of this kind she signified to me her acceptance of
me as a pupil....After that, she would receive me in varying
fashion, showing me pictures which passed like panoramas across
the walls of the room....

...At other times, times more rare, I would awake to find her
standing at the foot of my bed, and as I leaned upon my elbow,
her sign-language would begin, the harmonies of Nature would
fill the moonlit room, while the wondrous living pictures passed
across the wall. All this was perfectly objective to me. I was
fully awake to all the surroundings, to all the natural sounds of

the night, and I have taken my pet dog into my arms because it shivered and whimpered at sight of her. All the expressions of H.P.B.'s face became familiar to me. I can see her now, her old bedgown---what dingy old gown was ever so cherished?---folded about her, as she opened out space before me, and then, too, expanded into her own real being.

I have hardly more than half-a-dozen letters from her, and these contain no teaching; they bore upon external theosophic affairs and have this peculiarity. At night she would tell me to advise certain persons of certain things. I would obey, giving her as my authority, and a few days afterwards, but never long enough for the full voyage, would come her letter giving in writing the instructions previously heard at night. Thus I was enabled to prove that I really heard her wish over seas, for always the request concerned some sudden emergency which had just arisen a day, two days at most, before. I was able to check off my experience in this way, as I was also able to speak at times before an event occurred....

Vera Johnston[82]
(H.P.B.'s niece)
June, 1886, Elberfeld, Germany

In June, 1886, I stayed with my aunt in Elberfeld....It was her habit to read out in the afternoon what she had written of *The Secret Doctrine* in the preceding night....

Generally on coming down in the morning from the bedroom I occupied in the house of Madame Gebhard together with my mother, I found my aunt deep in her work....One day I saw evident traces of perplexity written on her face. Not wishing to disturb her I sat down quietly and waited for her to speak. She remained silent a long time with her eyes fixed on some point on the wall, and with a cigarette between her fingers, as was her custom. At last she called out to me:

"Vera," she said, "do you think you could tell me what is a pi?"

Rather astonished at such a question, I said I thought a pie was some kind of an English dish.

"Please don't make a fool of yourself," she said rather impatiently, "don't you understand I address you in your capacity of a mathematical pundit. Come and see this."

I looked at the page that lay before her on the table, and saw it was covered with figures and calculations, and soon became aware that the formula $\pi = 3.14159$ was put down wrongly throughout them all. It was written $\pi = 31.4159$. With great joy and triumph I hastened to inform her of her mistake.

"That's it!" she exclaimed. "This confounded...[decimal point] bothered me all the morning. I was rather in a hurry yesterday to put down what I saw, and to-day at the first glance at the page I intensely but vaguely felt there was something wrong, and do what I could I could not remember where the...[decimal point] actually was when I saw this number."

Knowing very little of Theosophy in general and my aunt's ways of writing in particular at that time, I of course was greatly struck with her not being able to correct such a slight mistake in the very intricate calculations she had written down with her own hand.

"You are very green," she said, "if you think that I actually know and understand all the things I write. How many times am I to repeat to you and your mother that the things I write are dictated to me, that sometimes I see manuscripts, numbers, and words before my eyes of which I never knew anything."...

Countess Constance Wachtmeister[83]
Oct., 1886---March, 1887, Ostend, Belgium

In October, 1886, I...[rejoined] H.P.B. in Ostend, and found her settled in comfortable enough quarters; she welcomed me with all the warmth of her genial nature....We recommenced our monotonous but interesting life, the thread being taken up from where it was last broken, and I watched with delight how the piles of manuscript for the *S.D.* were increasing. Our near vicinity to England caused people once more to come buzzing round H.P.B., and we received several visitors....

Towards the end of the winter [March, 1887] H.P.B. became very ill....

To my great distress, I now began to notice that...[H.P.B.] became drowsy and heavy in the middle of the day, and often was unable to work for an hour together. This increased rapidly, and as the doctor who attended her pronounced it to be an affection of the kidneys, I became alarmed, and sent a telegram to Madame Gebhard to tell her of my apprehensions, and to beg her to come and help me....I was...thankful when I received a cordial response to my telegram and knew that in a few hours I should see Madame Gebhard.

When she came I felt as if a great burden had been lifted off my shoulders. In the meanwhile H.P.B. was getting worse, and the Belgian doctor, who was kindness itself, tried one remedy after another, but with no good result. I began to get seriously alarmed and anxious as to what course I should adopt. H.P.B. was in a heavy, lethargic state, she seemed to be unconscious for hours together, and nothing could rouse or interest her. Finally, a bright inspiration came to me. In the London [Theosophical] group I knew there was a Doctor Ashton Ellis, so I telegraphed to him, described the state that H.P.B. was in, and entreated him to come without delay.

I sat by H.P.B.'s bed that night listening to every sound as I anxiously watched the hours go by, till at last, at 3 a.m., the joyful sound of a bell was heard. I flew to the door, opened it, and the doctor walked in. I eagerly told him all her symptoms, and described the remedies that had been applied, whereupon he went to her and made her drink some medicine that he had brought with him....

The next day there was a consultation between the two doctors. The Belgian doctor said that he had never known a case of a person with the kidneys attacked as H.P.B.'s were, living as long as she had done, and that he was convinced that nothing could save her....Mr. Ellis replied that it was exceedingly rare for anyone to survive so long in such a state. He further told us that he had consulted a specialist before coming to Ostend, who was of the same opinion, but advised that, in addition to the prescribed medicine, he should try massage, so as to stimulate the paralyzed organs....

The night passed quietly, and several times the following day Mr. Ellis...[massaged] her until he was quite exhausted; but she got no better, and to my horror I began to detect that peculiar faint odour of death which sometimes precedes dissolution. I hardly dared hope that she would live through the night, and while I was sitting alone by her bedside she opened her eyes and told me how glad she was to die, and that she thought the Master would let her be free at last. Still she was very anxious about her *Secret Doctrine.* I must be most careful of her manuscripts and hand all over to Col. Olcott with directions to have them printed. She had hoped that she would have been able to give more to the world, but the Master knew best. And so she talked on at intervals, telling me many things. At last she dropped off into a state of unconsciousness, and I wondered how it would all end.

It seemed to me impossible that she should die and leave her work unfinished; and then, again, the Theosophical Society....what would become of it? How could it be that the Master who was at the head of that Society would allow it to crumble away?...The thought came to me that the Master had told H.P.B. that she was to form a circle of students around her and that she was to teach them. How could she do that if she were to die? And then I opened my eyes and glanced at her and thought, was it possible that she who had slaved, suffered, and striven so hard should be allowed to die in the middle of her work?...

None of those who knew her, really understood her. Even to me, who had been alone with her for so many months, she was an enigma, with her strange powers, her marvellous knowledge, her extraordinary insight into human nature, and her mysterious life, spent in regions unknown to ordinary mortals, so that though her body might be near, her soul was often away in commune with others....

Such were the thoughts which passed through my mind, as I sat hour after hour that anxious night, watching her as she seemed to be getting weaker and weaker. A wave of blank despondency came over me, as I felt how truly I loved this noble woman, and I realized how empty life would be without her....My whole soul rose in rebellion at the thought of losing her....I gave a bitter cry and knew no more.

When I opened my eyes, the early morning light was stealing in, and a dire apprehension came over me that I had slept, and that perhaps H.P.B. had died during my sleep---died whilst I was untrue to my vigil. I turned round towards the bed in horror, and there I saw H.P.B. looking at me calmly with her clear grey eyes, as she said, "Countess, come here."

I flew to her side. "What has happened, H.P.B.---you look so different to what you did last night."

She replied, "Yes, Master has been here; He gave me my choice, that I might die and be free if I would, or I might live and finish *The Secret Doctrine*. He told me how great would be my sufferings and what a terrible time I would have before me in England (for I am to go there); but when I thought of those students to whom I shall be permitted to teach a few things, and of the Theosophical Society in general, to which I have already given my heart's blood, I accepted the sacrifice, and now to make it complete, fetch me some coffee and something to eat, and give me my tobacco box."

I flew off to do her errands and ran to tell Madame Gebhard the good news....

Archibald Keightley[84]
Feb.---April, 1887, Ostend, Belgium

In the early months of 1887 there were some few members of the T.S. in London who felt that if Theosophy did not receive some vital impulse, the centre there would be confined to a few individuals only who were pursuing and would continue to pursue their studies....There were many anxious discussions as to how a vital interest could be awakened in the truths of Theosophy, and how attention should be restored to the ethical philosophy....We all felt that we were working in the dark and that we were ignorant of the real basis upon which the philosophy rested.

Obviously we required a leader who might intelligently direct our efforts. We then determined each separately to write to H.P.

Blavatsky, who was then in Ostend, laying before the Founder of the T.S. and the Messenger of the Masters the position as each of us saw it. We asked her to reply in a collective letter giving us advice as to what to do. She replied, however, to each individual, writing letters of eight to twelve pages. The result of this was that we all wrote and asked her to come over and direct our efforts. She had told us that she was writing the *Secret Doctrine* and must finish that before undertaking other work.

Nevertheless we wrote to her that there was, we believed, urgent need of her directing presence, and that she could finish the *Secret Doctrine* in London as well as or better than in Ostend. After receiving her reply, which urged objections, Mr. Bertram Keightley went over to Ostend during the latter part of February or beginning of March and talked matters over with her. She agreed to come to London at the end of April provided we would find a house for her somewhere a little out of London in which she could work in peace. Soon after he returned I went over to Ostend rather unexpectedly to myself. I naturally went to call after leaving my luggage at the hotel. Madame Blavatsky received me with the greatest kindness, although previously to that occasion I was almost unknown to her. She insisted that I should transfer my things to her house and stay with her while in Ostend. At that time she was occupying the first floor of the house, with a Swiss maid to wait on her and Countess Wachtmeister to keep her company. I was at once introduced to the *Secret Doctrine* with a request to read, correct, and excise, a privilege I naturally did not avail myself of.

Madame Blavatsky at that time had never ventured out of her rooms since the previous November, and never came from her writing and bed-room into the dining-room until the windows had been closed and the room well warmed. Several attacks of inflammation of the kidneys had warned her that the slightest chill was dangerous to the completion of her work.

At the close of my visit I returned to England with renewed assurances of her arrival on May 1st, and under pledge to return and assist Madame Blavatsky on her journey to London. I had not been in London many hours when one of our members, Dr. Ashton Ellis, received a telegram from Countess Wachtmeister saying, as I recall its tenor, that Madame Blavatsky had had another inflammatory attack on the kidneys, that she was comatose, and that her life was in the utmost danger. Dr. Ellis went over to Ostend and attended her. He told me that he was extremely surprised, and so were the others who know her serious condition, to find her recovering in a few days. Her state then was so critical that she began arranging her affairs before the comatose attack came, burning up papers and having a will drawn up so as to be ready for the end. Later on she told me herself that her life was saved by the direct intervention of her Master. Her endurance manifested itself even at this point, for as soon as she could leave her bed she was at work on the *Secret Doctrine*.

In the middle of April Mr. [Bertram] Keightley again went over, and I followed him about the 25th or 26th. We were rather in consternation because Madame Blavatsky said she could not possibly leave in such weather as then prevailed, especially on account of her late serious illness. Her landlord said she must leave, for the rooms were let. Countess Wachtmeister had previously left for Sweden to attend to urgent business affairs there under promise to rejoin Madame Blavatsky in London. Staying in the house with us was a friend of Dr. Ellis who assisted in the removal.

The fated day came, and in place of being bright but cold, as had been the case two days before, the morning proved to be cold and foggy, with a steady drizzling rain falling and penetrating all it touched, the thermometer being about 40 degrees. We fully expected Madame Blavatsky would decline to move, and thought her justified in doing so. Nevertheless she appeared that morning in full marching order, the trunks were packed, and all was ready.

The carriage arrived and Madame Blavatsky was assisted into it, and off it drove to the wharf. It must be remembered that she had not had a window open in her room while she was in it (and would not scarcely allow it open while she was out) for six months. She kept her room at a temperature of over 70 deg., believing that anything under that would kill her. Moreover, she was almost crippled with rheumatism and could hardly walk, and was a constant martyr to sciatica. On getting to the wharf we found the tide low, and in consequence…there was only a narrow gangway leading at a very steep incline to the steamer's deck. Imagine our dismay. Madame Blavatsky, however, said nothing, but simply grasping the rails walked slowly and without assistance to the deck. We then took her to a cabin on deck where she sank on the sofa and only then betrayed the pain and exhaustion caused by her effort. The journey was uneventful so far as Dover, save that for the first time in her life Mme. Blavatsky knew what the preliminary qualms of sea-sickness meant and was much puzzled.

At Dover the tide was still lower, and as a result four very stalwart piermen had to carry her to the top. Then came the greatest difficulty, for the platform is low and the English railway carriage steps were high. It required the united efforts of all the party (and the piermen as well) to assist Madame Blavatsky in her crippled state into the carriage. The journey to London was uneventful, and with the help of an invalid chair and a carriage she was safely lodged in the house we had secured for her. Secretly I was afraid the journey would have serious results, but, whatever was the reason, she seemed to enjoy better health for some time after her arrival in England then she had for months previously.

The day after her arrival she was at work on the *Secret Doctrine* at 7 a.m....

Chapter 7

E N G L A N D

1887-1891

Bertram Keightley[85]
May, 1887---Oct., 1888, London

A day or two after our arrival at Maycot, H.P.B. placed the whole of the so-far completed MSS. [of *The Secret Doctrine*] in the hands of Dr. [Archibald] Keightley and myself, instructing us to read, punctuate, correct the English, alter, and generally treat it as if it were our own---which we naturally did *not* do, having far too high an opinion of her knowledge to take any liberties with so important a work.

But we both read the whole mass of MSS.---a pile over three feet high---most carefully through, correcting the English and punctuation where absolutely indispensable, and then, after prolonged consultation, faced the author in her den---in my case with sore trembling, I remember ---with the solemn opinion that the whole of the matter must be rearranged on some definite plan, since as it stood the book was another *Isis Unveiled*, only far worse, so far as absence of plan and consecutiveness were concerned.

After some talk, H.P.B. told us to go to Tophet and do what we liked. She had had more than enough of the blessed thing, had given it over to us, washed her hands of it entirely, and we might get out of it as best we could.

We retired and consulted. Finally, we laid before her a plan, suggested by the character of the matter itself, *viz.*, to make the work consist of four volumes….Further, instead of making the first

Bertram Keightley

volume to consist, as she had intended, of the history of some great Occultists, we advised her to follow the natural order of exposition, and begin with the Evolution of Cosmos, to pass from that to the Evolution of Man, then to deal with the historical part in a third volume treating of the lives of some great Occultists; and finally, to speak of Practical Occultism in a fourth volume, should she ever be able to write it.

This plan we laid before H.P.B., and it was duly sanctioned by her.

The next step was to read the MSS. through again and make a general re-arrangement of the matter pertaining to the subjects coming under the heading of Cosmogony and Anthropology, which were to form the first two volumes of the work. When this had been completed, and H.P.B. duly consulted, and her approval of what had been done obtained, the whole of the MSS. so arranged was typewritten out by professional hands, then reread, corrected, [and] compared with the original MSS....

It then appeared that the whole of the Commentary on the Stanzas [of Dzyan] did not amount to more than some twenty pages of the present work....So we seriously interviewed her, and suggested that she should write a proper commentary, as in her opening words she had promised her readers to do. Her reply was characteristic, "What on earth am I to say? What *do* you want to know? Why it's all as plain as the nose on your face!!!" We could not see it; she didn't---or made out she didn't---so we retired to reflect....

The solution was this: Each sloka [verse] of the stanzas was written (or cut out from the type-written copy) and pasted at the head of a sheet of paper, and then on a loose sheet pinned thereto were written all the questions we could find time to devise upon that sloka....H.P.B. struck out large numbers of them, made us write fuller explanations, or our own ideas---such as they were---of what her readers expected her to say, wrote more herself, incorporated the little she had already written on that particular sloka, and so the work was done.

But when we came to...sending the MSS. to the printers, the result was found to be such that the most experienced compositor would tear his hair in blank dismay. Therefore, Dr. Keightley and myself set to work with a type-writer, and alternately dictating and writing, made a clean copy of the first parts of volumes I and II.

Then work was continued till parts II. and III. of each volume were in a fairly advanced condition, and we could think of sending the work to press....

Of the further history of *The Secret Doctrine* there is not much more to say---though there were months of hard work before us. H.P.B. read and corrected two sets of galley proofs, then a page proof...correcting, adding, and altering up to the very last moment....

Of phenomena in connection with *The Secret Doctrine* ...quotations with full references, from books which were never in the house---quotations verified after hours of search, sometimes, at the British Museum for a rare book---of such, I saw and verified not a few.

In verifying them I found occasionally the curious fact that the numerical references were reversed, *e.g.,* p. 321 for p. 123, illustrating the reversal of objects when seen in the astral light....

Of the value of the work, posterity must judge finally. Personally, I can only place on record my profound conviction that when studied thoroughly but not treated as a revelation, when understood and assimilated but not made a text for dogma, H.P.B.'s *Secret Doctrine* will be found of incalculable value, and will furnish suggestions, clues, and threads of guidance, for the study of Nature and Man, such as no other existing work can supply.

———————

Charles Johnston[86]
Spring, 1887, London

I first met dear old "H.P.B.," as she made all her friends call her, in the spring of 1887. Some of her disciples had taken a pretty house in Norwood, where the huge glass nave and twin towers of the Crystal Palace glint about a labyrinth of streets and terraces. London was at its grimy best. The squares and gardens were scented with grape-clusters of lilac, and yellow rain of laburnums under soft green leaves. The eternal smoke-pall was thinned to a gray veil shining in the afternoon sun, with the great Westminster Towers and a thousand spires and chimneys piercing through. Every house had its smoke-wreath, trailing away to the east.

H.P.B. was just finishing her day's work, so I passed a half-hour upstairs with her volunteer secretary, a disciple who served her with boundless devotion....I had known him two years before....So we talked of old times, and of H.P.B.'s great book *The Secret Doctrine*, and he read me resonant stanzas [of Dzyan] about Universal Cosmic Night, when Time was not; about the Luminous Sons of Manvantaric Dawn; and the Armies of the Voice; about the Water Men Terrible and Bad, and the Black Magicians of Lost Atlantis; about the Sons of Will and Yoga and the Ring Pass-Not;

The Towers of Westminster

about the Great Day Be-With-Us, when all shall be perfected into one, re-uniting "thyself and others, myself and thee."

So the half-hour passed, and I went downstairs to see the Old Lady. She was in her writing-room, just rising from her desk, and clad in one of those dark blue dressing-gowns she loved. My first impression was of her rippled hair as she turned, then her marvellously potent eyes, as she welcomed me: "My dear fellow! I am so glad to see you! Come in and talk! You are just in time to have some tea!" And a hearty handshake.

Then a piercing call for "Louise," and her Swiss maid appeared, to receive a voluble torrent of directions in French, and H.P.B. settled herself snugly into an armchair, comfortably near her tobacco-box, and began to make me a cigarette. The cuffs of a Jaeger suit showed round her wrists, only setting off the perfect shape and delicacy of her hands, as her deft fingers, deeply stained with nicotine, rolled the white rice-paper round Turkish tobacco....

...H.P.B...with a quizzically humorous smile...[asked]: "Of course you have read the S.P.R. Report?---The Spookical Research Society---and know that I am a Russian spy, and the champion impostor of the age?"

"Yes, I read the Report. But I knew its contents already. I was at the meeting when it was first read, two years ago."

"Well," said H.P.B., again smiling with infinite humour, "and what impression did the frisky lambkin from Australia [Richard Hodgson] make upon your susceptible heart?"

"A very deep one. I decided that he must be a very good young man, who always came home to tea; and that the Lord had given him a very good conceit of himself. If he got an opinion into his head, he would plow away blandly, and contrary facts would be quite invisible....And all that Mr. Sinnett says in the *Occult World* seems to me absolutely unshaken by the whole Report...."

"I am glad you think so, my dear," she answered in her courtly way, "for now I can offer you some tea with a good conscience." Louise had laid a white cloth on the corner table, brought in a tray, and lit a lamp. The secretary soon joined us, receiving a tart little sermon on being unpunctual, which he was not. Then we came back to...the Psychical Researchers.

"They will never do much," said H.P.B. "They go too much on material lines, and they are far too timid....They were afraid of raising a storm if they said our phenomena were true. Fancy what it would have meant! Why it would practically have committed Modern Science to our Mahatmas and all I have taught about the inhabitants of the occult world and their tremendous powers. They shrank at the thought of it, and so they made a scapegoat of this poor orphan and exile." And her eyes were full of humourous pity for herself.

"It must have been something like that," I answered, "for there is simply no backbone in the Report itself. It is the weakest thing of the kind I have ever read. There is not a shred of real evidence in it from beginning to end."

"Do you really think so? That's right!" cried H.P.B.; and then she turned on her secretary, and poured in a broadside of censure, telling him he was greedy, idle, untidy, unmethodical, and generally worthless. When he ventured an uneasy defence, she

234

flared up and declared that he "was born a flapdoodle, lived a flapdoodle, and would die a flapdoodle." He lost his grip, and not unnaturally made a yellow streak of egg across her white tablecloth.

"There!" cried H.P.B., glaring at him with withering scorn, and then turning to me for sympathy in her afflictions. That was her way, to rate her disciples in the presence of perfect strangers. It speaks volumes for her, that they loved her still....

"There is one thing about the S.P.R. Report I want you to explain. What about the writing in the occult letters [of the Masters]?"

"Well, what about it?" asked H.P.B., immediately interested.

"They say that you wrote them yourself, and that they bear evident marks of your handwriting and style. What do you say to that?"

"Let me explain it this way," she answered, after a long gaze at the end of her cigarette. "Have you ever made experiments in thought-transference? If you have, you must have noticed that the person who received the mental picture very often colours it, or often changes it slightly, with his own thought, and this where perfectly genuine transference of thought takes place. Well, it is something like that with the precipitated letters. One of our Masters, who perhaps does not know English, and of course has no English handwriting, wishes to precipitate a letter in answer to a question sent mentally to him. Let us say he is in Tibet, while I am in Madras or London. He has the answering thought in his mind, but not in English words. He has first to impress that thought on my brain, or on the brain of someone else who knows English, and then to take the word-forms that rise up in that other brain to answer the thought. Then he must form a clear mind-picture of the words in writing, also drawing on my brain, or the brain of whoever it is, for the shapes. Then either through me or some Chela with whom he is magnetically connected, he has to precipitate these word-shapes on paper, first sending the shapes into the Chela's mind, and then driving them into the paper, using the magnetic force of the Chela to do the printing, and collecting the material, black or blue or red, as the case may be, from the astral light. As all things dissolve into the astral light, the will of the magician can draw them forth again. So he can draw forth colours of pigments to mark the figures in the letter, using the magnetic force of the Chela to stamp them in, and guiding the whole by his own much greater magnetic force, a current of powerful will.

"That sounds quite reasonable," I answered. "Won't you show me how it is done?"

"You would have to be clairvoyant," she answered, in a perfectly direct and matter-of-fact way, "in order to see and guide the currents. But this is the point: Suppose the letter [is] precipitated through me; it would naturally show some traces of my expressions, and even of my writing; but all the same, it would be a perfectly genuine occult phenomenon, and a real message from that Mahatma. Besides, when all is said and done, they exaggerate the likeness of the writings. And the experts are not infallible. We have had experts who were just as positive that I could not possibly have written those letters, and just as good experts, too. But the Report says nothing about them. And then there are letters, in just the same handwriting, precipitated when I was thousands of miles away. Dr. Hartmann received more than one at Adyar, Madras, when I was in London; I could hardly have written them....But you have seen some of the occult letters? What do you say?"

"Yes," I replied; "Mr. Sinnett showed me about a ream of them: the whole series that the *Occult World* and *Esoteric Buddhism* are based on. Some of them are in red, either ink or pencil, but far more are in blue. I thought it was pencil at first, and I tried to smudge it with my thumb; but it would not smudge."

"Of course not!" she smiled; "the colour is driven into the surface of the paper. But what about the writings?"

"I am coming to that. There were two: the blue writing, and the red; they were totally different from each other, and both were quite unlike yours. I have spent a good deal of time studying the relation of handwriting to character, and the two characters were quite clearly marked. The blue was evidently a man of very gentle and even character, but of tremendously strong will; logical, easy-going, and taking endless pains to make his meaning clear. It was altogether the handwriting of a cultivated and very sympathetic man."

"Which I am not," said H.P.B., with a smile; "that is Mahatma

Koothoomi; he is a Kashmiri Brahman by birth, you know, and has travelled a good deal in Europe. He is the author of the *Occult World* letters, and gave Mr. Sinnett most of the material of *Esoteric Buddhism*. But you have read all about it."

"Yes, I remember he says you shriek across space with a voice like Sarasvati's peacock. Hardly the sort of thing you would say of yourself."

"Of course not," she said; "I know I am a nightingale. But what about the other writing?"

"The red? Oh that is wholly different. It is fierce, impetuous, dominant, strong; it comes in volcanic outbursts, while the other is like Niagara Falls. One is fire, and the other is the ocean. They are wholly different, and both quite unlike yours. But the second has more resemblance to yours than the first."

"This is my Master," she said, "whom we call Mahatma Morya. I have his picture here."

And she showed me a small panel in oils. If ever I saw genuine awe and reverence in a human face, it was in hers, when she spoke of her Master. He was a Rajput by birth, she said, one of the old warrior race of the Indian desert, the finest and handsomest nation in the world. Her Master was a giant, six feet eight, and splendidly built; a superb type of manly beauty. Even in the picture, there is a marvellous power and fascination; the force, the fierceness even, of the face; the dark, glowing eyes, which stare you out of countenance; the clear-cut features of bronze, the raven hair and beard---all spoke of manhood strength. I asked her something about his age. She answered:

"My dear, I cannot tell you exactly, for I do not know. But this I will tell you. I met him first when I was twenty,---in 1851. He was in the very prime of manhood then. I am an old woman now, but he has not aged a day. He is still in the prime of manhood. That is all I can say. You may draw you own conclusions."

...Then she told me something about other Masters and adepts she had known....She had known adepts of many races, from Northern and Southern India, Tibet, Persia, China, Egypt; of various European nations, Greek, Hungarian, Italian, English; of certain races in South America, where she said there was a Lodge of adepts....

237

"...And now, my dear, it is getting late, and I am getting sleepy. So I must bid you goodnight!" And the Old Lady dismissed me with that grand air of hers which never left her, because it was a part of herself. She was the most perfect aristocrat I have ever known....

There was something in her personality, her bearing, the light and power of her eyes, which spoke of a wider and deeper life....That was the greatest thing about her, and it was always there; this sense of a bigger world, of deeper power, of unseen might; to those in harmony with her potent genius, this came as a revelation and incentive to follow the path she pointed out. To those who could not see with her eyes, who could not raise themselves in some measure to her vision, this quality came as a challenge, an irritant, a discordant and subversive force, leading them at last to an attitude of fierce hostility and denunciation.

When the last word is said, she was greater than any of her works, more full of living power than even her marvellous writings....

Archibald Keightley[87]
May, 1887---1889, London

It was no very long time before Mme. Blavatsky's presence began to be felt. People began to gather round her, and Maycot became the scene of the pilgrimage of a good many people....It was a remarkable experience to see those who came. Some had private interviews: others were received in company with us who lived in the house. And the method of treatment! At times argumentative: at others sarcastic: very rarely appealing for credence or justice: always the same driving energy which spared neither herself nor any other who might in any way further her Master's work....

The nominal day began for Mme. Blavatsky before 7 a.m. When it really began I do not know. The body had to have its sleep, for it could not be driven too hard. But I had reason to believe that many hours of the night were spent in writing, though this never interfered with her usual hour to get to her desk. She was invisible till she called for her midday meal. I say midday, but it was a very movable meal and might be called for at any hour between twelve and four, a proceeding which naturally disconcerted a cook. Woe betide any disturber of those hours of work, for the more quiet she was, the more seriously was she engaged.....Finally at 6.30 came for Mme. Blavatsky the evening meal, which was taken in company with the rest of us. The table cleared, came tobacco and talk, especially the former, though there was plenty of the latter. I wish I had the memory and the power to relate those talks. All things under the sun and some others, too, were discussed. Here was a mind stored with information gathered in very extensive travels, an experience of life and experience of things of an "unseen nature," and with it all an acuteness of perception which brought out the real and true....Of one thing Mme. Blavatsky was intolerant---cant and sham and of hypocrisy. For these she had no mercy; but for genuine effort, however mistaken, she would spare no trouble to give advice and readjustment. She was genuine in all her dealings, but I learned then and later that she at times had to remain silent in order that others might gain experience and knowledge, even if in gaining it they at times deceived themselves. I never knew her to state what was not true; but I knew she had sometimes to keep silence, because those who interrogated her had no right to the information. And in those cases, I afterwards learned that she was accused of deliberate untruth....

The evenings passed in such talks, and all the while she arranged her "patiences."...Among other things which I learned was the fact that while Solitaire occupied the brain, H.P.B. was engaged in very different work, and that Mme. Blavatsky could play Solitaire, take part in a conversation going on around her among us others, attend to what we used to call "upstairs" and also see what was going on in her own room and other places in the house and out of it, at one and the same time.

It was at one of these tobacco parliaments that Mme. Blavatsky stated her difficulty in getting her views expressed in the *Theosophist*. This was the magazine which she had started with Colonel Olcott in India. It was under his charge and he edited it in India and not unnaturally he conducted it on his own

239

lines. But with the commencement of Mme. Blavatsky's work in England a more immediate expression of *her* views became a matter of importance. So a new magazine was proposed and decided on and steps were taken to secure its publication. Oh, but there were discussions as to its title! "Truth," "Torch," and a variety of others were offered as suggestions and rejected. Then came the "Light-bringer" and finally "Lucifer," as an abbreviation. But this was most vehemently opposed by some as being too diabolical and too much opposed to *les convenances*. Perish the word! This secured its instant acceptance....

The Blavatsky Lodge was originally started as a body of people who were prepared to follow H.P.B. implicitly and a Pledge embodying this was drawn up. We all took it and the meetings began. Every Thursday evening they were held in Mme. Blavatsky's room, which was thrown into one with the dining room. Members flocked in, so that the rooms were too small, the interest being in the questions which were propounded for Mme. Blavatsky to answer. Some of the results were printed in "Transactions of the Blavatsky Lodge."...

The procedure under such circumstances is worth recalling. You would, as I did, present your thesis or remarks. It would be received vehemently, be opposed with a variety of eloquence---an eloquence calculated to upset your balance, and the impression given that you were a most evilly designing person, aiming to upset some of Mme. Blavatsky's most cherished plans of work. But with your sincerity of purpose becoming plain, there would come a change in Mme. Blavatsky. Her manner would change, even the expression of her face. "Sound and fury" evaporated, she became very quiet, and even her face seemed to become larger, more massive and solid. Every point you raised was considered and into her eyes---those wonderful eyes---came the look we learned to recognize. That look was one to be earned as a reward, for it meant that the heart had been searched and that guile was not found, also that H.P.B. was in charge....

It must be remembered that during all this time of stress and effort Mme. Blavatsky was still a sick woman, always suffering pain and often hardly able to walk. But her inflexible will and devotion got her from her bed to her writing table and enabled her to persist in the carrying through the press of the *Secret*

Doctrine, to edit *Lucifer*, write her Russian articles and those for *Lucifer*, the *Theosophist*, the *Path*,...to receive her visitors both in private and in public, and in addition to deal with an enormous private correspondence. It was at this time...I got a form of erysipelas with high fever, and had to stay in bed. It so happened that Mme. Blavatsky's physician was calling and he looked in on me. What was said I do not know, but as I lay in a kind of stupor I found that Mme. Blavatsky had made a progress up two flights of fairly steep stairs (she who never went up a step if it could be helped, on account of the pain so caused) and had arrived to judge for herself of her doctor's report of me. She sat and looked at me, and then she talked while she held a glass of water between her hands, and this water I afterwards drank: then she went downstairs again, bidding me to follow.

Down I went and was made to lie on the couch in her room and covered up. I lay there half asleep while she worked away at her writing, sitting at her table in her big chair, with her back towards me. How long I was there I do not know, but suddenly just past my head went a flash of deep crimson lightning. I started, not unnaturally, and was saluted through the back of the chair with "Lie down, what for do you take any notice?" I did so and went to sleep and, after I had been sent upstairs to bed, I again went to sleep and next morning was quite well, if a little shaky....This was the only time I saw the crimson light, though I have seen, and others saw, the pale blue light attached to some objects in the room and then flitting about. One of us rashly touched it one day when Mme. Blavatsky was in the next room. He got an electric shock and was also electrified by sounds of wrath from Mme. Blavatsky, greeting him by name and asking what on earth he meant by meddling with what he had no business to touch and by making an impertinently curious intrusion into matters with which he had no concern. I am sure he has not forgotten either the shock or rap to his knuckles or the rap to his curiosity. I know he remembered the shock to his arm for a long time.

The meetings of the Blavatsky Lodge were out of the ordinary. The discussions were informal and all sat round and asked questions of Mme. Blavatsky. All sorts and conditions of men and women were present and one part of our delight was for

Mme. Blavatsky to reply by the Socratic method---ask another question and seek information on her own account. It was a very effective method and frequently confounded the setter of the conundrum. If it was a genuine search for information which dictated the question, she would spare no pains to give all information in her power. But if the matter was put forward to annoy her or puzzle, the business resulted badly for the questioner. The meetings took up a lot of time, but Mme. Blavatsky enjoyed the contest of wits. All nations would be represented in those rooms on Thursday nights, and one could never tell who would be present. Sometimes there would be unseen visitors, seen by some but not by others of us. Results were curious. Mme. Blavatsky felt the cold very much and her room was therefore kept very warm, so much so that at the meetings it was unpleasantly hot very often. One night before the meeting time, I came downstairs to the find the room like an ice-house, though fire and lights were fully on. I called H.P.B.'s attention to this, but was greeted with a laugh and "Oh, I have had a friend of mine here to see me and he forgot to remove his atmosphere." Another time I remember that the rooms gradually filled until there was no vacant seat. On the sofa sat a distinguished Hindu, in full panoply of turban and dress. The discussion proceeded and apparently our distinguished guest was much interested, for he seemed to follow intelligently the remarks of each speaker. The President of the Lodge arrived that night very late, and coming in looked around for a seat. He walked up to the sofa and sat down---right in the middle of the distinguished Hindu, who promptly, and with some surprise, *fizzled and vanished*!

During this winter affairs had been moving in America and there had been a gradually increasing interest in things Theosophical....I was called to Mme. Blavatsky's room and asked "Arch, when can you start for America?"...I was off in three days...The voyage was an odd experience for me, as I had never been on an ocean trip before or to such a distance....On board in my cabin my attention was attracted to a number of little taps and cracks. These might naturally be due to the ship. But my attention was enforced to a series of little flashes of light, especially at night. The point to me was that these flashes and also these taps and cracks invariably associated themselves in my mind with the idea of H.P.B., and by this time I had begun to learn that most of these "happenings" meant something. Afterwards by letter, and later when I returned, I found she could tell me accurately what I had been doing during my journey to and from and throughout my stay in America. I was told that these taps and cracks and flashes were the coming and going of elemental forms of force which took a snapshot of me and my proceedings....

Walter R. Old[88]
Summer, 1887, London

...During the year 1887....I was in daily correspondence with members of the Theosophical Society,...and every day the fact of my not having seen [Madame Blavatsky] the chief mover in the occult renaissance of the 19th century, was growing more and more a source of annoyance to me....[Then] a letter from a London friend informed me that he had arranged for a few friends to meet at his house to discuss some of the problems in which we were mutually interested, and that if I would go up to town that evening, he would take me round to see "H.P.B." on the morrow.

I went...with the sole idea and purpose of seeing "H.P.B." That evening it seemed that Time stood still for the special purpose of laughing at my impatience. At last, however, the morning dawned and grew into a fine summer day, and towards noon I found myself with my friend at the house..., whence, he informed me, all the life of the Theosophical Society came. Entered, we were shown into the drawing-room, at least I presumed that was its appellation, though I have never seen, nor ever expect to see, another room like it. No, I was mistaken, for a few seconds later, in response to a familiar greeting from my friend, H.P.B. rose from her desk, where she had been hidden from view by an unusually large arm-chair, and came forward to receive us.

The largest and brightest blue eyes I have ever seen opened widely upon me as she took my hand and gave me welcome. All the confusion I had secretly predicted for myself fled from me on her first words. I felt at home and at ease with H.P.B. at once. "No, I will not be called 'Madame', not by my best friend, there was nothing said of that when I was christened, and if you please I will be simply H.P.B. Have a seat there; you smoke of course; I'll make you a cigarette. E-----, you flapdoodle, (this to my friend), if you can find my tobacco box on the place there, I'll mistake you for a gentleman." Then amid some laughter, as playful and buoyant as that of a child, she explained to me that E-----and she were "old friends" and that she was very fond of him, but that he often "took advantage of her old age and innocence", and amid some repartee the tobacco was produced, and H.P.B. made cigarettes for each of us. Then we settled down to more serious talk, H.P.B. asking me about my studies in Theosophy and western occultism, and telling me of the success of the Theosophical movement, and how the people said this and that, and how the papers said much more, and that all were wrong because they did not understand, and had forgotten their history books and could not see where the movement was going to. And then she asked me to tell her about myself, and gave me some practical advice, and soon afterwards I had taken leave of the most interesting person that I had ever seen.

...I was most pleasurably impressed with all that I had heard and seen during my brief visit to the home of the Theosophists, and the impression I most vividly recollect of H.P.B. herself, was of her surpassing kindliness of manner, her fearless candour, her remarkable vivacity, and above all the enthusiasm with which she spoke of the work which lay before the Theosophical Society. When, many months later, it was suggested that I should go to live at the London Headquarters, then in Lansdowne Road, I was only too glad to do so....

Alice L. Cleather[89]
1887, London

My husband and I, with our two children, were living at Eastbourne when H.P.B. came over to England from Ostend in 1887....I had met Mr. Bertram Keightley shortly after I joined the Theosophical Society, and from him received help and encouragement that was invaluable---as from an older to a younger member. He knew my keen desire to meet H.P.B., and kindly undertook to arrange it, if possible, while they were at Maycot, Norwood (a London suburb). But he warned me that it might be a difficult matter as "our old Lady" was apt to be---well, a little uncertain and capricious at times. I did not care the proverbial two pins what she was in those respects, if only she would *see me*. I had a profound conviction that I was approaching a crisis in my inner life, and that everything depended upon getting into touch with her. See her, therefore, I must and would.

We were not well off at this time, and a journey from Eastbourne to London, and back was not easy to compass. I had a small sum at "the bottom of a stocking," put by against a rainy day. This I now determined to use for my little pilgrimage. Indeed, I felt like a pilgrim, to an unknown goal; and I set out for London with no small excitement, and very definite high hopes. A friend had lent me a room for a couple of days, so I was spared that expense. Maycot was a small villa occupied at that time by Mrs. Kenningale Cook (a well-known novelist...) better known to Theosophists by her maiden name, Mabel Collins, as the scribe of *Light on the Path*.

I well remember Mr. Keightley telling me on our way out to Norwood that, in their frequent "arguments," she and H.P.B. could be "heard halfway down the road"---when the windows were open! We walked from Western Norwood station and, sure enough, when we got within about a hundred yards of Maycot, I heard loud and apparently angry voices floating---or rather ricochetting---towards us down the road. I was rather aghast, and Mr. Keightley's murmured remark that he was afraid "the old Lady" was in "one of her tempers" was not reassuring, particularly as he added that she would probably refuse to see me! *She did*: Nothing would induce her to, I could hear her saying so when Mr. Keightley went in (leaving me outside on the doorstep), and rating him soundly for bringing a total stranger to call at such an inopportune moment. In vain he reminded her that she herself had made the appointment, and that I had come up from the country on purpose to keep it. No, she was adamant; also angry (at least I thought so then). So I had to return sadly to London, and thence to Eastbourne, my "savings" gone, and my "high hopes" dashed to the ground. Truly I was greatly upset, as I imagined I must be "unworthy." All the same, I by no means abandoned my determination to see H.P.B. in the end---worthy or unworthy....

Later in the same year, 1887, I at last attained my heart's desire; and once more Mr. Keightley was the *Deus ex machina*. He obtained an invitation for me to 17, Lansdowne Road, and himself took me there late one afternoon. H.P.B. had moved into the West End of London from Maycot, and we had left Eastbourne for Harrow, a North-western suburb, so journeys were no longer a difficulty. When we were ushered into the well-known double drawing-room on the ground floor my attention immediately became riveted on the figure of a stout, middle-aged woman seated with her back to the wall before a card table, apparently engaged in playing Patience. She had the most arresting head and face I had ever seen, and when she lifted her eyes to mine, on Mr. Keightley presenting me, I experienced a distinct shock as her extraordinarily penetrating blue eyes literally "bored a hole" through my brain. She looked steadfastly at me for a few seconds (most uncomfortable ones for me) then, turning to Mr. Keightley, remarked indignantly: "You never told me she was like this!"---absolutely ignoring his assertion that he had repeatedly done so. Exactly what "like this" indicated I never subsequently discovered....

Reginald W. Machell[90]
Fall, 1887---1888, London

It was in…[1887] that I made the acquaintance of Madame Blavatsky in London and visited her at the house in Lansdowne Road, where she was then living.   In 1888 I joined the Theosophical Society and attended the meetings of the Blavatsky Lodge, which met at the house of the foundress of the Society in Lansdowne Road, at that time. Madame Blavatsky was present on all the occasions of my weekly visits, and took part in all the proceedings, answering questions as to the teachings of Theosophy, and incidentally speaking on a great range of topics more or less connected with the main subject of study, Theosophy.

The thing that had compelled my attention to this subject was my intense conviction of the absolute sincerity of the foundress of the Society, and of her power to expound the true teachings of Theosophy, as well as of her fitness to be a guide to one who aspired to lead a higher life. My conviction was based on my own personal observation and judgment of character, and not at all on anybody's evidence or opinions. So, when…I heard stories of a kind that did not agree with my own observations and conclusions, I was not influenced by them, but found support for my faith in Madame Blavatsky as a spiritual teacher in the internal evidence supplied by her works.…

The more I studied her works the stronger grew my faith in the reality of Madame Blavatsky's mission, and in her ability to transmit to the world the teachings intrusted to her for that purpose. It seemed to me that her devotion to the cause of Theosophy was absolute, and was wholly disinterested.

I saw that she suffered acutely from the slanders that were circulated about her former life, but I felt that no amount of calumny could turn her from the task which she had undertaken, and which she was carrying out under conditions of ill-health that seemed to make work of any kind impossible.

It was obvious that her self-sacrificing devotion to the cause of Theosophy could bring to herself no other reward than denunciation and vilification, on the one hand, and on the other the very doubtful support of those who were anxious to get from her some of the vast store of knowledge that was evidently at her command. While a few earnest followers honestly endeavored to lead the life and to follow the teacher, the majority of those who called themselves her followers were in reality seeking knowledge for their own gratification, rather than for the service of humanity. Some of these resented what they contemptuously called the "parrot-cry of Brotherhood," which the "old lady" was constantly insisting upon as the foundation of Theosophy, and which they considered "MERE ethics."

In spite of the constant failure of her professed followers to understand her, and the unscrupulous misrepresentations of avowed enemies, she never lost faith in the cause, nor wavered in her absolute devotion to the task she had undertaken. Suffering martyrdom both mentally and physically, she worked indefatigably, and her writing showed no trace of her physical condition, which was such as to make her life a wonder in itself and her literary achievement a marvel.

What need to refute attacks upon her character, when there remain such monuments to her nobility of soul and intellect as *The Secret Doctrine, The Voice of the Silence, Isis Unveiled,* and *The Key to Theosophy?*

William T. Stead[91]
1888, London

...It was in the year...[1887] that Madame Blavatsky took up her abode in London. Madame [Olga] Novikov was charmed by her powerful intellect, which commanded her homage altogether apart from her pretension to have explored with steady foot the bewildering mazes of the occult world. She was, besides, a great Russian patriot.

Madame Novikov wrote to me one day:---

"I made Madame Blavatsky translate the enclosed letter for you, as I thought it so very interesting. Don't you think so? By the bye, she is dying to see you; so, unless you commit a murder, shall you not go there with me some afternoon?"

I did not respond to the appeal. My interest in occult studies, which had been stimulated by a curious prediction made at the first seance I ever attended, in 1881, had languished under the stress of mundane pre-occupations. Madame Novikov repeated her invitation more insistently than before. Even then I do not think I should have consented to go had Madame Blavatsky not been a Russian. However, to make a long story short, I went. I was delighted with, and at the same time somewhat repelled, by Madame. Power was there, rude and massive, but she had the manners of a man, and a very unconventional man, rather than those of a lady. But we got on very well together, and Madame Blavatsky gave me her portrait, certifying that I might call myself what I pleased, but that she knew I was a good theosophist.

The pleasant relations thus established with Madame Blavatsky had unexpected results. When the *Secret Doctrine* came in for review to the *Pall Mall* office I shrank dismayed from the task of mastering its contents. I took it down to Mrs. [Annie] Besant, who had been for some time past attending seances and interesting herself in the other world, and asked her if she would review it. She grappled with the task, was fascinated by its contents, and when she finished her review she asked me if I could introduce her to the author. I did so with pleasure....

...There are those who imagine that because they can crack a joke about a teacup, they have disposed of Theosophy....Madame Blavatsky, they say, "was an impostor, a vulgar fraud. She was

249

exposed by the Coulombs, shown up by the Psychical Research Society...." They say all that, no doubt, but when all that is said and more besides, the problem of the personality of the woman remains full of interest, and even of wonder, to those who look below the surface of things.

Madame Blavatsky was a great woman....She was huge in body, and in her character, alike in its strength and weakness, there was something of the Rabelaisian gigantesque. But if she had all the nodosity of the oak, she was not without its strength; and if she had the contortions of the Sibyl, she possessed somewhat of her inspiration.

Of Madame Blavatsky the wonder-worker I knew nothing; I did not go to her seeking signs, and most assuredly no sign was given. She neither doubled a teacup in my presence...nor did she even cause the familiar raps to be heard. All these manifestations seemed as the mere trivialities, the shavings, as it were, thrown off from the beam of cedar wood which she was fashioning as one of the pillars in the Temple of Truth. I do not remember ever referring to them in our conversation, and it is slightly incomprehensible to me how any one can gravely contend that they constitute her claim to respect....

What Madame Blavatsky did was an immeasurably greater thing than the doubling of teacups. She made it possible for some of the most cultivated and skeptical men and women of this generation to believe---believe ardently, to an extent that made them proof against ridicule and disdainful of persecution, that not only does the invisible world that encompasses us contain Intelligences vastly superior to our own in knowledge of the Truth, but that it is possible for man to enter into communion with these hidden and silent ones, and to be taught of them the Divine mysteries of Time and of Eternity....Madame Blavatsky, a Russian, suspected of being a spy, converted leading Anglo-Indians to a passionate belief in her Theosophy mission....

Madame Blavatsky taught not merely that the Mahatmas existed, but that they were able and willing to enter into direct communication with men. Madame Blavatsky proclaimed herself as the directly commissioned messenger of the celestial hierarchy, charged by them to reveal the Path by which any one who was worthy and willing might enter into direct communion with these sublime Intelligences. I was but an outsider in the court of the Gentiles, a curious observer, and never a disciple. I cannot speak of these inner mysteries to which only the initiates are admitted....

But I can say of my own knowledge that she was undoubtedly a very gifted and original woman to converse with..., a fiery, impulsive, passionate creature, full of failings, and personally the very reverse of beautiful. There she was, a wonderful and powerful personality, the like of which I have never met either in Russia or in England. She was unique, but she was intensely human....

Bertram Keightley[92]
May-June, 1888, London

H.P.B. always wrote the Editorial [for *Lucifer*] herself, and also many other articles under more than one *nom de plume*, and she had a fancy for very often heading it with some quotation, and it used to be one of my troubles that she very seldom gave any reference for these, so that I had much work, and even visits to the British Museum Reading Room, in order to verify and check them, even when I did manage, with much entreaty, and after being most heartily "cussed," to extract some reference from her.

One day she handed me as usual the copy of her contribution, a story for the next issue headed with a couple of four line stanzas. I went and plagued her for a reference and would not be satisfied without one. She took the MS. and when I came back for it, I found she had just written the name "Alfred Tennyson" under the verses. Seeing this I was at a loss: for I knew my Tennyson pretty well and was certain that I had never read these lines in any poem of his, nor were they at all in his style. I hunted up my Tennyson, could not find them: consulted every one I could get at---also in vain. Then back I went to H.P.B. and told her all this and said that I was sure these lines could not be Tennyson's, and I dared not print them with his name attached, unless I could give an exact reference. H.P.B. just damned me and told me to get out

251

and go to Hell. It happened that the *Lucifer* copy *must* go to the printers that same day. So I just told her that I should strike out Tennyson's name when I went, unless she gave me a reference *before* I started. Just on starting I went to her again, and she handed me a scrap of paper on which were written the words: *The Gem*---1831. "Well, H.P.B.," I said, "this is worse than ever: for I am dead certain that Tennyson has never written any poem called *The Gem.*" All H.P.B. said was just: "Get out and be off."

So I went to the British Museum Reading Room and consulted the folk there; but they could give me no help and they one and all agreed that the verses could not be, and were not, Tennyson's. As a last resort, I asked to see Mr. Richard Garnett, the famous Head of the Reading Room in those days, and was taken to him. I explained to him the situation and he also agreed in feeling sure the verses were not Tennyson's. But after thinking quite a while, he asked me if I had consulted the Catalogue of Periodical Publications. I said no, and asked where that came in. "Well," said Mr. Garnett, "I have a dim recollection that there was once a brief-lived magazine called the *Gem*. It might be worth your looking it up." I did so, and in the volume for the year given in H.P.B.'s note, I found a poem of a few stanzas signed "Alfred Tennyson" and containing the two stanzas quoted by H.P.B. *verbatim* as she had written them down. And anyone can now read them in the second volume of *Lucifer*[*]: but I have never found them even in the supposedly most complete and perfect edition of Tennyson's Works.

----

[*][See H.P.B.'s **Collected Writings**. Vol. IX, pp 321-322 for a facsimile reproduction of the relevant pages from **The Gem**. 1831 containing Tennyson's poem.---Editor.]

William Kingsland[93]
June 2, 1888, London

I had the good fortune to meet...[Madame Blavatsky] for the first time on the 2nd June, 1888, when she was living at No. 17, Lansdowne Road, Notting Hill, and had gathered round her a considerable number of devoted workers. This visit was not, however, my first introduction to Theosophy, for I had for some two months previously been attending Mr. A.P. Sinnett's weekly gatherings at his own house; I had read his *Occult World*, and *Esoteric Buddhism*, and the early numbers of *The Theosophist* published in India. This literature opened out for me a new world of thought and endeavour....Theosophy struck a chord to which my inmost nature immediately responded. Here was disclosed not merely the possibility of a positive knowledge where science and philosophy and religion were only making guesses...but the whole cosmology and anthropology of this "Ancient Wisdom" appeared to me to be the only rational explanation of what we actually do know scientifically and historically of the world we live in, of our own nature as human beings, and of the literary records which have come down to us from a remote past. Underneath all this appeal to my rational faculty was an indefinable feeling---which so very many others have also experienced---that I was not now contacting this knowledge for the first time; that I was only recovering in my outer consciousness what was already familiar to my inner self....It was, therefore, with mind already eager for further enlightenment that I sought to know the remarkable woman who was the great pioneer of this Modern Movement for the revival of the old Occult teachings and traditions. It was, in fact the *teachings* and not the woman that attracted me. I desired to go to the fountain source; but I held very much in reserve any opinion I might be inclined to form as to the personality of a woman at that time accused of being a fraud and a charlatan....

...There was certainly in my case no emotional approach, and I held very largely in reserve any judgment I might feel inclined to pass as to her temperamental and most marked personal characteristics. I never asked her to perform, nor did I ever see her perform any occult phenomena. These phenomena, upon which so many placed their whole reliance, and which probably made for her more enemies than friends, always appeared to me to be of secondary importance to the teachings, though I might say that they appeared to me not merely to have been overwhelmingly vouched for, but also not inherently impossible in themselves. Psychical research has made great progress since that time, and it is hardly too much to say that their inherent possibility is now scientifically demonstrated....

The most that can be said for the remarkable powers which H.P. Blavatsky undoubtedly possessed from her childhood up, and which she undoubtedly did exhibit on many occasions, is, that they demonstrate the fact that these powers can be possessed and intelligently used, not in any "mediumistic" manner, but by the proper use of the trained will. But there is nothing new in this; it is an age-long knowledge in the East under the name of *Yoga*....

...I did not see how any of the phenomena she was reputed to have performed could be any evidence of the truth of the teachings, though they might possibly have gone to prove the existence of the Masters, as also the fact that every individual possesses unknown and undeveloped psychic faculties and powers....I did consider, however, in spite of the S.P.R. Report, that her phenomenal powers had been fully testified by a very large number of credible witnesses. I naturally held in reserve a great many conclusions when I first made her acquaintance; but I have never seen any reason to go back on my first favourable impressions; and I have since then made the philosophy which I learnt from her the basis of all my own literary work....

...The H.P. Blavatsky whom I knew personally was certainly not the "accomplished impostor" presented to us in the S.P.R. Report....If such a personality as is presented...ever existed, she must have utterly vanished by the time I came to know the author of *The Secret Doctrine*....

Nevertheless, the [S.P.R.] Report..[is] even now sometimes quoted as having definitely *proved* that the psychic phenomena associated with Mme. Blavatsky were entirely fraudulent; and also that the Masters or Mahatmas from whom she claimed to have received her teachings were her own invention, and do not, in fact, exist....The Report does not *prove* by any evidence that would be accepted in a court of law either the one or other of these assumptions....

...It is apparently thought by...detractors that if they only throw sufficient mud at the woman who gave the [Theosophical] teachings to the world they are thereby amply discrediting the teachings themselves....[As regards] the great work which Mme. Blavatsky accomplished in the literature which she gave to the world in *Isis Unveiled, The Secret Doctrine, The Key to Theosophy*, and *The Voice of the Silence*...it is by that literature and its gradual acceptance as being a fresh inflow of spiritual teaching at a time when the world was drifting into materialism, and not by the S.P.R. Report, that H.P. Blavatsky will be judged by posterity....The teachings and literary work which she gave to the world...will most assuredly as time goes on place her name amongst those of the world's great light-bringers.

Alice L. Cleather[94]
Oct.---Nov., 1888, London

In *Lucifer* for October, 1888, a notice had appeared to the effect that an "Esoteric Section of the Theosophical Society" was to be formed under H.P.B., and that those who wished to join and abide by its Rules should send in their names. Mrs. Chowne and I, also Colonel Chowne, if I remember rightly, at once responded; but for some time we heard nothing. Then, one day, Mrs. Chowne came down to Harrow to see me---I was ill at the time---bringing the E.S....Pledge from H.P.B. for me to write out and sign. She said that H.P.B. had told her that, on our sending in our signed Pledges, each one would be "tested" (*i.e.*, "examined for fitness") on inner planes, *by the Master*. Mrs. Chowne's exact words were, "taken out and tested." Our past lives would be called up, and upon what was there seen and known of our *real selves*, would depend whether or not we were accepted as candidates. She told me later that when she handed our signed Pledges to H.P.B. she had looked very seriously---almost solemnly---at her, and said:--- "It is a great trust that you have given me."

So we waited; days, even weeks passed, and nothing occurred. I had almost forgotten what Mrs. Chowne had warned me *might* happen, until, one Tuesday night, (it was Full Moon, I remember) I had the most wonderful experience, save one, that had ever happened to me. I knew I was myself, lying half awake, half asleep, in my own room at home. Yet I was also in an Egyptian Temple of extraordinary grandeur, and going through things quite unspeakable and most solemn. This experience began soon after 10 P.M., and almost exactly as a neighbouring church clock struck midnight I lost consciousness in an overpowering and almost terrible blaze of light, which seemed completely to envelope me. The next morning I recorded all I could remember in my diary, and on Thursday went up to Lansdowne Road as usual for the Lodge meeting. I was a little early, but H.P.B. at work in the inner room must have known who had arrived, for she called me in, and turning round, said most seriously: "Master told me *last night* that you are accepted." Nothing more; but I at once realised vividly that my experience the previous Tuesday night had indeed been my "testing." Thereupon I related the whole thing to H.P.B., who only nodded several times, but made no remark whatever about it.

Mrs. Chowne told me afterwards that she and her husband had had similar experiences, adding that only a few of the first applicants were so "tested"; that it did not, in fact, apply generally....

William Q. Judge[95]

Dec., 1888, London

Mme. Blavatsky...is living with the Countess Wachtmeister...in Holland Park, London, and is devoting herself to the most arduous labors in the cause of Theosophy. She scarcely ever leaves the house, and from 6:30 o'clock in the morning until evening is constantly engaged in writing articles for her magazine, *Lucifer*, or other theosophic publications, replying to correspondence, and preparing the matter for further forthcoming volumes of her gigantic work, *The Secret Doctrine*. In the evening she has many visitors of all sorts---inquirers, critics, skeptics, curiosity seekers, friends---and all are welcomed with such charming grace, friendliness, and simplicity that everyone is made to feel at home with her. By 10 o'clock generally all but intimate friends have retired, but they remain an hour or two later.

Notwithstanding that Mme. Blavatsky is beyond the vigor of middle age and for nearly three years past has been living in defiance of the leading London physicians, who gave her up long ago as hopelessly incurable of a deadly kidney disease that was liable to kill her at any moment, she never seems weary, but is the animated leader of conversation, speaking with equal ease in English, French, Italian and Russian, or dropping into Sanskrit and Hindustani as occasion requires. Whether working or talking, she seems to be constantly rolling, lighting, and smoking cigarettes of Turkish tobacco. As for her personal appearance, she hardly seems changed at all from what she was when in...[America] several years ago, except that she has grown somewhat stouter perhaps. The characteristics that are apparent in her countenance are, in equal blending, energy and great kindness....

Mme. Blavatsky now very seldom gives any manifestation of her occult powers, except to intimate friends; but I had, while over there, several evidences that she can do things quite inexplicable by any laws of "exact" science. Two years ago I lost, here in New York, a paper that was of considerable interest to me. I do not think anybody but myself knew that I had it, and I certainly mentioned to no one that I had lost it. One evening, a little over a fortnight ago, while I was sitting in Mme. Blavatsky's parlor with Mr. B. Keightley and several other persons, I happened to think of that paper. The Madame got up, went into the next room, and returning almost immediately, handed to me a sheet of paper. I opened it and found it an exact duplicate of the paper that I had lost two years before. It was actually a facsimile copy, as I recognized at once. I thanked her, and she said: "Well, I saw it in your head that you wanted it."

...The silvery bell sounds in the astral current that were heard over her head by so many person when she was here in New York, still continue to follow her, and it is beyond question to those familiar with her life and work that she is in constant receipt of the most potent aid from the adepts, particularly her teacher, the Mahatma Morya, whose portrait hangs in her study and shows a dark and beautiful Indian face, full of sweetness, wisdom and majesty. Of course it does not seem possible that he in Thibet instantaneously responds, either by a mental impression or a "precipitated" note to a mental interrogatory put by her in London, but it happens to be the fact that he does so all the same.

Her most intimate friends in London are the Countess Wachtmeister, the Keightleys, Mabel Collins...and Dr. Ashton Ellis. Mr. A.P. Sinnett drops in occasionally....

Fred J. Dick[96]
December, 1888, London

Prior to meeting Madame H.P. Blavatsky in London in 1888 I had been admitted, along with others in Dublin, to membership in the Theosophical Society by William Q. Judge, then on a visit to Ireland. At that time I had already become familiar with the details of many infamous attacks which had been fulminated against the honor and integrity of...H.P.B....

The pettiness and feebleness as to fact of all these, stood out in clear-cut contrast with the spiritual nobility of her writings in *Isis Unveiled* and the magazines edited by her, and such accusations but served to strengthen one's enthusiasm for the great principles which underlie the idea of man's essential solidarity---to the philosophic rationale of which, demonstrated by her work and her references to the lore and knowledge of countless Teachers throughout the long ages, she had devoted her life-energies and her very heart's blood.

Such attacks brought her unremitting suffering, as affecting the Cause she labored for; yet, for us beginners in the Science of Life, they showed well the inherent weaknesses of our complex nature, and enabled us better to realize the enormous import to the race of the message Theosophy holds out---a message delivered by H.P. Blavatsky in no uncertain terms, and in fact with a vigor, an eloquence, and an amplitude of historical and philosophic detail unrivaled in known history. While iconoclastically tearing to tatters most of the generally accepted beliefs and dogmas, scientific or otherwise, she stands revealed in her writings as a Master-builder possessed of a complete constructive philosophy of practical life and equally of cosmogenesis and anthropogenesis....

...Her main purpose was to permeate the world with the ideas and teaching of the *ancient Wisdom-Religion*, primal source of all the world-religions. It certainly was not to promulgate spiritualism, marvel-seeking, or psychism of any kind. Let her writings attest.

She brought to both east and west the truths so long obscured regarding the great laws of Karma, Reincarnation, and the dual nature of man, together with a spiritual philosophy so exalted as to furnish the keynote for many successive lives of...endeavor....

Bertram Keightley[97]
1888, London

...After a time, one learnt to realize that all...[H.P.B.'s] storming, "cussing" and general raising Cain over the smallest trifles, was just a "put-up job" and also an outlet and safety-valve for the over-pressure of nervous energy which flowed in such an intense stream through her whole nature.

I well remember one incident that cut deep and taught me a lesson I never forgot. The work for some time had been heavy and anxious; in addition I had just then many personal worries and difficulties, so that my nerves got badly frayed. One day H.P.B. sent upstairs for me before breakfast and when I came to her she just let loose and abused, scolded and scarified me, hitting just every one of my weakest and tenderest spots, scarifying every weakness and fault, and "telling me off" till at last she "got my goat" and suddenly I felt a surge of real red-hot anger rise within me. I may remark that the whole matter, about which H.P.B. was scolding and carrying on so angrily and almost viciously, was a matter with which I had nothing whatever to do, and of which even I knew absolutely nothing. But I could not get in a word of denial or explanation, even edgeways. Well, I felt my temper go and my eyes flash. On the moment, H.P.B., who seemed almost raving with fury, stopped dead-silent and absolutely quiet. There was not even a quiver or vibration of anger *from* H.P.B. in the air. She just looked me up and down and remarked coldly: "And you want to be an occultist." Then I saw and knew, and went off deeply ashamed: having learnt no small lesson.

Edmund Russell[98]
1888, London

...I knew...[H.P.B.] well in the last few years of her life and was often at her house in Lansdowne Road....

The whole world clamoured for her likeness. I persuaded her to go with me to a photographer. What a day! Wind and rain and

H.P.B. in 1889

scurries of autumn leaves. She had no out-of-door clothes. Everything was given away as soon as brought to her....

I never could have accomplished it without the aid of Countess Wachtmeister. Appointment made, the cab was kept waiting for hours. Unaccustomed to go out she would not move. "You want my death. I cannot step on the wet stones." Shawls, scarfs, fur were piled on. A sort of Russian turban tied over her head with a veil. Rugs spread from door to carriage. These were lifted and blown about by the storm so the Countess with the help of the coachman had to hold them down while I raised the umbrella over her head and helped her in. Afterwards the Countess told me that when she first came to London, wife of an Ambassador from Sweden, two powdered footmen in livery followed wherever she went. "If my poor husband could know the day had come when I held carpets for another woman to tread upon he would turn in his grave." This only smiling---she would have lain herself down for Madame to walk over.

Van der Weyde was a friend of mine. There disembarkation even more terrible! They don't unroll red carpets in Regent Street for nothing. "Come along, Your Majesty!" I said to keep up the illusion.

Once up the stairs she flatly refused [her photograph] to be taken. She was not an actress. What had I brought her to such a place for? Finally she was held as I knew she would be by the story of Van der Weyde's own experiments in the adaptation of electricity to photography....

"I will sit for you---only one---be quick---take me just as I am."

I bent over her and whispered: "Now let all the devil in you shine out of those eyes."

"Why, child, there is no devil in me."

She laughed, so the sitting was spoiled, but then all went well, and we got the famous likeness. She was pleased with it. I was not. She is there, but not all of her. I would have wished something at her writing-table---taken by chance---in the long folds of her seamless garment---vibrations of light all around. She really enjoyed the adventure I think, for she told of being "bossed" and "carried as a bundle" for a long time, especially of the "Come along, your Majesty."

Violet Tweedale[99]

1888---1889, London

I shall never forget that first interview with a much maligned woman [Madame Blavatsky], whom I rapidly came to know intimately and love dearly. She was seated in a great armchair, with a table by her side on which lay tobacco and cigarette paper. Whilst she spoke her exquisite taper fingers automatically rolled cigarettes. She was dressed in a loose black robe, and on her crinkly gray hair she wore a black shawl. Her face was pure Kalmuck, and a network of fine wrinkles covered it. Her eyes, large and pale green, dominated the countenance---wonderful eyes in their arresting, dreamy mysticism....

I have often heard Blavatsky called a charlatan, and I am bound to say that her impish behavior often gave grounds for this description. She was foolishly intolerant of the many smart West End ladies who arrived in flocks, demanding to see spooks, masters, elementals, anything, in fact, in the way of phenomena.

Madame Blavatsky was a born conjuror. Her wonderful fingers were made for jugglers' tricks, and I have seen her often use them for that purpose. I well remember my amazement upon the first occasion on which she exhibited her occult powers, spurious and genuine.

I was sitting alone with her one afternoon, when the cards of Jessica, Lady Sykes, the late Duchess of Montrose and the Honorable Mrs. S.----(still living) were brought into her. She said she would receive the ladies at once, and they were ushered in. They explained that they had heard of her new religion, and her marvelous occult powers. They hoped she would afford them a little exhibition of what she could do.

Madame Blavatsky had not moved out of her chair. She was suavity itself, and whilst conversing she rolled cigarettes for her visitors and invited them to smoke. She concluded that they were not particularly interested in the old faith which the young West called new; what they really were keen about was phenomena.

That was so, responded the ladies, and the burly Duchess inquired if Madame ever gave racing tips, or lucky numbers for Monte Carlo?

Madame disclaimed having any such knowledge, but she was willing to afford them a few moments' amusement. Would one of the ladies suggest something she would like done?

Lady Sykes produced a pack of cards from her pocket, and held them out to Madame Blavatsky, who shook her head.

"First remove the marked cards," she said.

Lady Sykes laughed and replied, "Which are they?"

Madame Blavatsky told her, without a second's hesitation. This charmed the ladies. It seemed a good beginning.

"Make that basket of tobacco jump about," suggested one of them.

The next moment the basket had vanished. I don't know where it went, I only know it disappeared by trickery, that the ladies looked for it everywhere, even under Madame Blavatsky's ample skirts, and that suddenly it reappeared upon its usual table. A little more jugglery followed and some psychometry, which was excellent, then the ladies departed, apparently well satisfied with the entertainment.

When I was once more alone with Madame Blavatsky, she turned to me with a wry smile and said, "Would you have me throw pearls before swine?"

I asked her if all she had done was pure trickery.

"Not all, but most of it," she unblushingly replied, "But now I will give you something lovely and real."

For a moment or two she was silent, covering her eyes with her hand, then a sound caught my ear. I can only describe what I heard as fairy music, exquisitely dainty and original. It seemed to proceed from somewhere just between the floor and the ceiling, and it moved about to different corners of the room. There was a crystal innocence in the music, which suggested the dance of joyous children at play.

"Now I will give you the music of life," said Madame Blavatsky.

For a moment or two there fell a trance-like silence. The twilight was creeping into the room, and seemed to bring with it a tingling expectancy. Then it seemed to me that something entered from without, and brought with it utterly new conditions, something incredible, unimagined and beyond the bounds of reason.

264

Some one was singing, a distant melody was creeping nearer, yet I was aware it had never been distant, it was only becoming louder.

I suddenly felt afraid of myself. The air about me was ringing with vibrations of weird, unearthly music, seemingly as much around me as it was above and behind me. It had no whereabouts, it was unlocatable. As I listened my whole body quivered with wild elation, and the sensation of the unforeseen.

There was rhythm in the music, yet it was unlike anything I had ever heard before. It sounded like a Pastorale, and it held a call to which my whole being wildly responded.

Who was the player, and what was his instrument? He might have been a flautist, and he played with a catching lilt, a luxurious abandon that was an incarnation of Nature. It caught me suddenly away to green Sicilian hills, where the pipes of unseen players echo down the mountain sides, as the pipes of Pan once echoed through the rugged gorges and purple vales of Hellas and Thrace.

Alluring though the music was, and replete with the hot fever of life, it carried with it a thrill of dread. Its sweetness was cloying, its tenderness was sensuous. A balmy scent crept through the room, of wile thyme, of herbs, of asphodel and the muscadine of the wine press. It enwrapt me like an odorous vapor.

The sounds began to take shape, and gradually mold themselves into words. I knew I was being courted with subtlety, and urged to fly out of my house of life....

My soul seemed to strain at the leash. Should I let go? Like a powerful opiate the allurement enfolded me, yet from out its thrall a small insistent voice whispered "Caution! Where will you be led: supposing you yield your will, would it ever be yours again?"

Now my brain was seized with a sense of panic and weakness. The music suddenly seemed replete with gay sinfulness and insolent conquest. It spoke the secrets which the nature myth so often murmurs to those who live amid great silences, of those dread mysteries of the spirit which yet invest it with such glory and wonderment.

With a violent reaction of fear I rose suddenly, and as I did so the whole scene was swept from out the range of my senses. I was back once more in Blavatsky's room with the creeping twilight and the far off hoarse roar of London stealing in at the open window. I glanced at Madame Blavatsky. She had sunk down in her chair, and she lay huddled up in deep trance. She had floated out with the music into a sea of earthly oblivion. Between her fingers she held a small Russian cross.

I knew that she had thrust me back to the world which still claimed me, and I went quietly out of the house into the streets of London.

On another occasion when I was alone with Madame Blavatsky she suddenly broke off our conversation by lapsing into another language, which I supposed to be Hindustanee. She appeared to be addressing some one else, and on looking over my shoulder I saw we were no longer alone. A man stood in the middle of the room. I was sure he had not entered by the door, window or chimney, and as I looked at him in some astonishment, he salaamed to Madame Blavatsky, and replied to her in the same language in which she had addressed him.

I rose at once to leave her, and as I bade her good-by she whispered to me, "Do not mention this." The man did not seem aware of my presence; he took no notice of me as I left the room. He was dark in color and very sad looking, and his dress was a long, black cloak and a soft black hat which he did not remove, pulled well over his eyes. I found out that evening that none of the general staff were aware of his arrival, and I saw him no more....

Annie Besant[100]
Spring 1889, London

...Since 1886 there had been slowly growing up a conviction that my philosophy was not sufficient; that life and mind were other than, more than, I had dreamed. Psychology was advancing with rapid strides; hypnotic experiments were revealing unlooked-for complexities in human consciousness....I studied the obscurer

Annie Besant

sides of consciousness, dreams, hallucinations....The phenomena of clairvoyance, clairaudience, thought-reading, were found to be real....I finally convinced myself that there was some hidden thing, some hidden power, and resolved to seek until I found, and by the early spring of 1889 I had grown desperately determined to find at all hazards what I sought. At last, sitting alone in deep thought as I had become accustomed to do after the sun had set, filled with an intense but nearly hopeless longing to solve the riddle of life and mind, I heard a Voice that was later to become to me the holiest sound on earth, bidding me take courage for the light was near. A fortnight passed, and then Mr. [W.T.] Stead gave into my hands two large volumes. "Can you review these? My young men all fight shy of them, but you are quite mad enough on these subjects to make something of them." I took the books; they were the two volumes of "The Secret Doctrine," written by H.P. Blavatsky.

Home I carried my burden, and sat me down to read. As I turned over page after page the interest became absorbing; but how familiar it seemed; how my mind leapt forward to presage the conclusions, how natural it was, how coherent, how subtle, and yet how intelligible. I was dazzled, blinded by the light in which disjointed facts were seen as parts of a might whole, and all my puzzles, riddles, problems, seemed to disappear....

I wrote the review, and asked Mr. Stead for an introduction to the writer, and then sent a note asking to be allowed to call. I received the most cordial of notes, bidding me come, and in the soft spring evening Herbert Burrows and I---for his aspirations were as mine on this matter---walked from Notting Hill Station, wondering what we should meet, to the door of 17, Lansdowne Road. A pause, a swift passing through hall and outer room, through folding-doors thrown back, a figure in a large chair before a table, a voice, vibrant, compelling. "My dear Mrs. Besant, I have so long wished to see you," and I was standing with my hand in her firm grip, and looking for the first time in this life straight into the eyes of "H.P.B." I was conscious of a sudden leaping forth of my heart---was it recognition? ---and then, I am ashamed to say, a fierce rebellion, a fierce withdrawal, as of some wild animal when it feels a mastering hand. I sat down, after some introductions that conveyed no ideas to me, and listened. She talked of travels, of various countries, easy brilliant talk, her eyes veiled, her exquisitely moulded fingers rolling cigarettes incessantly. Nothing special to record, no word of Occultism, nothing mysterious, a woman of the world chatting with her evening visitors. We rose to go, and for a moment the veil lifted, and two brilliant, piercing eyes met mine, and with a yearning throb in the voice: "Oh, my dear Mrs. Besant, if you would only come among us!" I felt a well-nigh uncontrollable desire to bend down and kiss her, under the compulsion of that yearning voice, those compelling eyes, but with a flash of the old unbending pride and an inward jeer at my own folly, I said a commonplace polite goodbye, and turned away with some inanely courteous and evasive remarks. "Child," she said to me long afterwards, "your pride is terrible; you are as proud as Lucifer himself."....

Once again I went, and asked about the Theosophical Society, wishful to join, but fighting against it. For I saw, distinct and clear---with painful distinctness, indeed---what that joining would mean. I had largely conquered public prejudice against me by my work on the London School Board....Was I to plunge into a new vortex of strife, and make myself a mark for ridicule---worse than hatred---and fight again the weary fight for an unpopular truth? Must I turn against Materialism, and face the shame of publicly confessing that I had been wrong, misled by intellect to ignore the Soul?...What would be the look in Charles Bradlaugh's eyes when I told him that I had become a Theosophist? The struggle was sharp and keen....And so it came to pass that I went again to Lansdowne Road to ask about the Theosophical Society. H.P. Blavatsky looked at me piercingly for a moment. "Have you read the report about me of the Society for Psychical Research?" "No, I never heard of it, so far as I know." "Go and read it, and if, after reading it, you come back---well." And nothing more would she say on the subject, but branched off to her experiences in many lands.

I borrowed a copy of the Report, read and re-read it. Quickly I saw how slender was the foundation on which the imposing structure was built. The continual assumptions on which conclusions were based; the incredible character of the allegations; and---most damning fact of all---the foul source from which the evidence was derived. Everything turned on the veracity of the Coulombs, and they were self-stamped as partners in the alleged frauds. Could I put such against the frank, fearless nature that I had caught a glimpse of, against the proud fiery truthfulness that shone at me from the clear, blue eyes, honest and fearless as those of a noble child? Was the writer of "The Secret Doctrine" this miserable impostor, this accomplice of tricksters, this foul and loathsome deceiver, this conjuror with trap-doors and sliding panels? I laughed aloud at the absurdity and flung the Report aside with the righteous scorn of an honest nature that knew its own kin when it met them, and shrank from the foulness and baseness of a lie. The next day saw me at the Theosophical Publishing Company's office at 7, Duke Street, Adelphi, where Countess Wachtmeister---one of the lealest of H.P.B.'s friends---was at work, and I signed an application to be admitted as fellow of the Theosophical Society.

On receiving my diploma I betook myself to Lansdowne Road, where I found H.P.B. alone. I went over to her, bent down and kissed her, but said no word. "You have joined the Society?"

"Yes," "You have read the report?" "Yes," "Well?" I knelt down before her and clasped her hands in mine, looking straight into her eyes. "My answer is, will you accept me as your pupil, and give me the honour of proclaiming you my teacher in the face of the world?" Her stern, set face softened, the unwonted gleam of tears sprang to her eyes; then, with a dignity more regal, she placed her hand upon my head. "You are a noble woman. May Master bless you."....

Herbert Burrows[101]
Spring, 1889, London

Beset with problems of life and mind that our materialism could not solve, dwelling intellectually on what are now to us the inhospitable shores of agnosticism, Annie Besant and I ever craved more light. We had read the *Occult World*, and in bye-gone years we had heard---who had not?---of the strange woman whose life seemed to be a contradiction of our most cherished theories, but as yet the philosophy of the book was to us but assertion, the life of the woman a career which we had no means of examining. Sceptical, critical, trained by long years of public controversy to demand the most rigid scientific proof of things which were outside our experience, Theosophy was to us an unknown, and, as it then seemed, an impossible land. And yet it fascinated, for it promised much, and with talking, with reading, the fascination grew. With the fascination also grew the desire to know, and so, on an ever-to-be remembered evening, with a letter of introduction from Mr. W.T. Stead, then editor of the *Pall Mall Gazette*, as our passport, we found ourselves face to face, in the drawing room of 17, Lansdowne Road, with the woman whom we afterwards learned to know and to love as the most wonderful woman of her time.

I was not foolish enough to look for miracles. I did not expect to see Madame Blavatsky float, nor did I crave for materialised teacups, but I did want to hear about Theosophy, and

H.P.B.'s Drawing Room, 17 Lansdowne Rd.

I did not hear much. She whom we were there to see was a stout, unwieldy lady, playing Russian "Patience," and keeping up a stream of conversation on nearly every subject except the one which was just then nearest our minds. No attempt at proselyting, no attempt to "fix" us (we were *not* hypnotised!) but all the while the wonderful eyes were flashing light, and, in spite of the bodily infirmity which was even then painfully apparent, there was a reserve of power which gave the impression that we were seeing, not the real woman, but only the surface character of some one who had endured much, and who knew much.

I tried to keep an open impartial mind, and I believe I succeeded. I was genuinely anxious to learn, but I was critical and on the watch for the slightest attempt at hoodwinking. When I afterwards discovered something of H.P.B.'s extraordinary insight, I was not surprised to find that she had gauged accurately and unerringly my mental attitude on this my first visit, and it is an attitude which she never really discouraged. If those who talk so foolishly about her magnetising people could but know how she continually impressed upon us the absolute duty of proving all things and holding fast only to that which is good!

To go once was to go again, and so it came that after a few visits I began to see light. I caught glimpses of a lofty morality, of a self-sacrificing zeal, of a coherent philosophy of life, of a clear and definite science of man and his relation to a spiritual universe. These it was which attracted me---not phenomena, for I saw none. For the first time in my mental history I had found a teacher who could pick up the loose threads of my thought and satisfactorily weave them together, and the unerring skill, the vast knowledge, the loving patience of the teacher grew on me hour by hour. Quickly I learned that the so-called charlatan and trickster was a noble soul, whose every day was spent in unselfish work, whose whole life was pure and simple as a child's, who counted never the cost of pain or toil if these could advance the great cause to which her every energy was consecrated. Open as the day to a certain point, she was the incarnation of kindness---silent as the grave if need be, she was sternness personified at the least sign of faithlessness to the work which was her life. Grateful, so grateful for every affectionate attention, careless, so careless of all that concerned herself, she bound us to her, not simply as wise teacher, but as loving friend. Once I was broken down through long bodily and mental strain and the wheels of my life ran so heavily that they nearly stopped. Through it all her solicitude was untiring and one special proof of it that she gave, too personal to mention here, would have been thought of, perhaps, but by one in a million.

Perfect---no; faults---yes; the one thing she would hate most of all would be the indiscriminate praise of her personality. But when I have said that she was sometimes impetuous as a whirlwind, a very cyclone when she was really roused, I have told nearly all. And I have often thought it was more than possible that some of these outbursts were assumed for a special object. Lately they had almost vanished. Her enemies sometimes said she was rough and rude. We who knew her, knew that a more unconventional woman, in the very realest sense of the word, never lived. Her absolute indifference to all outward forms was a true indifference based upon her inner spiritual knowledge of the verities of the universe. Sitting by her when strangers came,

272

as they did come from every corner of the earth, I have often watched with the keenest amusement their wonder at seeing a woman who always said what she thought. Given a prince and she would probably shock him, given a poor man and he would have her last shilling and her kindliest word....

Annie Besant[102]
July, 1889, Fontainebleau, France

...I was called away to Paris to attend, with Herbert Burrows, the great Labour Congress held there from July 15th to July 20th, and spent a day or two at Fontainebleau with H.P. Blavatsky, who had gone abroad for a few weeks' rest.   There I found her translating the wonderful fragments from "The Book of the Golden Precepts," now so widely known under the name of "The Voice of the Silence." She wrote it swiftly, without any material copy before her....I sat in the room while she was writing it. I know that she did not write it referring to any books, but she wrote it down steadily, hour after hour, exactly as though she were writing either from memory or from reading it where no book was....and in the evening made me read it aloud to see if the "English was decent."   Herbert Burrows was there, and Mrs. Candler, a staunch American Theosophist, and we sat round H.P.B. while I read.   The translation was in perfect and beautiful English, flowing and musical; only a word or two could we find to alter, and she looked at us like a startled child, wondering at our praises---praises that any one with the literary sense would endorse if they read that exquisite prose poem.

A little earlier in the same day I had asked her as to the agencies at work in producing the taps so constantly heard at Spiritualistic *Seances*. "You don't use spirits to produce taps, " she said; "see here." She put her hand over my head, not touching it, and I heard and felt slight taps on the bone of my skull, each sending a little electric thrill down the spine. She then carefully explained how such taps were producible at any point desired by the operator, and how interplay of the current to which they were due might be caused otherwise than by conscious human volition. It was in this fashion that she would illustrate her verbal teachings, proving by experiment the statements made as to the existence of subtle forces controllable by the trained mind. The phenomena all belonged to the scientific side of her teaching, and she never committed the folly of claiming authority for her philosophic doctrines on the ground that she was a wonder-worker. And constantly she would remind us that there was no such thing as "miracle"; that all the phenomena she had produced were worked by virtue of a knowledge of nature deeper than that of average people, and by the force of a well-trained mind and will; some of them were what she would describe as "psychological tricks," the creation of images by force of imagination, and in pressing them on others as a "collective hallucination"; others, such as the moving of solid articles, either by an astral hand projected to draw them towards her, or by using an Elemental; others by reading in the Astral light and so on....

G.R.S. Mead[103]
Aug., 1889---1891, London

...It was not until the beginning of August, 1889, that I came to work permanently with H.P.B. She was away [from London] in Jersey [an island off the southern coast of England]....A pressing telegram came from H.P.B., and I started for Jersey. What a warm greeting there was in the porch of that honeysuckle-covered house, and what a fuss to have everything comfortable for the new comer!

It has often been a surprise to me that the chief of the accusations and slanders brought against H.P.B. have been those of fraud and concealment....According to my experience, she was ever over-trustful of others and quite prodigal in her frankness. As an instance, no sooner had I arrived than she gave me the run of all her papers, and set me to work on a pile of correspondence that would otherwise have remained unanswered till doomsday; for if she detested anything, it was answering letters. I then was initiated into the mysteries of *Lucifer*, and soon had my hands

274

G.R.S. Mead

full with transmission of directions, alterations, and counter-directions to Bertram Keightley, who was then Sub-editor, for in those days H.P.B. *would* not let one word go into *Lucifer* until she had seen and reseen it, and she added to and cut up the proofs until the last moment.

One day, shortly after my arrival, H.P.B. came into my room unexpectedly with a manuscript and handed it to me, saying, "Read that, old man, and tell me what you think of it." It was the MS. of the third part of the *Voice of the Silence*, and while I read she sat and smoked her cigarettes, tapping her foot on the floor, as was often her habit. I read on, forgetting her presence in the beauty and sublimity of the theme until she broke in upon my silence with, "Well?" I told her it was the grandest thing in all our theosophical literature, and tried, contrary to my habit, to convey in words some of the enthusiasm that I felt. But even then H.P.B.

was not content with her work, and expressed the greatest apprehension that she had failed to do justice to the original in her translation, and could hardly be persuaded that she had done well. This was one of her chief characteristics. Never was she confident of her own literary work, and cheerfully listened to all criticisms, even from persons who should have remained silent. Strangely enough she was always most timorous of her best articles and works and most confident of her polemical writings.

When we returned to Lansdowne Road...both Dr. Archibald Keightley and Bertram Keightley left for abroad, the former on a voyage round the world, the latter to lecture in the United States. And so their duties came mostly to me, and I gradually began to see a great deal of her alone at her work owing to the necessity of the case.

Let me see if I can give some idea of how the work was done.

To begin with there was *Lucifer*, of which she was then sole editor. In the first place H.P.B. never read an MS., she required to see it in proof and then mostly "averaged" its contents. What she *was* particular about was the length of the copy, and she used to laboriously count the number of words in each paper, and would never be persuaded of the accuracy of my count when I in my turn "averaged" the length. If I suggested that mine was the most expeditious method, she would proceed to tell me some home truths about Oxford and Cambridge education, and I often thought she used to continue her primitive methods of arithmetical computation on purpose to cure me of my impatience and my confidence in my own superiority. Another great thing was the arranging of the different articles. In those days she would never entrust this to any other hand, and the measuring of everything was a painful operation.

Getting *Lucifer* through the press was invariably a rush, for she generally wrote her leader the last thing and, having been used to it, considered the printers, if anybody, were to blame if it did not appear in time....

The first hour in the morning after breakfast...will ever remain with me a pleasant recollection. Everything was so unconventional. I used to sit on the arm of her great armchair and obediently smoke the cigarette she offered, while she opened the letters, told me what she wanted done and signed diplomas and certificates, the latter under great pressure, however, for she detested such mechanical work....

Though H.P.B. left much of her correspondence to me, still it was not without a distinct supervision, for she would suddenly call for a reply that had not yet gone out or for the copy of an old letter, without any warning, and if there were any mistakes, the lecture I received was not reassuring to my discomfiture. One thing she was always impressing upon me, and this was to develope a sense of the "fitness of things", and she was merciless if this law of harmony were broken, leaving no loop-hole of escape, and listening to no excuse, with her over-powering reason and knowledge, which in spite of its apparently disconnected expression, always went home; although, indeed, the minute afterward, she was again the affectionate friend and elder brother, shall I even say, comrade, as she alone knew how to be....

Rev. B. Old[104]
Nov., 1889, London

My first recollection of H.P.B. is in connection with my brother Walter ("Sepharial," astrological nom-de-plume). He was very much interested in Theosophy....Walter resigned his banking position and went to London to become a helper at the Theosophical Headquarters....My mother was extremely anxious about his connection with The Theosophical Society, and naturally thought he had made a great mistake on leaving a very profitable Bank employment for a non-paid secretarial position. So I was sent to see what they were doing with him....

I have a description of...[H.P.B.'s] personal appearance as she struck me on first meeting her at Lansdowne Road, [November] 1889....This is taken from a personal diary which I used to write up....

"After arriving in London...we went to Lansdowne Road and my brother introduced Mme. H.P. Blavatsky. Imagine an elderly woman, stout and phlegmatic, in an unconventional armchair..., draped in a loose black gown which hid her immense proportions.

A large head almost leonine and masculine in its bold outlines....Imagine two grey eyes soft as a gazelle's, very prominent, and having a far-away vision....Further peculiarity in the personality of H.P.B. were her hands, fingers long and tapering, soft and agile...; turned outward at the ends the nails were thin and beautifully shaped...."

...I told my mother when I got home from my first visit that Walter was all right. If he got nothing in the nature of a salary, he certainly was getting wisdom and happiness. He had full scope for the study of Astrology in an excellent atmosphere and environment....

She was quite a character and a very remarkable one at that; she certainly had powers beyond the ordinary which she used on special occasions. Of one such occasion, I happened to be a silent witness, and on this occasion my brother Walter was the subject. He had been thinking about some astrological problem and came into the sitting-room looking serious and harassed. H.P.B. and I were having a chat; she evidently sensed something from my brother, so in a masterful way directed him to sit down on the sofa and rest himself. Then she turned to me and softly said: "Don't be alarmed, I am going to show him what he wants to know." She only touched his thumb with the ring she had upon her finger, and he instantly fell asleep as in a trance, just as one sees a sensitive go into a trance during a performance of hypnotism. In a very short time, he was awakened and she said to him: "Do you understand what you saw?" He said: "Yes, and it is the answer to my astrological problem in Hebrew letters of fire." "Yes," she said, "that is right. But at present you must not go over by yourself." Then she again turned to me and said that she had been away from her body three times during my brother's trance or sleep....

Henry S. Olcott[105]

July, 1890, London

It was in [July] 1890 that H.P.B. and her staff settled in the...Headquarters, 19 Avenue Road, St. John's Wood, London, and it was here that in the following year she died....It was a large house, standing in its own grounds, which formed a pleasant garden, with bits of lawn, shrubbery, and a few tall trees. Mounting the front steps, one entered a vestibule and short hall, from each side of which doors opened into rooms. The front one on the left was H.P.B.'s working-room, and her small bedchamber adjoined it. From this inner room a short passage led into a rather spacious chamber, which was built for and occupied by the Esoteric Section. To the right of the hall on entering was an artistically furnished dining-room, which was also used for the reception of visitors. Back of this was a small room, then used as a general work-room....A door cut through the north wall of the dining-room gave access to the new hall of the Blavatsky Lodge; while one cut in the south wall of H.P.B.'s room led into the office of the General Secretary of the European Section [of the Theosophical Society]. The upper stories of the house were sleeping apartments. The meeting-hall of the Blavatsky Lodge was of corrugated iron, the walls and ceiling sheathed with unpainted wood. Mr. R. Machell, the artist, had covered the two sloping halves of the ceiling with the symbolic representations of six great religions and of the zodiacal signs. At the south end was a low platform for the presiding officer and the lecturer of the evening. The hall had a seating capacity of about 200. On the opening night [July 3, 1890] the room was crammed, and many were unable to gain admission. The speakers were Mrs. Besant, Mr. Sinnett, a Mrs. Woolff (of America), and Mr. [Bertram] Keightley. H.P.B. was present but said nothing, on account of the critical state of her health.

H.P.B.'s work-room was crammed with furniture, and on the walls hung a large number of photographs of her personal friends and of members of the Esoteric Section. Her large writing-desk faced a window through which she could see the front grassplot and trees, while the view of the street was shut out by a high brick wall. Avenue Road was a veritable beehive of workers, with no place for drones, H.P.B. herself setting the example of tireless literary drudgery, while her strong auric influence enwrapped and stimulated all about her....

19 Avenue Road, London

Alice L. Cleather[106]
July, 1890---May, 1891, London

...[In July, 1890] H.P.B. and the Lansdowne Road household...[moved] into Mrs. Besant's house in Avenue Road....A lecture hall had been added to...[the] house (a large detached one, standing in a garden) for the meetings of the Blavatsky Lodge, both public and private. It was also used for the meetings of the E.S....[Esoteric Section]. This hall was at the side of the house furthest from H.P.B.'s quarters, and she did not appear as frequently, nor was she as accessible as was the case at Lansdowne Road. Failing health had much to say to this, but before she became almost entirely confined to her own rooms she would sometimes be present at the Lodge meetings. On such occasions her presence was both an inspiration and a "terror." Once, when Mrs. Besant was in the chair, and a rather lengthy and stupid paper was being read, the whole room could hear H.P.B.'s stage whisper of agonized appeal:---"Oh stop her, Annie---*stop her!*"

To the E.S. meetings H.P.B. rarely, if ever, came (in person, at least); and, on the formation of the Inner Group of the E.S. [in August, 1890], she was seen even less often outside her own rooms, save in her bath chair, in the garden at the back of the house.

...The twelve members of the Inner Group...were six men and six women...: Countess [Constance] Wachtmeister...Mrs. [Isabel] Cooper-Oakley...Miss Emily Kislingbury...Miss Laura Cooper...Mrs. [Annie] Besant...[Mrs. Alice Cleather herself]...Dr. Archibald Keightley...Mr. Herbert Coryn...Mr. Claude Wright...[Mr. G.R.S.] Mead...Mr. [E.T.] Sturdy...[and] Mr. Walter Old....

The Inner Group was formed, and held its weekly meetings at 19, Avenue Road, in a room which had been specially built for it, leading out of H.P.B.'s bedroom; into it no one but herself and her twelve pupils ever entered. We had each our own place, and our own chair; and H.P.B. sat with her six men pupils on her right, and the six women on her left hand side, in semi-circular formation, during our instructions.[*]

Esther Windust[107]
July, 1890---May, 1891, London

The first time that I saw...[H.P.B.] has made an ineffaceable impression on me. An acquaintance invited me to go with her to a meeting of members and associates to Avenue Road, London. It was a regular evening meeting...."One should see this woman" she said, "as there is told so much about her, good and bad, but most people look on her as a fraud."

So I went---without much enthusiasm---to see an interesting woman, and with a strong resolution to look well out of my eyes!...

The hall was not full, and we sat more or less in the middle

----

[*][H.P.B.'s instructions to the Inner Group are now available under the title **The Inner Group Teachings of H.P. Blavatsky to Her Personal Pupils (1890-91)**: A Reconstruction of the Teachings by H.J. Spierenburg. San Diego. California. Point Loma Publications. Inc.. 1985.---Editor.]

and could well see the podium on which stood two easy chairs, and at the side a stand for the speaker. Soon two ladies appeared, Mrs. Besant, who shortly before had become president of the Blavatsky Lodge, and another lady, not tall, but stout. "Look, that must be Mme. Blavatsky" whispered my cicerone. I could only say "Sh", and pulled a little away....

I had seen many people in many lands, stars in their own firmament, art, theatre, politics, literature, etc.---but this---never! This small, simple woman with a shawl on her shoulders, who filled the big chair, looked smaller than she was because of her stout body....But at that moment I only saw her face with those clear, blue eyes, and the hands on the lap. I studied art at that time, and never in my life had I seen such perfect hands. But this was not even of so much importance. What overwhelmed me was the force and the impersonal love that surrounded her and radiated from her, and which gave me the impression of moving, flimsy light in which faces and forms appeared and disappeared, and even scenes that came up and then disappeared again. Later, much later, I believe, I recognized many of those faces. I knew nothing then of Auras, and sat looking, fascinated. I knew then that I sat in the presence of someone greater, enormously greater, than ever I had dreamt.

Scenes out of Egypt appeared and disappeared, and also from other Southern or Eastern countries, which I had never seen. I remember that I thought of her as a living Sphinx, in contact, conscious intimate contact, with the occult Mysteries of the olden time. The Light remained, though the mysterious images of persons dissolving changed. I had never seen such a thing, and the impression was formidable. I heard little of the lecture. Walter Old...gave a lecture about the Sun, and after the lecture one could put questions, and when the audience did not do it, the speaker himself put questions to H.P.B.

Later I attended many lectures, but that one remains for me a landmark. I joined the Theosophical Society and became a member of the Blavatsky Lodge, but my life was changed, it could not be the same. I had a look into another world. Had I not been so impossibly shy, I would have written to H.P.B. and visited her to put questions. But I did not dare, and when I had to go to the continent some months later, I was very glad to get an invitation to come to Avenue Road that gave me the opportunity to take leave of her before my departure to France. But once in the room I took a chair near the door. When H.P.B. came in I was very glad, but could only sit and look, overwhelmed at the remembrance of what I had seen that first evening, and now by the feeling of the enormous majesty of that small figure, the Messenger sent out by the Great White Lodge to bring help to the suffering humanity of the West.

I believe that I would have remained sitting in that chair till the end of the evening, without saying a word to any one, if...Countess Wachtmeister had not come to me and, with a soft urge...had taken me with her to talk to H.P.B.

When at last I took leave, very much under the impression of her charm, she looked at me with kind eyes and said, after the good wishes for the journey: "Come to see us as soon as you get back!" I was delighted, and at the same time on the point of tears, for I knew at once that I would never see her again in that body....

Countess Constance Wachtmeister[108]
March---April, 1891, London

Things are going pretty well here [at 19, Avenue Road]. The Thursday evenings are continued, though H.P.B. is seldom present; in fact, we rarely see her now. She shuts herself up for days together. She is having a room built out into the garden, leading from her own room; and then, I expect, she will shut herself away altogether. As she grows weaker, she finds it trying to have so many people buzzing around her....

H.P.B. is certainly growing more and more feeble, and she feels that to be able to do any work at all she must be quite alone, so as to enable her to concentrate her energies. Her present sitting-room is a passage room to the E.S. [Esoteric Section], and she cannot have that quiet and solitude that are necessary; and so the inner room, now being built, will be closed to all outsiders, relations included....She says that her body is now so broken and shattered that it is only by being much alone that she can keep it together; and I expect the day will come when she will shut herself up altogether, and only occasionally see those in the house. As it is, we never go near her except in the evening....

G.R.S. Mead[109]
April, 1891, London

One of the greatest proofs to me of H.P.B.'s extraordinary gifts and ability, if proof were needed in the face of the manifest sincerity of her life-work, was the way in which she wrote her articles and books. I knew every book she had in her small library, and yet day after day she would produce quantities of MS. abounding in quotations, which were seldom inaccurate. I remember almost the last day she sat at her desk, going into her room to query two Greek words in a quotation, and telling her they were inaccurate. Now though H.P.B. could in her early years speak modern Greek and had been taught ancient Greek by her grandmother, she had long forgotten it for all purposes of accuracy, and the correction of the words I objected to required precise scholarship. "Where did you get it from, H.P.B.?" I asked. "I'm sure I don't know, my dear," was her somewhat discouraging rejoinder, "I saw it!" adding that she was certain that she was right, for now she remembered when she wrote the particular passage referred to. However, I persuaded her that there was some mistake, and finally she said, "Well, of course you are a great Greek pundit, I know, but you're not going to sit upon me always. I'll try if I can see it again, and now get out," meaning that she wanted to go on with her work, or at any rate had had enough of me. About two minutes afterwards, she called me in again and presented me with a scrap of paper on which she had written the two words quite correctly, saying, "Well, I suppose you'll be a greater pundit than ever after this!"...

Laura M. Cooper[110]
April 21---May 8, 1891, London

It was on Tuesday, the 21st of April, that I went to stay at Headquarters for the few days, which, owing to the unexpected events that followed, turned into a visit of some weeks. H.P.B. seemed in her usual state of health, and on Thursday, the 23rd, attended the Lodge and remained chatting with the friends who surrounded her for some time after the proceedings of the evening were over; she then adjourned to her room where, according to their habit, members who live at Headquarters [at 19, Avenue Road] followed to sit with her while she took her coffee before retiring for the night....Saturday, she was very bright....My sister, Mrs. [Isabel] Cooper-Oakley, and I, with one or two others, remained talking with her until eleven o'clock, when she retired with a cheery "Good night all", apparently in her usual health. The next morning, however, H.P.B.'s maid came early to my room to tell me she had passed a very restless night and had been seized with shivering attacks...The doctor was immediately sent for, and the day passed with H.P.B. alternately in a heavy sleep, or in a state of restlessness. Late in the afternoon Dr. Mennell came, pronounced the illness to be influenza; the fever was very high, her temperature being 105....From that memorable Sunday night, April 26th, began the succession of misfortunes, the illness of one member of the household after another, which culminated in the passing away of our beloved H.P.B....Towards the end of Thursday the 30th, H.P.B. began to suffer very much from her throat, and as the hours went by she had increasing difficulty in swallowing; her cough became very troublesome and her breathing very laboured. On Friday morning she was no better, and when Dr. Mennell arrived he found a quinsy had formed in the right side of the throat; hot poultices were applied and some relief was gained....The morning of Sunday, May 3rd, found H.P.B. very ill indeed, for the pain of swallowing made it very difficult for her to take the necessary amount of nourishment, and her weakness increased in consequence....How bravely she struggled against her illness only those who were with her can realise. On Wednesday, the 6th of May, she partially dressed and walked into the sitting-room, remained there for her luncheon, resting for some time on the sofa; in the evening Dr. Mennell found her going on fairly well, all fever had entirely left her, but the great weakness and the difficulty in breathing caused him considerable anxiety....That Wednesday night was the turning point in her illness....On Thursday [May 7th]...H.P.B. rallied and about three in the afternoon dressed, and with very little assistance walked into the sitting room; when there she asked for her large armchair to be brought her...The chair was turned facing into the room and when H.P.B. was sitting in it she had her card table with the cards drawn in front of her, and she tried to "make a patience"; notwithstanding all these brave efforts it was quite apparent that she was suffering intensely....Dr. Mennell came shortly after 5 o'clock and was much surprised to find her sitting up, and he congratulated her and praised her courage; she said, "I do my best, Doctor"; her voice was hardly above a whisper and the effort to speak was exhausting, as her breath was very short....She handed Dr. Mennell a cigarette she had managed with difficulty to prepare for him; it was the last she ever made....The night that followed, her last with us, was a very suffering one; owing to the increased difficulty in breathing H.P.B. could not rest in any position; every remedy was tried without avail, and finally she was obliged to remain seated in her chair propped with pillows. ...About 4 a.m. H.P.B. seemed easier....[But] about 11:30 [a.m. on May 8th] I was aroused by Mr. Wright, who told me to come at once as H.P.B. had changed for the worse, and the nurse did not think she could live many hours; directly I entered her room I realised the critical condition she was in. She was sitting in her chair and I knelt in front of her and asked her to try and take the stimulant; though too weak to hold the glass herself she allowed me to hold it to her lips, and she managed to swallow the contents; but after that we could only give a little nourishment in a spoon. The nurse said H.P.B. might linger some hours, but suddenly there was a further change, and when I tried to moisten her lips I saw the dear eyes were already becoming dim, though she retained full consciousness to the last. In life H.P.B. had a habit of moving one foot when she was thinking intently, and she continued that movement almost to the moment she ceased to breathe. When all hope was over the nurse left the room, leaving C.F. Wright, W.R. Old and myself with our beloved H.P.B; the two former knelt in

286

H.P.B. at 19, Avenue Road

front, each holding one of her hands, and I at her side with one arm round her supported her head; thus we remained motionless for many minutes, and so quietly did H.P.B. pass away that we hardly knew the second she ceased to breathe; a great sense of peace filled the room, and we knelt quietly there....

Henry S. Olcott[111]
May 9 & 10, 1891, Sydney, Australia

My first intimation of H.P.B.'s death was received by me "telepathically" from herself, and this was followed by a second similar message. The third I got from one of the reporters present at my closing lecture in Sydney, who told me, as I was about leaving the platform, that a press message had come from London announcing her decease. In my Diary entry for 9th May, 1891, I say: "Had an uneasy foreboding of H.P.B.'s death." In that of the following day it is written: "This morning I feel that H.P.B. is dead...." The last entry for that day says: "Cablegram, H.P.B. dead." Only those who saw us together, and knew of the close mystical tie between us, can understand the sense of bereavement that came over me upon receipt of the direful news.

Julia Keightley[112]
May, 1891, Pennsylvania

A few days after Madame Blavatsky died, H.P.B. awoke me at night. I raised myself, feeling no surprise, but only the sweet accustomed pleasure. She held my eyes with her leonine gaze. Then she grew thinner, taller, her shape became masculine; slowly then her features changed, until a man of height and rugged powers stood before me, the last vestige of her features melting into his, until the leonine gaze, the progressed radiance of her glance alone remained. The man lifted his head and said: "Bear

288

witness!'" He then walked from the room, laying his hand on the portrait of H.P.B. as he passed. Since then, he has come to me several times, with instructions, in broad daylight while I was busily working, and once he stepped out from a large portrait of H.P.B....

"MADAME BLAVATSKY"
New York Tribune, May 10, 1891

Few women in our time have been more persistently misrepresented, slandered, and defamed than Madame Blavatsky, but though malice and ignorance did their worst upon her, there are abundant indications that her life-work will vindicate itself, that it will endure, and that it will operate for good. She was the founder of the Theosophical Society, an organization now fully and firmly established, which has branches in many countries, East and West....For nearly twenty years she had devoted herself to the dissemination of doctrines the fundamental principles of which are of the loftiest ethical character....

Madame Blavatsky held that the regeneration of mankind must be based upon the development of altruism. In this she was at one with the greatest thinkers, not alone of the present day, but of all time....

In another direction..., she did important work. No one in the present generation, it may be said, has done more towards reopening the long sealed treasures of Eastern thought, wisdom, and philosophy. No one certainly has done so much towards elucidating that profound wisdom-religion wrought out by the ever-cogitating Orient, and bringing into the light those ancient literary works whose scope and depth have so astonished the Western World....Her own knowledge of Oriental philosophy and esotericism was comprehensive. No candid mind can doubt this after reading her two principal works. The tone and tendency of all her writings were healthful, bracing, and stimulating. The lesson which was constantly impressed by her was assuredly that which the world most needs, and has always needed, namely the necessity of subduing self and of working for others....

The work of Madame Blavatsky has already borne fruit, and destined, apparently, to produce still more marked and salutary effects in the future.....Thus Madame Blavatsky has made her mark upon the time, and thus, too, her works will follow her....Some day, if not at once, the loftiness and purity of her aims, the wisdom and scope of her teachings, will be recognized more fully, and her memory will be accorded the honor to which it is justly entitled.

———————

APPENDIX A

H.P.B. Speaks

When, years ago, we first travelled over the East, exploring the penetralia of its deserted sanctuaries, two saddening and ever-recurring questions oppressed our thoughts: *Where, Who, What is GOD? Who ever saw the IMMORTAL SPIRIT of man, so as to be able to assure himself of man's immortality?*

It was while most anxious to solve these perplexing problems that we came into contact with certain men, endowed with such mysterious powers and such profound knowledge that we may truly designate them as the sages of the Orient. To their instructions we lent a ready ear....[113]

I...[have] known Adepts, the "Brothers," not only in India and beyond Ladakh, but in Egypt and Syria,---for there are "Brothers" there to this day....Whether they were called Rosicrucians, Kabalists, or Yogis---Adepts were everywhere Adepts---silent, secret, retiring, and who would never divulge themselves entirely to anyone, unless one did as I did---passed seven and ten years probation and given proofs of absolute devotion, and that he, or she, would keep silent even before a prospect and a threat of death. I fulfilled the requirements and am what I am....All I was allowed to say was---the truth: There is beyond the Himalayas a nucleus of Adepts, of various nationalities; and the Teschu Lama [the Panchen Lama of Shigatse, Tibet] knows them, and they act together, and some of them are with him and yet remain unknown in their true character even to the average lama....My Master [Morya] and Mahatma K.H. and several others I know personally are there, coming and going, and they are all in communication with Adepts in Egypt and Syria, and even Europe....[114]

For thousands of years, one initiate after another...has explored and re-explored the invisible Universe, the worlds of the interplanetary regions, during long periods when his conscious soul, united to the spiritual soul and to the ALL, free and almost omnipotent, left his body. It is not only the initiates belonging to the "Great Brotherhood of the Himalayas" who give us these doctrines....

The mysteries of life as well as of death, of the visible and invisible worlds, have been fathomed and observed by initiated adepts in all epochs and in all nations. They have studied these during the solemn moments of union of their divine monad with the universal Spirit, and they have recorded their experiences. Thus by comparing and checking the *observations* of one with those of another, and finding none of the contradictions so frequently noticed in *communications* of *mediums*, but on the contrary, having been able to ascertain that the visions of adepts who lived 10,000 years ago are invariably corroborated and verified by those of modern adepts, to whom the writings of the former never do become known until later---the truth has been established. A definite science, based on personal observation and experience, corroborated by continuous demonstration, containing irrefutable proofs, for those who study it, has thus been established....

By the training of faculties we all possess, but which they alone have developed to perfection,...[the Adepts] have entered in spirit these various [psycho-spiritual] planes and states. For long ages, one generation of Adepts after another has studied the mysteries of being, of life, death, and re-birth, and all have taught in their turn some of the facts so learned....[115]

...[In] 1851...I saw my Master *bodily* and personally for the first time....

...I saw Master in my visions ever since my childhood. In the year of the first Nepaul Embassy...[I] saw and recognised him [in London]. Saw him twice. Once he came out of the crowd, then He ordered me to meet Him in Hyde Park....

...I venerate the Masters, and worship MY MASTER---the sole creator of my inner Self which but for His calling it out, awakening it from its slumber, would have never come to conscious being---not in *this* life, at all events....

...I am enough of an occultist to know that before we find the Master within our own hearts and seventh principle---we need an outside Master....He is a Saviour, he who leads you to finding the Master within yourself. It is ten years already that I preach the inner Master and God and never represented our Masters as Saviours in the Christian sense....[116]

...I have lived at different periods in Little Tibet as in Great Tibet, and...these combined periods form more than seven years....I have stopped in Lamaistic convents;...I have visited Tzi-gadze [Shigatse], the Tashi-Lhunpo territory and its neighbourhood, and...I have been further in, and in such places of Tibet as have never been visited by any other European....[117]

...[In 1870] I was...in Mah[atma] K.H.'s house. I was sitting in a corner on a mat and he walking about the room in his riding dress...."*I remind can't*"---I pronounced in answer to a question of His about a dead aunt. He smiled and said "Funny English you use." Then I felt ashamed, hurt *in my vanity*, and began thinking..."now I am here and speaking *nothing but English*...I can perhaps learn to speak better with Him."....

Then...*three months after*...I was standing before Mah. K.H....As Master [Morya] was not at home, I took to him a few sentences I was studying in Senzar in his sister's room and asked him to tell me if I translated them correctly---and gave him a slip of paper with these sentences written in English. He took and read them, and correcting the interpretation read them over and said "Now your English is becoming better--- *try to pick out of my head even the little I know of it*." And he put his hand on my forehead in the region of memory and squeezed his fingers on it....and since that day He did so with my head daily, for about two months....

...[Then] I am going away with Master who is sending me off, back to Europe. I am bidding good-bye to his sister and her child and all the chelas. I listen to what the Masters tell me. And then come the parting words of Mah. K.H. laughing at me as He always did and saying "Well, if you have not learned much of the Sacred Sciences and practical Occultism...you have learned, at any rate, a little English. You speak it now *only a little worse* than I do!" and he laughed.[118]

I am here in this country [America] sent by my Lodge on behalf of Truth in modern spiritualism, and it is my most sacred duty to unveil what is, and expose what is not. Perhaps did I arrive here one hundred years too soon....

I pray you, do not take me to be a "blind fanatic," for, if I am the latter, I am not the former. When I became a spiritualist, it was not through the agency of the ever-lying, cheating mediums, miserable instruments of the undeveloped Spirits of the lower Sphere, the ancient Hades. My belief is based on something older than the Rochester knockings, and springs out from the same source of information that was used by Raymond Lully, Picus della Mirandola, Cornelius Agrippa, Robert Fludd, Henry More...etc., all of whom have ever been searching for a system that should disclose to them the "deepest depths" of the Divine nature, and show them the real tie which binds all things together. I found at last, and many year ago, the cravings of my mind satisfied by this theosophy taught by the Angels....[119]

I was sent to America on purpose and sent to the Eddies. There I found Olcott...I was ordered to let him know that spiritual phenomena without the philosophy of Occultism were dangerous and misleading. I proved to him that all that mediums could do through spirits others could do at will without any spirits at all; that bells and thought-reading, raps and physical phenomena, could be achieved by anyone who had a faculty of acting in his physical body through the organs of his astral body; and I had that faculty ever since I was four years old, as all my family know. I could make furniture move and objects fly apparently, and my astral arms that supported them remained invisible; all this ever before I knew even of Masters....[120]

You cannot imagine in what a charmed world of pictures and visions I live. I am writing *Isis*...I sit with my eyes open and to all appearances see and hear everything real and actual around me, and yet at the same time I see and hear that which I write. I feel short of breath; I am afraid to make the slightest movement for fear the spell might be broken. Slowly century after century, image after image, float out of the distance and pass before me as if in a magic panorama; and meanwhile I put them together in my mind....Races and nations, countries and cities, which have for long disappeared in the darkness of the prehistoric past, emerge and then vanish...Hoary antiquity makes way for historical periods; myths are explained to me....Every event which is at all remarkable, every newly-turned page of this many-colored book of life, impresses itself on my brain with photographic exactitude. My own reckonings and calculations appear to me later on as separate colored pieces of different shapes in the game which is called *casse-tete* (puzzles) I gather them together and try to match them one after the other, and at the end there always comes out a geometrical whole...Most assuredly it is not I who do it all, but my Ego, the highest principle which lives in me. And even this with the help of my Guru and teacher who helps me in everything. If I happen to forget something I have just to address him, or another of the same kind, in my thought, and what I have forgotten rises once more before my eyes----sometimes whole tables of numbers passing before me, long inventories of events. They remember everything. They know everything. Without them, from whence could I gather my knowledge....[121]

Do not be afraid that I am off my head. All that I can say is that someone positively *inspires me*....More than this: someone enters me. It is not I who talk and write: it is something within me, my higher and luminous Self, that thinks and writes for me. Do not ask me, my friend, what I experience, because I could not explain it to you clearly. I do not know myself! The one thing I know is...I have become a sort of storehouse of somebody else's knowledge.....*Someone* comes and envelops me as a misty cloud and all at once pushes me out of myself, and then I am not "I" any more ---Helena Petrovna Blavatsky---but someone else. Someone strong and powerful, born in a totally different region of the world; and as to myself it is almost as if I were asleep, or lying by not quite conscious,---not in my own body but close by, held only by a thread which ties me to it. However, at times I see and hear everything quite clearly: I am perfectly conscious of what my body is saying and doing---or at least its new possessor. I even understand and remember it all so well that afterwards I can repeat it and even write down *his* words....At such a time I see awe and fear on the faces of Olcott and others, and follow with interest the way in which *he* half-pityingly regards them out of my own eyes and teaches them with my physical tongue. Yet not with my mind but his own, which enwraps my brain like a cloud....[122]

It seems strange to you that some Hindu Sahib is so free and easy in his dealings with me. I can quite understand you: a person not used to that kind of phenomenon ---which, though not quite unprecedented, is yet perfectly ignored----is sure to be incredulous....You ask whether he is likely to indulge in wanderings inside other people as well as me. I am sure I don't know....Admit that man's soul---his real living soul - --is a thing perfectly separate from the rest of the organism; that this perisprit is not stuck with paste to the physical "innards" and that this soul...is capable of acting freely and independently. In the case of the uninitiated profane, it acts during their sleep: in the case of an initiated adept, it acts at any moment he chooses according to his will...What mediums accomplish unconsciously, under the influence of outside powers which take possession of them, can be accomplished by Adepts consciously at their own volition.....As to the Sahib, I have known him a long time. Twenty-five year ago he came to London with the Prince of Nepaul....[Here in New York City] he appeared repeatedly, not only to me but also to other people, and to Olcott....I always recognize and know the Master, and often talk to him without seeing him. How is it that he hears me from everywhere, and that I also hear his voice across seas and oceans twenty times a day? I do not know, but it is so. Whether it is he personally that enters me I really cannot say with confidence: if it is not he, it is his power, his influence....

...The Master...is quite commonly seen by perfect strangers. Sometimes he looks just as if he were a living man, as merry as possible....He will soon take us all to India, and there we shall see him in his body just like an ordinary person....[123]

I am very busy [writing] on *Secret D*[octrine]. The thing at N.Y. is repeated--- only far clearer and better. I begin to think it *shall vindicate* us. Such pictures, panoramas, scenes, *antediluvian* dramas with all that! Never saw or heard better....

There's a new development and scenery, every morning. I *live two lives again*. Master finds that it is too difficult for me to be looking consciously into the astral light for my S.D. and so, it is now about a fortnight, I am made to see all I have to as though in my dream. I see large and long rolls of paper on which things are written and I recollect them....[124]

...We may claim to have placed before the thinking public a logical, coherent, and philosophical scheme of man's origin, destiny, and evolution---a scheme pre-eminent above all for its rigorous adherence to justice. And, that we may broaden our criterion of truth, our research extends to an inquiry into the nature of the less known forces, cosmic and psychical....

In one word, our whole aim and desire are to help, in at least some degree, toward arriving at correct scientific views upon the nature of man, which carry with them the means of reconstructing for the present generation the deductive metaphysical or transcendental philosophy which alone is the firm, unshakable foundation of every religious philosophy.

Theosophy, the universal solvent, is fulfilling its mission; the opalescent tints of the dawn of modern psychology are blending together, and will all be merged into the perfect daylight of truth, when the sun-orb of Eastern esotericism has mounted to its noon-stage. For many a long year the "great orphan," Humanity, has been crying aloud in the darkness for guidance and for light. Amid the increasing splendours of a progress purely material, of a science that nourished the intellect, but left the spirit to starve, Humanity, dimly feeling its origin and presaging its destiny, has stretched out towards the East empty hands that only a *spiritual* philosophy can fill. Aching from the divisions, the jealousies, the hatreds, that rend its very life, it has cried for some sure foundation on which to build the solidarity it senses, some metaphysical basis from which its loftiest social ideals may rise secure. Only the Masters of the Eastern wisdom can set that foundation, can satisfy at once the intellect and the spirit, can guide Humanity safely through the night to "the dawn of a larger day."

Such is the goal which Theosophy has set itself to attain....[125]

If Theosophy...strikes deep root into the minds and hearts of men, if its doctrines of Reincarnation and Karma, in other words, of Hope and Responsibility, find a home in the lives of the new generations, then, indeed, will dawn the day of joy and gladness for all who now suffer and are outcast. For real Theosophy is ALTRUISM, and we cannot repeat it too often. It is brotherly love, mutual help, unswerving devotion to Truth. If once men do but realize that in these alone can true happiness be found, and never in wealth, possessions, or any selfish gratification, then the dark clouds will roll away, and a new humanity will be born upon earth. Then the GOLDEN AGE will be there, indeed.

But if not, then the storm will burst, and our boasted western civilization and enlightenment will sink in such a sea of horror that its parallel History has never yet recorded.[126]

There *is* a road, steep and thorny, beset with perils of every kind, but yet a road, and it leads to the very heart of the Universe: I can tell you how to find those who will show you the secret gateway that opens inward only, and closes fast behind the neophyte for evermore. There is no danger that dauntless courage cannot conquer; there is no trial that spotless purity cannot pass through; there is no difficulty that strong intellect cannot surmount. For those who win onwards there is reward past all telling---the power to bless and save humanity; for those who fail, there are other lives in which success may come.[127]

The world is not prepared yet to understand the philosophy of Occult Sciences ---let them assure themselves first of all that there are beings in an invisible world, whether "Spirits" of the dead or *Elementals*; and that there are hidden powers in man, which are capable of making a *God* of him on earth.

When I am dead and gone people will, perhaps, appreciate my disinterested motives. I have pledged my word to help people on to *Truth* while living and---will keep my word. Let them abuse and revile me. Let some call me a MEDIUM and a Spiritualist, and others an *impostor*. The day will come when posterity will learn to know me better.[128]

APPENDIX B

The Mahatmas Speak

One or two of us hoped that the world had so far advanced intellectually, if not intuitionally, that the Occult doctrine might gain an intellectual acceptance, and the impulse given for a new cycle of occult research....So casting about we found in America the man [H.S. Olcott] to stand as leader---a man of great moral courage, unselfish, and having other good qualities. He was far from being the best, but...he was the best one available. With him we associated [H.P.B.] a woman of most exceptional and wonderful endowments. Combined with them she had strong personal defects, but just as she was, there was no second to her living fit for this work. We sent her to America, brought them together---and the trial began.---**Morya.**[129]

...Imperfect as may be our visible agent---and often most unsatisfactory and imperfect she is---yet...[H.P.B.] is the best available at present, and her phenomena have for about half a century astounded and baffled some of the cleverest minds of the age....---**Koot Hoomi.**[130]

I am painfully aware of the fact that the habitual incoherence of...[H.P.B.'s] statements---especially when excited---and her strange ways make her in your opinion a very undesirable transmitter of our messages. Nevertheless..., once...you have learned the truth; once told...this unbalanced mind, the seeming incongruity of her speeches and ideas, her nervous excitement, all that in short which is so calculated to upset the feelings of sober minded people, whose notions of reserve and manners are shocked by such strange outbursts of what they regard as her temper, and which so revolt you,---once...*you know* nothing of it is due to any fault of hers, you may, perchance, be led to regard her in quite a different light....I am empowered to allow you a glimpse behind the veil. This state of hers is intimately connected with her occult training in Tibet, and due to her being sent out alone into the world to gradually prepare the way for others. After nearly a century of fruitless search, our chiefs [Adept Superiors] had to avail themselves of the only opportunity to send out a European *body* upon European soil to serve as a connecting link between that country and our own....Remember...the fact of the *seven* principles in the *complete* human being. Now, no man or woman, unless he be an initiate of the "fifth circle," can leave the precincts of *Bod-Lhas* and return back into the world in his integral whole....One at least of his seven satellites has to remain behind for two reasons; the first to form the necessary connecting link, the wire of transmission---the second as the safest warranter that certain things will never be divulged. She is no exception to the rule....The bearing and status of the remaining *six* [principles] depend upon the inherent qualities, the psycho-physiological peculiarities of the person....---**Koot Hoomi.**[131]

Spirit is strong but flesh is weak; so weak sometimes that it even overpowers the strong spirit "which knows all truth." And now, having almost shaken off its control this poor body [of H.P.B.'s] raves....If you are ever to learn any lesson about man's duality and the possibility through occult science of awakening from its dormant state to an independent existence the invisible but real *I am*, seize this chance. Observe and learn....I can now only act thro'...[H.P.B.] upon very rare occasions and under the greatest precautions....---**Koot Hoomi.**[132]

...If...[H.P.B.] ever became guilty of real, *deliberate* deception...it was when in the presence of [occult] phenomena produced she kept constantly denying---except in the matter of such trifles as bells and raps---that she had anything to do with their production *personally*....Yes; in that, and in that alone, she became constantly guilty of *deceiving* her friends. She could never be made to realize the utter uselessness, the danger of such a zeal; and how mistaken she was in her notions that she was adding to our glory, whereas, by attributing to us very often phenomena of the most childish nature, she but lowered us in the public estimation and sanctioned the claim of her enemies that she was "but a medium"! But it was of no use. In accordance with our rules, M[orya] was not permitted to forbid her such a course, in so many words. She had to be allowed full and entire freedom of action, the liberty of *creating causes* that became in due course of time her scourge, her public pillory. He could at best forbid her producing phenomena, and to this last extremity he resorted as often as he could, to her friends' and theosophists' great dissatisfaction....Is it lack of intellectual perceptions in her? Certainly not. It is a psychological disease, over which she has little if any control at all. Her impulsive nature...is always ready to carry her beyond the boundaries of truth, into the regions of exaggeration; nevertheless without a shadow of suspicion that she is thereby deceiving her friends....She can and did produce [occult] phenomena, owing to her natural powers combined with several long years of regular training, and her phenomena are sometimes better, more wonderful and for more perfect than those of some high, initiated chelas [disciples]....Thus, while fathering upon us all manner of foolish, often clumsy and *suspected* phenomena, she has most undeniably been *helping* us in many instances, saving us sometimes as much as two-thirds of the power used, and when [we] remonstrated---for often we are unable to prevent her doing it on her end of the line---answering that she had no need of it, and that her only joy was to be of some use to us. And thus she kept on killing herself inch by inch, ready to give---for our benefit and glory, as she thought---her life-blood drop by drop, and yet invariably denying before witnesses that she had anything to do with it. Would you call this sublime, albeit foolish self-abnegation--- "dishonest"? We do not....

...Most undeniably she is given to exaggeration in general, and when it becomes a question of "puffing up" those she is devoted to, her enthusiasm knows no limit....We cannot help feeling at times angry with, oftener---laughing at, her. Yet the feeling that dictates all this ridiculous effusion is too ardent, too sincere and true, not to be respected or even treated with indifference. I do not believe I was ever so profoundly touched by anything I witnessed in all my life, as I was with the poor old creature's ecstatic rapture, when meeting us recently both in our natural bodies, one---after three years, the other---nearly two years absence and separation in [the] flesh. Even our phlegmatic M. was thrown off his balance by such an exhibition---of which he was the chief hero. He had to use his *power*, and plunge her into a profound sleep, otherwise she would have burst some blood-vessel...in her delirious attempts to flatten her nose against his riding mantle besmeared with the Sikkim mud!...You can never know her as we do, therefore---none of you will ever be able to judge her impartially or correctly. You see the surface of things....In your opinion H.P.B. is, at best, for those who like her despite herself---a quaint, strange woman, a psychological riddle; impulsive and kindhearted, yet not free from the vice of untruth. We, on the other hand, under the garb of eccentricity and folly---we find a profounder wisdom in her *inner* Self than you will ever find yourselves able to perceive....---**Koot Hoomi.**[133]

One of the most valuable effects of Upasika's [H.P.B.'s] mission is that it drives men to self-study and destroys in them blind servility for persons....We employ agents ---the best available. Of these for the past thirty years the chief [agent] has been the personality known as H.P.B. to the world (but otherwise to us). Imperfect and very troublesome, no doubt, she proves to some, nevertheless, there is no likelihood of our finding a better one for years to come....---**Koot Hoomi.**[134]

APPENDIX C

Why Did Madame Blavatsky
Perform Psychic Phenomena?

[The following extracts from the writings of H.P.B. and her Masters help to answer the above question and also give valuable insights concerning the value and worth of psychic phenomena in the light of Theosophy, Occultism, and the Spiritual Path.--- Editor.]

From its very beginning the world has seen in Theosophy nothing but certain marvellous phenomena, in which two-thirds of the non-spiritualists do not believe. Very soon the [Theosophical] Society came to be regarded as a body pretending to the possession of "miraculous" powers. The world never realised that the Society taught absolute disbelief in *miracle* or even the possibility of such; that in the Society there were only a few people who possessed such psychic powers and but few who cared for them. Nor did it understand that the [occult] phenomena were never produced publicly, but only privately for friends, and merely given as an accessory, to prove by direct demonstration that such [psychic] things could be produced without dark rooms, spirits, mediums, or any of the usual paraphernalia [of Spiritualism].....---**H.P. Blavatsky.**[135]

"Occult phenomena"...failed to produce the desired effect, but they were, in no sense of the word, "miracles." It was supposed that intelligent people, especially men of science, would, at least, have recognized the existence of a new and deeply interesting field of enquiry and research when they witnessed physical effects produced at will, for which they were not able to account. It was supposed that theologians would have welcomed the proof, of which they stand so sadly in need in these agnostic days, that the soul and the spirit are not mere creations of their fancy, due to ignorance of the physical constitution of man, but entities quite as real as the body, and much more important. These expectations were not realized. The [occult] phenomena were misunderstood and misrepresented, both as regards their nature and their purpose.

In the light which experience has now thrown upon the matter the explanation of this unfortunate circumstance is not far to seek. Neither science nor religion acknowledges the existence of the Occult, as the term is understood and employed in theosophy; in the sense, that is to say, of a super-material, but not super-natural, region, governed by law; nor do they recognize the existence of latent powers and possibilities in man. Any interference with the every-day routine of the material world is attributed, by religion to the arbitrary will of a good or an evil autocrat, inhabiting a supernatural region inaccessible to man, and subject to no law, either in his actions or constitution, and for a knowledge of whose ideas and wishes mortals are entirely dependent upon inspired communications delivered through an accredited messenger....

When people see wonders, nowadays, the sentiment excited in their minds is no longer veneration and awe, but curiosity. It was in the hope of arousing and utilizing this spirit of curiosity that occult phenomena were shown. It was believed that this manipulation of forces of nature which lie below the surface...would have led to enquiry into the nature and the laws of those forces, unknown to science, but perfectly known to occultism. That the phenomena did excite curiosity in the minds of those who witnessed them, is certainly true, but it was, unfortunately, for the most part of an idle kind. The greater number of the witnesses developed an insatiable appetite for phenomena for their own sake, without any thought of studying the philosophy or the science of whose truth and power the phenomena were merely trivial and, so to say, accidental illustrations. In but a few cases the curiosity which was awakened gave birth to the serious desire to study the philosophy and the science themselves and for their own sake....

...Modern science...labours under disabilities with respect to the investigation of the Occult quite as embarrassing as those of Religion; for, while Religion cannot grasp the idea of natural law as applied to the supersensuous universe, Science does not allow the existence of any supersensuous universe at all to which the reign of law could be extended; nor can it conceive the possibility of any other state of consciousness than our present terrestrial one....So it calmly proceeded at once to pooh-pooh the phenomena; and, when obliged to express some kind of opinion, it did not hesitate, without examination, and on hearsay reports, to attribute them to fraudulent contrivances---wires, trapdoors, and so forth....

Never were the phenomena presented in any other character than that of instances of a power *over perfectly natural though unrecognized forces*, and incidentally over matter, possessed by certain individuals who have attained to a larger and higher knowledge of the Universe than has been reached by scientists and theologians, or can ever be reached by them, by the roads they are now respectively pursuing. Yet this power is latent in all men, and could, in time, be wielded by anyone who would cultivate the knowledge and conform to the conditions necessary for its development. Nevertheless, except in a few isolated and honourable instances, never was it received in any other character than as would-be miracles, or as works of the Devil, or as vulgar tricks....And from all sides, theosophy and theosophists were attacked with a rancour and bitterness, with an absolute disregard alike of fact and logic, and with malice, hatred and uncharitableness that would be utterly inconceivable, did not religious history teach us what mean and unreasoning animals ignorant men become when their cherished prejudices are touched; and did not the history of scientific research teach us, in its turn, how very like an ignorant man a learned man can behave, when the truth of his theories is called in question.

An occultist can produce phenomena, but he cannot supply the world with brains, nor with the intelligence and good faith necessary to understand and appreciate them. Therefore, it is hardly to be wondered at, that *word* [from the Masters] came to abandon phenomena and let the ideas of Theosophy stand on their own merits.---**H.P. Blavatsky**.[136]

The goal of the aspirant for spiritual wisdom is entrance upon a higher plane of existence; he is to become a new man,...and if he succeeds, his capabilities and faculties will receive a corresponding increase of range and power....This is how it is that the Adept becomes endowed with marvellous powers that have been so often described, but the main point to be remembered is, that these powers are the natural accompaniments of existence on a higher plane of evolution, just as the ordinary human faculties are the natural accompaniments of existence on the ordinary human plane.

Many persons seem to think that adeptship is not so much the result of radical development as of additional construction; they seem to imagine that an Adept is a man, who, by going through a certain plainly defined course of training, consisting of minute attention to a set of arbitrary rules, acquires first one power and then another; and, when he has attained a certain number of these powers is forthwith dubbed an adept. Acting on this mistaken idea, they fancy that the first thing to be done towards attaining adeptship is to acquire "powers"---clairvoyance and the power of leaving the physical body and travelling to a distance are among those which fascinate the most.

To those who wish to acquire such powers for their own private advantage, we have nothing to say; they fall under the condemnation of all who act for purely selfish ends....---**H.P. Blavatsky.**[137]

...The Theosophical Society has to fight all who under its cover seek to obtain magical powers to use for their own selfish ends and to the hurt of others. Many are those who joined our Society for no other purpose than curiosity. Psychological [occult] phenomena were what they sought, and they were unwilling to yield one iota of their own pleasures and habits to obtain them. These very quickly went away empty-handed. The Theosophical Society has never been and never will be a school of promiscuous Theurgic rites. But there are dozens of small occult Societies which talk very glibly of Magic, Occultism, Rosicrucians, adepts, etc....Under cover of the philosophy of the Wisdom-Religion [Theosophy] they manage to get up a mystical jargon which for the time is effective and enables them, by the aid of a very small amount of clairvoyance, to fleece the mystically inclined but ignorant aspirants to the occult, and lead them like sheep in almost any direction....But woe to those who try to convert a noble philosophy into a den for disgusting immorality, greediness of selfish power, and money-making under the cloak of Theosophy.---**H.P. Blavatsky.**[138]

...The Society was not founded as a nursery for forcing a supply of Occultists ---as a factory for the manufacture of Adepts. It was intended to stem the current of materialism, and also that of spiritualistic phenomenalism....It had to guide the spiritual awakening that has now begun, and not to pander to psychic cravings which are but another form of materialism....---**H.P. Blavatsky.**[139]

Psychism, with all its allurements and all its dangers, is necessarily developing among you, and you must beware lest the Psychic outruns the Manasic and Spiritual development. Psychic capacities held perfectly under control, checked and directed by the Manasic principle, are valuable aids in development. But these capacities running riot, controlling instead of controlled, using instead of being used, lead the Student into the most dangerous delusions and the certainty of moral destruction.---**H.P. Blavatsky.**[140]

As the preparation for the new cycle proceeds, as the forerunners of the new sub-race make their appearance on the American continent, the latent psychic and occult powers in man are beginning to germinate and grow....Understand once for all that there is nothing "spiritual" or "divine" in *any* of these manifestations....Ethics of Theosophy are more important than any divulgement of psychic laws and facts. The latter relate wholly to the material and evanescent part of...man, but the Ethics sink into and take hold of the real man---the reincarnating Ego....---**H.P. Blavatsky.**[141]

Without ever becoming a "Mahatma," a Buddha or a Great Saint, let...[the aspirant] study the [Theosophical] philosophy and the "Science of the Soul,: and he can become one of the modest benefactors of humanity, without any superhuman powers. *Siddhis* (or the Arhat powers) are .only for those who are able to "lead the life," to comply with the terrible sacrifices required for such a training, and to comply with them *to the very letter*....Know at once and remember always, that *true Occultism or Theosophy* is the "Great Renunciation of SELF," unconditionally and absolutely, in thought as in action. It is ALTRUISM...."Not for himself, but for the world, he lives"....His personality must disappear, and he has to become *a mere beneficent force in Nature*....---**H.P. Blavatsky.**[142]

...Try to break thro' that great *maya* [illusion] against which occult students, the world over, have always been warned by their teachers---the hankering after [occult] phenomena. Like the thirst for drink and opium, its grows with gratification. The Spiritualists are drunken with it...If you cannot be happy without phenomena you will never learn our [Theosophical] philosophy...I tell you a profound truth in saying that if you...but choose wisdom all other things will be added unto it---in time. It adds no force to our metaphysical truths that our letters are dropped from space on to your lap or come under your pillow. If our philosophy is wrong a *wonder* will not set it right.---**Morya.**[143]

...Men who join the [Theosophical] Society with the one selfish object of reaching power, making occult science their only or even chief aim may as well not join it---they are doomed to disappointment...How many times had we to repeat, that he who joins the Society with the sole object of coming in contact with us and if not of acquiring at least of assuring himself of the reality of such powers and of our objective existence---was pursuing a mirage?...It is he alone who has the love of humanity at heart, who is capable of grasping thoroughly the idea of a regenerating practical Brotherhood who is entitled to the possession of our secrets. He alone, such a man---will never misuse his powers, as there will be no fear that he should turn them to selfish ends. A man who places not the good of mankind above his own good is not worthy of becoming our *chela* [disciple]---he is not worthy of becoming higher in knowledge than his neighbour. If he craves for phenomena let him be satisfied with the pranks of spiritualism...We are in the midst of a conflicting people, of an obstinate, ignorant people seeking to know the truth yet not able to find it, for each seeks it only for his own private benefit and gratification, without giving one thought to others...---**Morya.**[144]

...You can do immense good by helping to give the Western nations a secure basis upon which to reconstruct their crumbling faith. What they need is the evidence that Asiatic psychology alone supplies. Give this and you will confer happiness of mind on thousands. The era of blind faith is gone; that of enquiry is here. Enquiry that only unmasks error, without discovering anything upon which the soul can build, will but make iconoclasts. Iconoclasm from its very destructiveness can give nothing, it can only raze. But man can not rest satisfied with bare negation. Agnosticism is but a temporary halt.

This is the moment to guide the recurrent impulse which must soon come, and which will push the age toward extreme atheism, or drag it back to extreme sacerdotalism, if it is not led to the primitive and soul-satisfying philosophy of the Aryans. He who observes what is going on today, on the one hand among the Catholics, who are breeding miracles as fast as the white ants do their young, on the other, among the free thinkers, who are converting by masses into agnostics---will see the drift of things. The age is revelling at a debauch of phenomena. The same marvels that spiritualists quote in opposition to the dogmas of eternal perdition and atonement, the catholics swarm to witness as the strongest proof of their faith in miracles. The skeptic make game of both. All are blind and there is no one to lead them! You and your colleagues may help furnish the materials for a needed universal religious philosophy; one impregnable to scientific assault because itself the finality of absolute science; and, a religion, that is indeed worthy of the name, since it includes the relations of man physical to man psychical, and of the two to all that is above and below them...[The Theosophical Society] is no miracle-mongering...club, nor specially given to the study of phenomenalism. Its chief aim is to extirpate current superstitions and skepticism, and, from long sealed ancient fountains to draw the proof that man may shape his own future destiny, and know for a certainty that he can live hereafter, if he only wills; and that all "phenomena" are but manifestations of natural law, to try to comprehend which is the duty of every intelligent being...
---**Koot Hoomi.**[145]

REFERENCES

1. *Incidents in the Life of Madame Blavatsky*, compiled from Information supplied by her Relatives and Friends and edited by A.P. Sinnett, London, George Redway, 1886, pp. 18-20. Further references to this title abbreviated: *Incidents*.

2. *Incidents*, pp. 26-28.

3. Collated from: Vera P. de Zhelihovsky, "Helena Petrovna Blavatsky," *Lucifer* [London], November, 1894, pp. 203, 204, 203; and *Incidents*, pp. 30-35, 37-39.

4. *Incidents*, pp. 54-55.

5. Constance Wachtmeister, *Reminiscences of H.P. Blavatsky and "The Secret Doctrine"*, London, Theosophical Publishing Society, 1893, pp. 56-57. Further references to this title abbreviated: C. Wachtmeister, *Reminiscences*.

6. Collated from: Vera P. de Zhelihovsky, "Helena Petrovna Blavatsky, " *Lucifer* [London], November, 1894, pp. 205-206; and *Incidents*, pp. 86, 87-91.

7. *Incidents*, pp. 91-97.

8. *Incidents*, pp. 115-116, 134-135, 143, 146-151, 150, 152.

9. *Report of the Result of an Investigation into the Charges against Madame Blavatsky Brought by the Missionaries of the Scottish Free Church of Madras, and Examined by a Committee appointed for that Purpose by the General Council of the Theosophical Society*, Madras, India, The Theosophical Society, 1885, pp. 94-95. Further references to this title abbreviated: *T.S. Report*.

10. *Incidents*, pp. 158-163, 167-168 with additions and corrections from the original English translation of Vera P. de Zhelihovsky's account.

11. Emma Coulomb, *Some Account of My Intercourse with Madame Blavatsky from 1872 to 1884; with Additional Letters and a Full Explanation of the Most Marvellous Theosophical Phenomena*, Madras, India, Higginbotham and Co., 1884, pp. 3-4.

12. "Ghost Stories Galore: A Night of Many Wonders at Second Hand in the Eighth Avenue Lamasery," *The New York World*, April 21, 1878, p. 9.

13. Henry S. Olcott, *Old Diary Leaves: The True Story of the Theosophical Society*, [Volume I (1874-1878)], New York, G.P. Putnam's Sons, 1895, pp. 21-22. Further references to this volume abbreviated: ODL, Vol. I.

14. Elizabeth G.K. Holt, "A Reminiscence of H.P. Blavatsky in 1873," *The Theosophist* [Adyar, Madras, India], December, 1931, pp. 257-266.

15. ODL, Vol. I, pp. 1-10.

16. ODL, Vol. I, pp. 10-11, 40-42, 17.

17. *Incidents,* pp. 186-199.

18. "Rosicrucianism in New York," *The Liberal Christian* [New York], September 4, 1875.

19. *Some Unpublished Letters of Helena Petrovna Blavatsky,* with an Introduction and Commentary by Eugene Rollin Corson, London, Rider & Co., 1929, collated from pp. 45-46, 24-26, 118, 26-28, 33, 35, 36-37, 47, 118.

20. Collated from: Henry S. Olcott, "The First Leaf of T.S. History," *The Theosophist* [Adyar, Madras, India], November, 1890, pp. 65-66, 67-70; and Henry S. Olcott, *A Historical Retrospect---1875-1896---of the Theosophical Society,* Madras, India, The Theosophical Society, 1896, pp. 2-3.

21. ODL, Vol. I, pp. 202-204, 205, 208-212, 236-237, 243-247.

22. Alexander Wilder, "How 'Isis Unveiled' Was Written," *The Word,* [New York], May, 1908, pp. 77-87.

23. Olcott's letter is quoted in: Theodore Besterman, *Mrs. Annie Besant: A Modern Prophet,* London, Kegan Paul, Trench, Trubner & Co., Ltd., 1934, pp. 148-154.

24. ODL, Vol. I, pp. 377, 379-381.

25. Collated from *Religio-Philosophical Journal* [Chicago, Illinois], January 12, 1878, p. 6; and *H.P.B.: In Memory of Helena Petrovna Blavatsky,* by Some of Her Pupils, London, Theosophical Publishing Society, 1891, pp. 11-13. Further references to the latter title abbreviated: *H.P.B.: In Memory.*

26. *Theosophical Review* [London], January, 1902, pp. 387-388, 386, 387.

27. "H.P. Blavatsky's Adieux," *The New York Daily Graphic,* December 10, 1878, p. 266.

28. *Light* [London], August 30, 1884, p. 360.

29. Henry S. Olcott, *Old Diary Leaves: The Only Authentic History of the Theosophical Society,* Second Series, 1878-1883, London, The Theosophical Publishing Society, 1900, pp. 4-6. Further references to this volume abbreviated: ODL, Vol. II.

30. George Wyld, *Notes of My Life,* London, Kegan, Paul, Trench, Truber & Co., 1903, pp. 71-73.

31. Collated from: ODL, Vol. II, pp. 8-25; and A.O. Hume, *Hints on Esoteric Theosophy, No. 1: Is Theosophy a Delusion? Do the Brothers Exist?,* Calcutta, India, The Calcutta Central Press Co., Ld., April, 1882, pp. 78, 80. Further references to this volume abbreviated: *Hints.*

32. Collated from: *Incidents,* pp. 221-222, 224, 226, 234; and A.P. Sinnett, *The Occult World,* London, Trubner & Co., 1881, pp. 42-48. Further references to the latter title abbreviated: OW.

33. "Voyage with Mme. Blavatsky: The Summary Manner in Which She Silenced a Skeptical First Officer," *The Philadelphia Inquirer,* May 11, 1891; reprinted in *The Canadian Theosophist* [Toronto, Canada], January-February, 1990, pp. 1-2.

34. ODL, Vol. II, pp. 151-205.

35. Anagarika Dharmapala, "On the Eightfold Path," *Asia* [New York], September, 1927, pp. 720-722.

36. *The Theosophical Forum* [Point Loma, California], April 15, 1933, pp. 241-243. Reprinted in Damodar K. Mavalankar, *Damodar: The Writings of a Hindu Chela*, edited by Sven Eek, Point Loma, California, Theosophical University Press, 1940, pp. 256-259. Further references to this title abbreviated: *Damodar*, 1940. Also reprinted in an enlarged, revised edition entitled *Damodar and the Pioneers of the Theosophical Movement*, compiled and annotated by Sven Eek, Adyar, Madras, India, The Theosophical Publishing House, 1965, pp. 55-58. Further references to this latter title abbreviated: *Damodar*, 1965.

37. ODL, Vol. II, pp. 206-208, 213, 215, 225.

38. *Damodar*, 1940, pp. 260-264; reprinted in *Damodar*, 1965, pp. 58-62.

39. OW, pp. 66-84.

40. OW, pp. 88-90.

41. OW, pp. 92-95.

42. OW, pp. 108-113.

43. *Hints*, pp. 103, 104-105.

44. *T.S. Report*, p. 70.

45. *Incidents*, pp. 236-239, 241-243.

46. *Hints*, pp. 97-98.

47. Collated from *Light* [London], June 24, 1882, p. 301; and *Light* [London], January 30, 1886, pp. 50-51.

48. Alice Gordon, "Instantaneous Transmission of Another Letter," *Psychic Notes* [Calcutta, India], March 30, 1882, pp. 60-61.

49. ODL, Vol. II, pp. 363-367.

50. Collated from *T.S. Report*, pp. 89, 60-61.

51. S. Ramaswamier, "How a 'Chela' Found His Guru," *The Theosophist* [Bombay, India], December, 1882, pp. 67-69.

52. *Incidents*, pp. 255, 257-258.

53. Collated from *The Path* [New York], April, 1890, p. 8; and *The Path* [New York], June, 1892, pp. 71-75.

54. *The Theosophist* [Adyar, Madras, India], May, 1907, pp. 633-634; reprinted in *Damodar*, 1965, pp. 307-309.

55. Collated from: ODL, Vol. II, pp. 463-466; and Henry S. Olcott, *Old Diary Leaves: The Only Authentic History of the Theosophical Society*, 1883-1887, Third Series, Adyar, Madras, India, The Theosophical Publishing House, 1929, pp. 11, 18. Further references to this latter title abbreviated: ODL, Vol. III.

56. William T. Brown, *Some Experiences in India*, London, The London Lodge of the Theosophical Society, 1884, pp. 5-7, 10-11, 12, 13, 15-17.

57. ODL, Vol. III, pp. 37-39, 43-45.

58. Damodar K. Mavalankar, "A Great Riddle Solved," *The Theosophist* [Adyar, Madras, India], December, 1883---January, 1884, pp. 61-62; reprinted in *Damodar*, 1940, pp. 213-216; *Damodar*, 1965, pp. 334-336.

59. T.S. Report, pp. 79-80.

60. Collated from: Franz Hartmann, *Report of Observations Made During a Nine Month Stay at the Headquarters of The Theosophical Society at Adyar (Madras), India*, Madras, India, Printed at the Scottish Press, by Graves, Cookson, and Co., 1884, pp. 11-12, 13-15, 28-30; and Franz Hartmann, Supplement to *The Theosophist* [Adyar, Madras, India], April, 1884, p. 65.

61. Collated from W.Q. Judge's letters in *The Word* [New York], April, 1912, pp. 17-19, 22.

62. A.P. Sinnett, *The Early Days of Theosophy in Europe*, London, Theosophical Publishing House, 1922, pp. 54-56. Further references to this title abbreviated: *Early Days*.

63. Archibald Keightley, "Reminiscences of H.P. Blavatsky," *The Theosophical Quarterly* [New York], October, 1910, p. 110.

64. *H.P.B.: In Memory*, pp. 52-55; also reprinted in *Echoes of the Orient: The Writings of William Quan Judge*, compiled by Dara Eklund, San Diego, California, Point Loma Publications, 1980, Volume II, pp. 17-20.

65. *Incidents*, pp. 266-269.

66. Collated from: *H.P.B.: In Memory*, p. 69; and Francesca Arundale, *My Guest: H.P. Blavatsky*, Adyar, Madras, India: Theosophical Publishing House, 1932, pp. 29-37, 40-42. Further references to the latter title abbreviated: *My Guest*.

67. L.C.L. [Laura C. Langford, the former Laura C. Holloway], "The Mahatmas and Their Instruments," *The Word* [New York], July, 1912, pp. 204-206.

68. *Henry Sidgwick: A Memoir* by A.S. and E.M.S., London, Macmillan and Co., Limited, 1906, pp. 384-385.

69. *My Guest*, pp. 44-46.

70. *Incidents*, pp. 279-286.

71. Quoted in: Beatrice Hastings, *Solovyoff's Fraud*, Edmonton, Alberta, Canada, Edmonton Lodge of the Theosophical Society in Canada, 1988, pp. 27-29.

72. Laura C. Holloway, "Blavatsky's Mesmerism," *Current Literature* [New York], March, 1889, pp. 243-244.

73. C.W. Leadbeater, *How Theosophy Came To Me*, Adyar, Madras, India, The Theosophical Publishing House, 1930, in 1948 reprinting, pp. 57, 59-62. Further references to this title abbreviated: *How Theosophy*.

74. *H.P.B.: In Memory*, pp. 14-15.

75. *How Theosophy*, pp. 68, 71, 73-77.

76. *H.P.B.: In Memory*, pp. 15-17.

77a. Richard Hodgson, "Account of Personal Investigations in India, and Discussion of the Authorship of the 'Koot Hoomi' Letters," *Proceedings of the Society for Psychical Research* [London], Volume III, 1885, collated from pages 207, 261, 262, 313-314, 317.

77b. *The Theosophist* [Adyar, Madras, India], September, 1932, pp. 732-734.

78. Charles Johnston, "The Theosophical Movement," *The Theosophical Quarterly* [New York], July, 1907, pp. 17-18.

79. Collated from: *Early Days*, pp. 79, 83; and *Incidents*, pp. 302-303.

80. C. Wachtmeister, *Reminiscences*, pp. 16-21, 22-23, 32-33, 43-45, 49-50, 55-56, 59-61.

81. C. Wachtmeister, *Reminiscences*, pp. 121-125. [NOTE; This article is signed R.S. but research indicates that the author was Julia W. Keightley.]

82. C. Wachtmeister, *Reminiscences*, pp. 107-108.

83. Collated from: *H.P.B.: In Memory*, p. 20; and C. Wachtmeister, *Reminiscences*, pp. 71-76.

84. Archibald Keightley, "From Ostende to London," *The Path* [New York], November, 1892, pp. 245-248.

85. C. Wachtmeister, *Reminiscences*, pp. 90-95.

86. Charles Johnston, "Helena Petrovna Blavatsky," *The Theosophical Forum* [New York], April, May, June, and July, 1900; reprinted in H.P.B.'s *Collected Writings*, Vol. VIII, pp. 392-409.

87. Archibald Keightley, "Reminiscences of H.P. Blavatsky," *The Theosophical Quarterly* [New York], October, 1910, pp. 113-119.

88. *H.P.B.: In Memory*, pp. 38-39.

89. Alice Leighton Cleather, *H.P. Blavatsky As I Knew Her*, Calcutta, Thacker, Spink & Co., 1923, pp. 2-4. Further references to this title abbreviated: Cleather, *As I Knew Her*.

90. Katherine Tingley, *Helena Petrovna Blavatsky: Foundress of the Original Theosophical Society in New York, 1875*, Point Loma, California, The Woman's International Theosophical League, 1921, pp. 34-35. Further references to this title abbreviated: Tingley, *H.P.B.*

91. Collated from: William T. Stead's "Note" in *The M.P. For Russia: Reminiscences & Correspondence of Madame Olga Novikoff*, edited by W.T. Stead, London, Andrew Melrose, 1909, Vol. One, pp. 130-131; and William T. Stead, *The Review of Reviews* [London], June, 1891, pp. 548-550.

92. Bertram Keightley, *Reminiscences of H.P.B.*, Adyar, Madras, India, Theosophical Publishing House, 1931, pp. 21-23. Further references to this title abbreviated: B. Keightley, *Reminiscences*.

93. William Kingsland, *The Real H.P. Blavatsky: A Study in Theosophy, and a Memoir of a Great Soul*, London, John M. Watkins, 1928, collated from pp. 18-19, 24, 259, 258, 259, 261.

94. Cleather, *As I Knew Her*, pp. 15-16.

95. "Blavatsky Still Lives and Theosophy is in a Flourishing Condition," *New York Times*, January 6, 1889, p. 10; also reprinted in *Echoes of the Orient: The Writings of William Quan Judge*, compiled by Dara Eklund, San Diego, California, Point Loma Publications, Inc., 1987, Vol. III, pp. 138-141.

96. Tingley, *H.P.B.*, pp. 35-36.

97. B. Keightley, *Reminiscences*, pp. 25-27.

98. Edmund Russell, "Isis Unveiled," *Theosophical Outlook* [San Francisco, California], April 26, 1919, pp. 129-134.

99. Violet Tweedale, *Ghosts I Have Seen and Other Psychic Experiences*, New York, Frederick A. Stokes Company, 1919, pp. 51, 56-61.

100. *Annie Besant: An Autobiography*, London, T. Fisher Unwin, 1893, pp. 308-313. Further references to this title abbreviated: Besant, *Autobiography*.

101. *H.P.B.: In Memory*, pp. 31-35.

102. Collated from: Besant, *Autobiography*, pp. 321-323; and Annie Besant, *The Masters*, Adyar, Madras, India, The Theosophical Publishing House, 1912; 1977 reprint, pp. 32-33.

103. *H.P.B.: In Memory*, pp. 31-35.

104. Rev. B. Old, "Memories of H.P.B.---Over 50 Years Ago," *The Theosophist* [Adyar, Madras, India], November, 1941, pp. 107, 109, 107, 108.

105. Henry S. Olcott, *Old Diary Leaves: The Only Authentic History of the Theosophical Society*, Fourth Series, 1887-1892, Adyar, Madras, India, The Theosophical Publishing House, 1931, pp. 254-256. Further references to this volume abbreviated: ODL, Vol. IV.

106. Cleather, *As I Knew Her*, pp. 21-24.

107. Esther Windust, "Personal Reminiscences of H.P.B." *Eirenicon* [Hyde, Chesire, England], Winter Solstice, 1950, No. 97, pp. 1-2; also reprinted in *The Canadian Theosophist* [Toronto, Canada], May 15, 1951, pp. 33-34.

108. "Extracts from Countess Wachtmeister's Letters as to H.P.B.'s Last Days," *The Theosophist* [Adyar, Madras, India], May, 1929, pp. 124-125.

109. *H.P.B.: In Memory*, p. 34.

110. *H.P.B.: In Memory*, pp. 3-7.

111. ODL, Vol. IV, p. 300.

112. C. Wachtmeister, *Reminiscences*, p. 127.

113. H.P. Blavatsky, *Isis Unveiled: A Master-Key to the Mysteries of Ancient and Modern Science and Theology*, New York, J.W. Bouton, 1877, Vol. I, p. vi.

114. *The Path* [New York], March, 1896, pp. 369-370.

115. Collated from: H.P. Blavatsky, *Collected Writings*, Wheaton, Illinois, The Theosophical Publishing House, Vol. V, pp. 50-51 (Further references to volumes in the *Collected Writings* Series abbreviated: H.P.B., *C.W.* with the appropriate volume number); and H.P. Blavatsky, *The Key to Theosophy*, London, The Theosophical Publishing Company, Limited, 1889, p. 217. Further references to the latter title abbreviated: H.P.B., *Key*.

116. Collated from: H.P.B., *C.W.*, Vol. VII, p. 247; *The Letters of H.P. Blavatsky to A.P. Sinnett*, etc., transcribed, compiled, and with an Introduction by A.T. Barker, Pasadena, California, Theosophical University Press, 1973, pp. 151, 104 (Further references to this title abbreviated: HPB-APS Letters); and *The Path* [New York], March, 1896, p. 367.

117. H.P.B., *C.W.*, Vol. VI, p. 272.

118. *The Mahatma Letters to A.P. Sinnett from the Mahatmas M. & K.H.*, transcribed, compiled, and with an Introduction by A.T. Barker, Pasadena, California, Theosophical University Press, 1975, Facsimile of the Second Edition, pp. 478-479 (Further references to this Second edition abbreviated: ML, 2nd Ed.); also in: *The Mahatma Letters to A.P. Sinnett from the Mahatmas M. & K.H.*, transcribed and compiled by A.T. Barker, Adyar, Madras, India, The Theosophical Publishing House, 1962, Third and Revised Edition, p. 471. Further references to this Third edition abbreviated: ML, 3rd Ed.

119. *Some Unpublished Letters of Helena Petrovna Blavatsky*, with an Introduction and Commentary by Eugene Rollin Corson, London, Rider & Co., 1929, pp. 127-128.

120. *The Path* [New York], March, 1896, p. 369.

121. *The Path* [New York], January, 1895, pp. 300-301.

122. *The Path* [New York], December, 1894, p. 266.

123. Collated from: *The Path* [New York], January, 1895, pp. 298-299, 300.

124. Collated from: HPB-APS Letters, pp. 244, 194.

125. H.P.B., *C.W.*, Vol. XII, pp. 307-308.

126. H.P.B., *C.W.*, Vol. XI, p. 202.

127. H.P.B., *C.W.*, Vol. XIII, p. 219.

128. H.P.B., *C.W.*, Vol. I, p. 73.

129. ML, 2nd Ed., p. 263; ML, 3rd Ed., p. 259.

130. ML, 2nd Ed., pp. 9-10; ML, 3rd Ed., pp. 9-10.

131. ML, 2nd Ed., pp. 203-204; ML, 3rd Ed., pp. 201-202.

132. HPB-APS Letters, p. 7.

133. ML, 2nd Ed., pp. 311-314; ML, 3rd Ed., pp. 307-309.

134. *Letters from the Masters of the Wisdom, 1870-1900*, First Series, transcribed and compiled by C. Jinarajadasa, Adyar, Madras, India, The Theosophical Publishing House, 1973, pp. 44-45.

135. H.P.B., *Key*, pp. 273-274.

136. H.P.B., *C.W.*, Vol. IX, pp. 46-50.

137. H.P.B., *C.W.*, Vol. VI, pp. 332-333.

138. H.P.B., *C.W.*, Vol. XI, pp. 164-165.

139. H.P.B, *C.W.*, Vol. IX, p. 244.

140. H.P.B., *C.W.*, Vol. XIII, p. 173.

141. H.P.B., *C.W.*, Vol. XII, pp. 154-156.

142. H.P.B., *C.W.* Vol. IX, p. 254.

143. ML, 2nd Ed., p. 262; ML, 3rd Ed., p. 258.

144. ML, 2nd Ed., pp. 251-252; ML, 3rd Ed., pp. 248-249.

145. Quoted in OW, pp. 137-139.

THE BLAVATSKY BIBLIOGRAPHY

[This bibliography is a unique listing of Blavatsky-related books, audio cassettes and videos (VHS) *in-print* as of October, 1991. However, this listing does *not* contain every edition or title available; in many cases, the compiler has included only what in his judgment were the "best" editions, etc.

The titles are arranged under five major categories: (1) H.P. Blavatsky's Life; (2) H.P. Blavatsky's Writings; (3) The Study of *The Secret Doctrine*; (4) The Mahatmas and Their Letters; and (5) Introductory Studies in Theosophy. If the reader wants to learn more about H.P.Blavatsky's life and her Theosophical teachings, please refer to the section on "Introductory Studies in Theosophy," pp. 327-328. It is suggested that these 27 titles be read in the order given.

Many of the items in this bibliography can be purchased through your local bookstore. If you cannot obtain a particular title, try to order it by mail from: The Wizards Bookshelf, Box 6600, San Diego, California, 92106, U.S.A.; or Quest Book Shop, 306 W. Geneva, Wheaton, Illinois, 60187, U.S.A.; or Los Angeles Center for Theosophic Studies, P.O. Box 3727, Los Angeles, California, 90078, U.S.A.---Editor.]

H.P. BLAVATSKY'S LIFE

Biographies

Fuller, Jean Overton. *Blavatsky and Her Teachers: An Investigative Biography*. London: East-West Publications, 1988. 270 pp. [Written by long-time Theosophist. Contains several important discoveries, but marred by numerous mistakes, unwarranted speculations, and misleading conclusions.]

Kingsland, William. *The Real H.P. Blavatsky: A Study in Theosophy, and a Memoir of a Great Soul*. London: Theosophical Publishing House, LTD, 1985. (First Edition, 1928) xiv + 322 pp. [Good introductory biography. Author personally knew H.P.B.]

Meade, Marion. *Madame Blavatsky: The Woman Behind the Myth*. New York: G.P. Putnam's Sons, 1980. 528 pp. [Out-of-Print] [The definitive, hostile biography of H.P.B. Contains numerous errors, unwarranted speculations, misleading conclusions; poorly researched; unreliable.]

Murphet, Howard. *When Daylight Comes: A Biography of Helena Petrovna Blavatsky*. Wheaton, Illinois: The Theosophical Publishing House, 1975. xxxi + 277 pp. [Good introduction to H.P.B.'s life; should be read first before going on to other H.P.B. biographies.]

Ryan, Charles J. *H.P. Blavatsky and the Theosophical Movement: A Brief Historical Sketch*. Second and Revised Edition. Edited by Grace F. Knoche. Pasadena, California: Theosophical University Press, 1975. (First Edition, 1937) xviii + 358 pp. [Good introductory biography.]

Special Studies on H.P.B.

Barborka, Geoffrey A. *H.P. Blavatsky, Tibet and Tulku.* Adyar, Madras, India: The Theosophical Publishing House, 1966. xxii + 476 pp.

Burnier, Radha. *Who Was H.P.B.?* Wheaton, Illinois: The Department of Education, The Theosophical Society in America, 1986. 1 *audio* cassette, 27 minutes.

Gomes, Michael. *The Dawning of the Theosophical Movement.* Wheaton, Illinois: The Theosophical Publishing House, 1987. x + 248 pp.

Hanson, Virginia, ed. *H.P. Blavatsky and The Secret Doctrine.* Second Edition. Wheaton, Illinois: The Theosophical Publishing House, 1988. xvii + 240 pp. [Contains 21 articles.]

Harris, Iverson L. *Mme. Blavatsky Defended: Refutation of Falsehoods, Slanders, and Misrepresentations Published by The National Broadcasting Company, Truman Capote, Walter Winchell, The John Birch Society, Time Magazine, and Others.* San Diego, California: Point Loma Publications, 1971. 174 pp.

Price, Leslie. *Madame Blavatsky Unveiled?: A New Discussion of the Most Famous Investigation of The Society for Psychical Research.* London: Theosophical History Centre, 1986. 44 pp.

Reminiscences of H.P.B.

Cleather, Alice Leighton. *H.P. Blavatsky As I Knew Her.* Vernon, British Columbia, Canada: The H.P.B. Lending Library, 1979. (First Edition, 1923) ix + 76 pp.

Judge, William Quan. *The Esoteric She: Articles on Madame Blavatsky's Life, Work and Teachings.* Compiled and edited by Daniel H. Caldwell. San Diego, California: Point Loma Publications, 1991. 108 pp.

Leadbeater, C.W. *How Theosophy Came to Me.* Adyar, Madras, India: The Theosophical Publishing House, 1975. (First Edition, 1930) vii + 136 pp.

Mavalankar, Damodar K. *Damodar and the Pioneers of the Theosophical Movement.* Compiled and annotated by Sven Eek. Adyar, Madras, India: The Theosophical Publishing House, 1965. xvi + 720 pp.

Olcott, Henry Steel. *Old Diary Leaves: The History of The Theosophical Society.* Adyar, Madras, India: The Theosophical Publishing House, 1972-1975.

> First Series, 1874-1878. xiv + 490 pp. 1974. (First Edition, 1895)
> Second Series, 1878-1883. xii + 476 pp. 1974. (First Edition, 1900)
> Third Series, 1883-1887. viii + 460 pp. 1972. (First Edition, 1904)
> Fourth Series, 1887-1892. viii + 537 pp. 1975. (First Edition, 1910)

Sinnett, A.P. *The Occult World.* Ninth edition. London: Theosophical Publishing House, 1969. (First Edition, 1881) xv + 181 pp.

Sinnett, A.P. *Incidents in the Life Of Madame Blavatsky.* New York: Ayer Co., 1976. (First Edition, 1886) xii + 324 pp.

Sinnett, A.P. *Autobiography of Alfred Percy Sinnett*. London: Theosophical History Centre, 1986. 65 pp.

Solovyoff, Vsevolod S. *A Modern Priestess of Isis*. New York: Ayer Co., 1976. (First Edition, 1895) xix + 366 pp.

Some of Her Pupils. *H.P.B.: In Memory of Helena Petrovna Blavatsky*. London: Theosophical Publishing House, Ltd., 1991. (First Edition, 1891) 96 pp.

Wachtmeister, Countess Constance and others. *Reminiscences of H.P. Blavatsky and the Secret Doctrine*. Second Edition. Wheaton, Illinois: The Theosophical Publishing House, 1976. (First Edition, 1893) xiv + 141 pp.

Major Attacks Against H.P.B. and Their Rebuttals

THE COULOMB---HODGSON---S.P.R. ATTACK:

Coulomb, Emma. *Some Account of My Intercourse with Madame Blavatsky from 1872 To 1884: With Additional Letters and a Full Explanation of the Most Marvellous Theosophical Phenomena*. London: Published for the Proprietors of the "Madras Christian College Magazine" by Elliot Stock, 1885. ii + 112 pp. [Out-of-Print]

Society for Psychical Research. "Report of the Committee Appointed to Investigate Phenomena Connected with The Theosophical Society," *Proceedings of the Society for Psychical Research*, Vol. III, London, 1885, pp. 201-400. Reprinted in: Webb, James, ed. *The Society for Psychical Research Report on The Theosophical Society*. New York: Ayer Co., 1976. [Most of this "Report" is written by Richard Hodgson; hostile.]

REBUTTALS:

Endersby, Victor. *The Hall of Magic Mirrors*. New York: Carlton Press, Inc., 1969. 351 pp.

Harrison, Vernon. "J'Accuse: An Examination of the Hodgson Report of 1885," *Journal of the Society for Psychical Research*, London, April, 1986, pp. 286-310.

Jinarajadasa, C. *Did Madame Blavatsky Forge the Mahatma Letters?* (First Edition, 1934) 55 pp. Reprinted in: Kelly, Aidan, ed. *Theosophy II: Controversial and Polemical Pamphlets*. New York: Garland Publishing, 1990.

Kingsland, William. *Was She A Charlatan? A Critical Analysis of the 1885 Report of the Society for Psychical Research on the Phenomena connected with Mme. H.P. Blavatsky*. (First Edition, 1927) 60 pp. Reprinted in: Webb, James, ed. *The Society for Psychical Research Report on the Theosophical Society*. New York: Ayer Co., 1976.

Waterman, Adlai E. *Obituary---The "Hodgson Report" on Madame Blavatsky, 1885-1960: Re-examination Discredits the Major Charges Against H.P. Blavatsky*. Adyar, Madras, India: The Theosophical Publishing House, 1963. xx + 92 pp. [The definitive rebuttal of Hodgson's charges against H.P.B.]

THE SOLOVYOFF---S.P.R. ATTACK:

Solovyoff, Vsevolod S. *A Modern Priestess of Isis*. Abridged and Translated on

Behalf of the Society for Psychical Research from the Russian by Walter Leaf. New York: Ayer Co., 1976. (First Edition, 1895) xix + 366 pp.

REBUTTAL:

Hastings, Beatrice. *Solovyoff's Fraud: A Critical Analysis of the Book A Modern Priestess of Isis*. Edmonton, Alberta, Canada: Edmonton Lodge of the Theosophical Society in Canada, 1988. (First published, 1943-1944) 76 pp.

Historical Studies on the Theosophical Movement

Campbell, Bruce F. *Ancient Wisdom Revived: A History of the Theosophical Movement*. Berkeley, California: University of California Press, 1980. x + 249 pp. [Negative toward H.P.B.; omits vital information on controversies surrounding H.P.B.]

Cooper, John. *The Theosophical Movement and Its Importance*. Wheaton, Illinois: The Department of Education, The Theosophical Society in America, 1990. 1 *video* cassette, VHS, 60 minutes.

Godwin, Joscelyn. *The Beginnings of Theosophy in France*. London: Theosophical History Centre, 1989. 39 pp.

Gomes, Michael. *The Dawning of the Theosophical Movement*. Wheaton, Illinois: The Theosophical Publishing House, 1987. x + 248 pp.

Greenwalt, Emmett A. *California Utopia: Point Loma: 1897---1942*. Revised Edition. San Diego, California: Point Loma Publications, Inc., 1978. (First Edition, 1955) xvii + 244 pp.

Leslie-Smith, Leslie. *100 Years of Modern Occultism: A Review of the Parent Theosophical Society*. London: Theosophical History Centre, 1987. 70 pp.

Mills, Joy. *100 Years of Theosophy: A History of The Theosophical Society in America*. Wheaton, Illinois: The Theosophical Publishing House, 1987. xv + 215 pp.

Ransom, Josephine, comp. *A Short History of The Theosophical Society*. Adyar, Madras, India: The Theosophical Publishing House, 1989. (First Edition, 1938) xii + 591 pp.

Ryan, Charles J. *H.P. Blavatsky and The Theosophical Movement: A Brief Historical Sketch*. Edited by W. Emmett Small and Helen Todd. San Diego, California: Point Loma Publications, Inc., 1975. (First Edition, 1937.) xxii + 441 pp. [With 7 Appendices.]

Santucci, James A. *Theosophy and The Theosophical Society*. London: Theosophical History Centre, 1985. 35 pp.

The Theosophical Movement. Los Angeles, California: The Cunningham Press, 1951. xiii + 351 pp.

The Theosophical Society in America: An Illustrated History. Wheaton, Illinois: The Department of Education, The Theosophical Society in America, 1986. 1 *video* cassette, VHS, 38 minutes.

H.P. BLAVATSKY'S WRITINGS

Major Works
(1877-1892)

1877   *Isis Unveiled: A Master-Key to the Mysteries of Ancient and Modern Science and Theology.* (First Edition, New York, 1877) 2 volumes.

Collected Writings Edition. Wheaton, Illinois: The Theosophical Publishing House, 1972. Edited by Boris de Zirkoff. 2 Volumes: Vol. I---Science, [63] pp. + xlv + 657 pp; Vol. II---Theology, iv + 848 pp. [Includes historical introduction, large index and bibliography.]

Theosophical University Press Edition. Pasadena, California: Theosophical University Press, 1988. Facsimile of the Original Edition. 2 Volumes: Vol. I---xlv + 628 pp.; Vol. II---iv + 708 + 53 pp. [Available in hardbound edition or quality paperback.]

Theosophy Company Edition. Los Angeles, California: The Theosophy Company, 1982. A Photographic facsimile reproduction of the Original Edition. 2 Volumes Bound in One Book: Vol. I---xlv + 628 pp.; Vol. II ---iv + 708 pp.

1883   *From the Caves and Jungles of Hindostan.*

Collected Writings Edition. Translated from the Russian. 1883-1886. Wheaton, Illinois: The Theosophical Publishing House, 1975. lv + 719 pp.

1888   *The Secret Doctrine: The Synthesis of Science, Religion, and Philosophy.* (First Edition, London, 1888) 2 volumes.

Collected Writings Edition. Edited by Boris de Zirkoff. Adyar, Madras, India: The Theosophical Publishing House, 1978-1979. 3 Volumes: Vol. I---Cosmogenesis, [84] + xlvii + 696 pp.; Vol. II---Anthropogenesis, v + xx + 817 pp.; Vol. III---General Index and Bibliography, vii + 520 pp.

Theosophical University Press Edition. Pasadena, California: Theosophical University Press, 1988. Centennial Edition. Photographic Facsimile of the original edition. 2 Volumes: Vol. I---xlvii + 676 pp; Vol. II---xiv + 798 + xxxi pp. [Available in hardbound edition or quality paperback.]

Theosophy Company Edition. Los Angeles, California: The Theosophy Company, 1982. A Facsimile of the Original Edition. 2 Volumes Bound in One Book: Vol. I---xlvii + 676 pp; Vol. II---xiv + 798 + xxx pp.

An Abridgement of The Secret Doctrine. Edited by Elizabeth Preston and Christmas Humphreys. Wheaton, Illinois: The Theosophical Publishing House, 1967. xxxii + 260 pp.

1889   *The Key to Theosophy: Being a Clear Exposition, in the Form of Question and Answer, of the Ethics, Science, and Philosophy for the*

Study of Which the Theosophical Society has been Founded. (First Edition, London, 1889)

Theosophical University Press Edition. Pasadena, California: Theosophical University Press, 1987. Unabridged, verbatim reprinting of the original edition of 1889, including the Glossary (which appeared in H.P.B.'s second edition), and a new Index. xii + 373 + 53 pp.

The Key to Theosophy: An Abridgement. Edited by Joy Mills. Wheaton, Illinois: The Theosophical Publishing House, 1981. xv + 176 pp.

1889   *The Voice of the Silence: Being Chosen Fragments from the "Book of the Golden Precepts" for the Daily Use of Lanoos (Disciples).* Translated and annotated by "H.P.B." (First Edition, London, 1889)

Theosophical University Press Edition. Pasadena, California: Theosophical University Press, 1976. A Verbatim Reproduction of the original edition of 1889. xi + 97 pp.

The "Peking" Edition. Vernon, British Columbia, Canada: The H.P.B. Lending Library, 1978. (This edition first published 1927 in Peking, China.) With Notes and Comments by Alice Leighton Cleather and Basil Crump. xi + 129 pp. [Frontispiece to this edition was written by the Tibetan Panchen Lama Lobzang Tub-ten Chogyi Nyima (1883-1937).]

1890   *Gems From the East: A Birthday Book of Precepts and Axioms.* Compiled by H.P.B. (First Edition, London, 1890)

Theosophical University Press Edition. Pasadena, California: Theosophical University Press, 1983. 320 pp.

1890   *Transactions of the Blavatsky Lodge of the Theosophical Society: Discussions on the Stanzas of the First Volume of The Secret Doctrine.* [With a Section on "Dreams."] (First Edition, London, issued in two parts, 1890 and 1891)

Theosophical University Press Edition. Pasadena, California: Theosophical University Press, 1946. 118 pp.

Collected Writings Edition. Published in H.P.B.'s *Collected Writings*, Volume X, pp. 298-406 and pp. 246-264. Wheaton, Illinois: The Theosophical Publishing House, 1974.

1892   *Nightmare Tales.* (First Edition, London, 1892)

Health Research Edition. Mokelumne Hill, California: Health Research, 1971. 139 pp.

Collected Writings Edition. Not available in a separate volume; scattered through several volumes. See Vol. VI, pp. 354-355 of *Collected Writings* for a listing of and historical data on H.P.B.'s "Nightmare Tales."

1892   *The Theosophical Glossary.* (First Edition, London, 1892)

Theosophy Company Edition. Facsimile of the Original Edition. Los Angeles, California: The Theosophy Company, 1973. 389 pp.

H.P.B.'s Articles
(1874-1891)

Collected Writings. Volumes I---XV.

Compiled and edited by Boris de Zirkoff. Wheaton, Illinois: The Theosophical Publishing House, 1966-1991.

[The most complete, *definitive* collection of H.P.B.'s articles and miscellaneous writings; arranged in chronological order covering the years 1874 through 1891.]

Vol. I	(1874-1878)	lxxx + 570 pp.
Vol. II	(1879-1880)	xlvi + 590 pp.
Vol. III	(1881-1882)	xxxviii + 583 pp.
Vol. IV	(1882-1883)	xliv + 718 pp.
Vol. V	(1883)	xxxii + 416 pp.
Vol. VI	(1883-1885)	liv + 481 pp.
Vol. VII	(1886-1887)	xxxiv + 433 pp.
Vol. VIII	(1887)	xxviii + 507 pp.
Vol. IX	(1888)	xxx + 487 pp.
Vol. X	(1888-1889)	xxxvi + 461 pp.
Vol. XI	(1889)	xxxvi + 632 pp.
Vol. XII	(1889-1890)	xxx + 859 pp.

[This volume includes H.P.B.'s *Esoteric Section Instructions* (I, II and III) and other documents pertaining to her Esoteric School; see pp. 477-713 therein. Unfortunately, the text of the 3 E.S. Instructions is *not* verbatim with the original copies; there are deletions and alterations from the original text. Also other E.S. documents signed by H.P.B. (as well as the complete, unedited text of H.P.B.'s "Inner Group Teachings") are *not* included in this volume.]

Vol. XIII	(1890-1891)	xxxii + 465 pp.
Vol. XIV	(Miscellaneous)	xlviii + 733 pp.
Vol. XV	(Cumulative Index)	xiii + 633 pp.

[NOTE: In addition to the above listed *numbered* volumes, some of H.P.B.'s major works have also been published in the *Collected Writings* Series as separate, *unnumbered* volumes. See the previous two pages of this bibliography for information on these titles.]

Other Collections and Compilations of H.P.B.'s Writings

[Most of H.P.B.'s writings published in these compilations are also available in the *Collected Writings* Series. However, a few of H.P.B.'s writings are *not* published in the *C.W.* Series. Such material has been noted in annotations below. Titles preceded by an asterisk [*] are major contributions to the Blavatsky literature and are highly recommended.]

The Beacon Light. Santa Barbara, California: Concord Grove Press, 1984. 79 pp. [8 articles]

The Buddhism of H.P. Blavatsky. Compiled and Annotated by H.J. Spierenburg. San Diego, California: Point Loma Publications, 1991. xiv + 335 pp.

The Circle of Wisdom: A Blavatsky Quotation Book. Compiled by Winifred A. Parley. Wheaton, Illinois: The Theosophical Publishing House, 1978. 144 pp.

Dynamics of the Psychic World: Comments by H.P. Blavatsky on Magic, Mediumship, Psychism, and the Powers of the Spirit. Compiled with notes by Lina Psaltis. Wheaton, Illinois: The Theosophical Publishing House, 1972. xviii + 132 pp.

Five Years of Theosophy: Mystical, Philosophical, Theosophical, Historical and Scientific Essays, Selected from "The Theosophist." Los Angeles, California: The Theosophy Company, 1981. 575 pp. (Reprint of the 1885 edition.)
[A selection of articles published in *The Theosophist*, 1879-1884; many of the articles are from H.P.B.'s pen; also articles by other Theosophical contributors.]

Foundations of Esoteric Philosophy: From the Writings of H.P. Blavatsky. Arranged with a Foreword and Notes by Ianthe H. Hoskins. London: The Theosophical Publishing House LTD, 1980. 68 pp.

Fundamentals of Theosophy. [Collated from H.P.B.'s writings.] Los Angeles, California: The Theosophy Company, n.d. 22 pp.

Gods and Elementals: Articles by H.P. Blavatsky. Los Angeles, California: The Theosophy Company, n.d. 55 pp. [2 articles]

Gupta Vidya. Santa Barbara, California: Concord Grove Press, 1979. 79 pp. [16 selections]

H.P.B. Speaks. Edited by C. Jinarajadasa. Adyar, Madras, India: The Theosophical Publishing House, 1950-1951.
    Volume I: viii + 248 pp.
    Volume II: xvi + 181 pp.
[These two volumes contain various letters of H.P.B. to correspondents, extracts from her Scrapbooks and other rare items.]

H.P. Blavatsky to the American Conventions, 1888-1891. With a Historical Perspective by Kirby Van Mater. Pasadena, California: Theosophical University Press, 1979. x + 74 pp.

The Inner Group Teachings of H.P. Blavatsky to Her Personal Pupils (1890-91): A Reconstruction of the Teachings by H.J. Spierenburg. San Diego, California: Point Loma Publications, Inc., 1985. xxiii + 188 pp. [Very valuable material not included in Volume XII of the *Collected Writings* Series. Unfortunately, the most complete, authentic text of H.P.B.'s "Inner Group Teachings" has never been published although several copies of this text are extant.]

Karma and Reincarnation: A Collation from the Writings of Helena P. Blavatsky. Los Angeles, California: The Theosophy Company, n.d. 16 pp.

*The Letters of H.P. Blavatsky to A.P. Sinnett and Others Miscellaneous Letters. Transcribed, Compiled, and with an Introduction by A.T. Barker. Pasadena, California: Theosophical University Press, 1973. (First Edition, 1925) xv + 404 pp.

*Madame Blavatsky on How to Study Theosophy. Notes made by Robert Bowen. Adyar, Madras, India: The Theosophical Publishing House, 1979. 17 pp. [Not included in H.P.B.'s *Collected Writings* Series.]

A Modern Panarion: A Collection of Fugitive Fragments from the Pen of H.P. Blavatsky. Reprint of the original 1895 edition. Los Angeles, California: The Theosophy Company, 1981. v + 504 pp. [A compilation of H.P.B.'s articles covering the years 1874-1882.]

*The New Testament Commentaries of H.P. Blavatsky. Compiled and Annotated by H.J. Spierenburg. San Diego, California: Point Loma Publications, 1987. xiv + 343 pp.

Spiritual Evolution: Articles by H.P. Blavatsky. Los Angeles, California: The Theosophy Company, n.d. 39 pp. [5 articles]

Studies in Occultism. Pasadena, California: Theosophical University Press, 1980. 212 pp. [These 12 articles appeared in *Lucifer*, 1887-1891.]

Teachers and Disciples: Articles by H.P. Blavatsky. Los Angeles, California: The Theosophy Company, n.d. 40 pp. [8 articles]

*Theosophical Articles. Reprinted from Original Sources. Los Angeles, California: The Theosophy Co., 1981.
     Volume I: 511 pp.
     Volume II: 531 pp.
     Volume III: 500 pp. (Including index for all 3 vols.)
     [A compilation of 165 articles from H.P.B.'s pen covering 1879-1891; these articles are also printed in 37 separate pamphlets available from same publisher.]

Theosophical Articles and Notes. Reprinted from Original Sources. Los Angeles, California: The Theosophy Co., 1985. 314 pp.
     [Only some of the material in this volume comes from H.P.B. One unique H.P.B. document (not available in the *Collected Writings* Series) is found on pp. 298-300.]

*The Theosophist: A Monthly Journal Devoted to Oriental Philosophy, Art, Literature, and Occultism, Embracing Mesmerism, Spiritualism and Other Secret Sciences. Conducted [and edited] by H.P. Blavatsky, Bombay, India. Volume I: (October, 1879--September, 1880). A Centennial Reissue. San Diego, California: Wizards Bookshelf, 1979. 318 + iv pp.
     [Contains many of H.P.B.'s original articles and editorial notes plus articles by other contributors. Approximately 260 articles.]

What is Theosophy?: Its Nonsectarian Spirit. [Collated from H.P.B.'s writings.] Los Angeles, California: The Theosophy Company, n.d. 20 pp.

THE STUDY OF THE SECRET DOCTRINE

Texts

The Secret Doctrine: The Synthesis of Science, Religion, and Philosophy. (First Edition, London, 1888) 2 volumes.

Collected Writings Edition. Edited by Boris de Zirkoff. Adyar, Madras, India: The Theosophical Publishing House, 1978-1979. 3 Volumes: Vol. I---Cosmogenesis, [84] + xlvii + 696 pp.; Vol. II---Anthropogenesis, v + xx + 817 pp.; Vol. III---General Index and Bibliography, vii + 520 pp.

Theosophical University Press Edition. Pasadena, California: Theosophical University Press, 1988. Centennial Edition. Photographic Facsimile of the original edition. 2 Volumes: Vol. I---xlvii + 676 pp; Vol. II---xiv + 798 + xxxi pp. [Available in hardbound edition or quality paperback.]

Theosophy Company Edition. Los Angeles, California: The Theosophy Company, 1982. A Facsimile of the Original Edition. 2 Volumes Bound in One Book: Vol. I---xlvii + 676 pp; Vol. II---xiv + 798 + xxx pp.

Abridgements

An Invitation to The Secret Doctrine. Pasadena, California: Theosophical University Press, 1988. 112 pp. [Selections from *The Secret Doctrine*, reproduced from the 1888 edition.]

An Abridgement of The Secret Doctrine. Edited by Elizabeth Preston and Christmas Humphreys. Wheaton, Illinois: The Theosophical Publishing House, 1967. xxxii + 260 pp.

The History of the Writing of The Secret Doctrine

De Zirkoff, Boris. *Rebirth of the Occult Tradition: How The Secret Doctrine of H.P. Blavatsky Was Written.* Adyar, Madras, India: The Theosophical Publishing House, 1977. 78 pp.

Gomes, Michael. "The Making of The Secret Doctrine." Article published in: Hanson, Virginia, ed. *H.P. Blavatsky and The Secret Doctrine.* Second Edition. Wheaton, Illinois: The Theosophical Publishing House, 1988, pp. 31-44.

Van Mater, Kirby. "The Writing of *The Secret Doctrine*." Article published in: *An Invitation to The Secret Doctrine.* Pasadena, California: Theosophical University Press, 1988, 17 pp., including facsimiles of letters from Masters K.H. and M.

Wachtmeister, Countess Constance and others. *Reminiscences of H.P. Blavatsky and The Secret Doctrine.* Second Edition. Wheaton, Illinois: The Theosophical Publishing House, 1976. (First Edition, 1893) 141 pp.

Commentaries and Studies on The Secret Doctrine

Algeo, John. *Getting Acquainted with The Secret Doctrine: A Study Course.* Revised Edition. Wheaton, Illinois: The Department of Education, The Theosophical Society in America, 1990. 66 pp.

Algeo, John. *Senzar: The Mystery of the Mystery Language.* London: The Theosophical History Centre, 1988. 32 pp.

Ashish, Sri Madhava. *Man, Son of Man: In the Stanzas of Dzyan.* Wheaton, Illinois: The Theosophical Publishing House, 1970. xv + 352 pp.

Barborka, Geoffrey A. *The Divine Plan: Written in the Form of a Commentary on H.P. Blavatsky's Secret Doctrine.* Adyar, Madras, India: The Theosophical Publishing House, 1964. xxvii + 564 pp. [Highly recommended; excellent in-depth study of the basic *Secret Doctrine* concepts.]

Barborka, Geoffrey A. *The Peopling of the Earth: A Commentary on Archaic Records in The Secret Doctrine.* Wheaton, Illinois: The Theosophical Publishing House, 1975. xiv + 233 pp.

Barborka, Geoffrey A. *The Story of Human Evolution: Written in the Form of a Commentary on The Stanzas of Dzyan---Second Series.* Adyar, Madras, India: The Theosophical Publishing House, 1980. x + 147 pp.

Benjamin, Elsie. *The Stanzas of Dzyan: Notes for Study and Discussion on Cosmogenesis and Anthropogenesis.* San Diego, California: Point Loma Publications, Inc., 1981. 45 pp.

Blavatsky, H.P. *Transactions of the Blavatsky Lodge of the Theosophical Society: Discussions on the Stanzas of the First Volume of The Secret Doctrine.* Pasadena, California: Theosophical University Press, 1946. (First Edition, 1890, 1891) 118 pp.

Gardner, Edward L. *The Wider View: Studies in The Secret Doctrine.* Adyar, Madras, India: The Theosophical Publishing House, 1962. viii + 144 pp.

Hanson, Virginia, ed. *H.P. Blavatsky and The Secret Doctrine.* Second Edition. Wheaton, Illinois: The Theosophical Publishing House, 1988. xvii + 240 pp. [Contains 21 articles.]

Heindel, Max. *Blavatsky and The Secret Doctrine.* Introduction by Manly Hall. San Diego, California: Wizards Bookshelf, 1991. (First Edition, 1933.) 95 pp.

Judge, William Q. *Hidden Hints in The Secret Doctrine.* Los Angeles, California: The Theosophy Company, n.d. 23 pp.

Lancri, Salomon. *Selected Studies in The Secret Doctrine.* Translated by Ianthe H. Hoskins. London: Theosophical Publishing House Limited, 1977. 86 pp.

McDavid, William Doss. *An Introduction to Esoteric Principles.* Second Edition. Wheaton, Illinois: The Department of Education, The Theosophical Society in America, 1990. ix + 91 pp.

Mills, Joy. *The Important Principles of The Secret Doctrine*. Wheaton, Illinois: The Department of Education, The Theosophical Society in America, 1986. 3 *audio* cassettes, 227 minutes.

Nicholson, Shirley. *Ancient Wisdom---Modern Insight*. Wheaton, Illinois: The Theosophical Publishing House, 1985. xvii + 198 pp.

Noia, Beverly B. *An Intuitive Approach to The Seven Stanzas of Dzyan*. Wheaton, Illinois: The Department of Education, The Theosophical Society in America, 1989. 29 pp.

Plummer, Gordon L. *The Mathematics of the Cosmic Mind: A Study in Mathematical Symbolism*. Second Edition. Wheaton, Illinois: The Theosophical Publishing House, 1970. xv + 224 pp.

Prem, Sri Krishna and Ashish, Sri Madhava. *Man, the Measure of All Things: In the Stanzas of Dzyan*. Wheaton, Illinois: The Theosophical Publishing House, 1969. 360 pp.

Reigle, David. *The Books of Kiu-te or The Tibetan Buddhist Tantras: A Preliminary Analysis*. San Diego, California: Wizards Bookshelf, 1983. 68 pp.

Report of Proceedings, Secret Doctrine Centenary, October 29-30, 1988. Pasadena, California: The Theosophical Society, 1989. 121 pp.

Sellon, Emily. *Some Metaphysics from The Secret Doctrine*. Wheaton, Illinois: The Department of Education, The Theosophical Society in America, 1984. 2 *audio* cassettes, 118 minutes.

Sinnett, A.P. *Esoteric Buddhism*. Reprint of the Fifth (1885) Edition. San Diego, California: Wizards Bookshelf, 1981. xxvii + 244 pp.

Symposium on H.P. Blavatsky's Secret Doctrine Held at San Diego, California, Sat. & Sun, July 21-22, 1984: Proceedings. San Diego, California: Wizards Bookshelf, 1984. 110 pp. [17 papers from 4 countries.]

Taimni, I.K. *Man, God and the Universe*. Wheaton, Illinois: The Theosophical Publishing House, 1974. xliii + 447 pp.

Trew, Corona and Smith, E. Lester, eds. *This Dynamic Universe*. Wheaton, Illinois: The Theosophical Publishing House, 1983. viii + 167 pp.

Two Students. *Theosophical Gleanings: Or Notes on The Secret Doctrine*. Wheaton, Illinois: The Theosophical Publishing House, 1978. 76 pp.

Tyberg, Judith M. *Sanskrit Keys to the Wisdom-Religion: An Exposition of the Philosophical and Religious Teachings embodied in the Sanskrit Terms used in Theosophical and Occult Literature*. Second Edition. San Diego, California: Point Loma Publications, Inc., 1984. xvii + 163 pp.

Van Pelt, Gertrude W. *Archaic History of the Human Race: As Recorded in The Secret Doctrine by H.P. Blavatsky*. San Diego, California: Point Loma Publications, Inc., 1979. 52 pp.

Warcup, Adam. *Cyclic Evolution: A Theosophical View*. London: The Theosophical Publishing House, 1986. viii + 144 pp.

THE MAHATMAS AND THEIR LETTERS

Texts

The Mahatma Letters to A.P. Sinnett from the Mahatmas M. & K.H. Transcribed and Compiled by A.T. Barker. Third and Revised Edition. Edited by Christmas Humphreys and Elsie Benjamin. Adyar, Madras, India: The Theosophical Publishing House, 1979. (First Edition, 1923; Third Edition, 1962) xliii + 524 pp.

The Mahatma Letters to A.P. Sinnett from the Mahatmas M. & K.H. Transcribed, Compiled, and with an Introduction by A.T. Barker. Facsimile Reprint of the 2nd [1926] Edition. Pasadena, California: Theosophical University Press, 1975. xlvii + 542 pp. [Available in hardbound edition or quality paperback.]

Letters from the Masters of the Wisdom---1870-1900. First Series. Transcribed and Compiled by C. Jinarajadasa. Adyar, Madras, India: The Theosophical Publishing House, 1988. (First Edition, 1919) 124 pp.

Letters from the Masters of Wisdom. Second Series. Transcribed and Annotated by C. Jinarajadasa. Adyar, Madras, India: The Theosophical Publishing House, 1977. (First Edition, 1925) 189 pp.

Introductions, Commentaries and Special Studies

Barborka, Geoffrey A. *The Mahatmas and Their Letters.* Adyar, Madras, India: The Theosophical Publishing House, 1973. xix + 422 pp.

Conger, Margaret. *Combined Chronology for Use with The Mahatma Letters to A.P. Sinnett and The Letters of H.P. Blavatsky to A.P. Sinnett.* Pasadena, California: Theosophical University Press, 1973. (First Edition, 1939) xiii + 47 pp.

Farthing, Geoffrey A., comp. *When We Die: A Comprehensive Description, in Outline, of the Processes and Subjective States in the Period between Lives, with Some Information about Spiritualistic and Psychic Phenomena.* [Compiled from *The Mahatma Letters*.] London: Theosophical Publishing House, 1968. ix + 51 pp.

Hanson, Virginia. *An Introduction to The Mahatma Letters: Today's Encounter with the Wisdom of the Ages.* Adyar, Madras, India: The Theosophical Publishing House, 1977. 25 pp.

Hanson, Virginia. *An Introduction to The Mahatma Letters: A Study Course.* Wheaton, Illinois: The Department of Education, The Theosophical Society in America, 1983. 97 pp.

Hanson, Virginia. *Masters and Men: The Human Story in The Mahatma Letters.* Quest Paperback Edition. Wheaton, Illinois: The Theosophical Publishing House, 1980. xx + 323 pp.

Hanson, Virginia and Linton, George E. *An Introduction to the Study of The Mahatma Letters.* Wheaton, Illinois: The Department of Education, The Theosophical Society in America, 1984. 5 *audio* cassettes, 450 minutes.

Harrison, Vernon. "J'Accuse: An Examination of the Hodgson Report of 1885," *Journal of the Society for Psychical Research*, London, April, 1986, pp. 286-310. [In his 1885 report, Richard Hodgson accused Madame Blavatsky of writing the "Koot Hoomi" letters. In this 1986 analysis, Dr. Harrison, an acknowledged handwriting expert, examines the "K.H." letters and comes to the conclusion that H.P.B. did *not* write them.]

Jinarajadasa, C. *Did Madame Blavatsky Forge the Mahatma Letters?* (First Edition, 1934) 55 pp. Reprinted in: Kelly, Aidan, ed. *Theosophy II: Controversial and Polemical Pamphlets.* New York: Garland Publishing, 1990.

Jinarajadasa, C. *The "K.H." Letters to C.W. Leadbeater.* Adyar, Madras, India: The Theosophical Publishing House, 1980. (First Edition, 1941.) 109 pp.

Jinarajadasa, C. *The Story of The Mahatma Letters.* Adyar, Madras, India: The Theosophical Publishing House, 1946. 26 pp.

Johnson, Paul. *In Search of the Masters: Behind the Occult Myth.* South Boston, Virginia: Published by the author, 1990. 305 pp. [Highly speculative with numerous unwarranted conclusions not supported by evidence; poor research methodology; interesting reading but only creates another "myth" concerning the Masters.]

Linton, George E. and Hanson, Virginia, eds. *Readers' Guide to The Mahatma Letters to A.P. Sinnett.* Second Edition. Adyar, Madras, India: The Theosophical Publishing House, 1988. xviii + 430 pp.

The Mahatmas and Their Letters. Wheaton, Illinois: The Department of Education, The Theosophical Society in America, 1989. 1 *video* cassette, VHS, 42 minutes.

Mills, Joy. *The Mahatma Letters to Mr. A.P. Sinnett.* Wheaton, Illinois: The Department of Education, The Theosophical Society in America, 1987. 2 *audio* cassettes, 157 minutes.

Robson, Arthur. *The Eternal Truths of Life.* Adyar, Madras, India: The Theosophical Publishing House, 1952. 296 pp.

Sinnett, A.P. *The Occult World.* Ninth edition. London: The Theosophical Publishing House, 1969. (First Edition, 1881) xv + 181 pp.

Sinnett, A.P. *Esoteric Buddhism.* Reprint of the Fifth (1885) Edition. San Diego, California: Wizards Bookshelf, 1981. (First Edition, 1883) xxvii + 244 pp. [First simple exposition of Theosophy in modern times; based on teachings contained in Sinnett's correspondence with the Mahatmas K.H. and M.]

INTRODUCTORY STUDIES IN THEOSOPHY

(1) Winner, Anna Kennedy. *The Basic Ideas of Occult Wisdom.* Wheaton, Illinois: The Theosophical Publishing House, 1970. 113 pp.

(2) Ryan, Charles J. *What Is Theosophy?: A General View of Occult Doctrine.* San Diego, California: Point Loma Publications, Inc., 1975. viii + 83 pp.

(3) *Foundations of Esoteric Philosophy: From the Writings of H.P. Blavatsky.* Arranged with a Foreword and Notes by Ianthe H. Hoskins. London: The Theosophical Publishing House LTD, 1980. 68 pp.

(4) Murphet, Howard. *When Daylight Comes: A Biography of Helena Petrovna Blavatsky.* Wheaton, Illinois: The Theosophical Publishing House, 1975. xxxi + 277 pp.

(5) Hanson, Virginia, ed. *H.P. Blavatsky and the Secret Doctrine.* Second Edition. Wheaton, Illinois: The Theosophical Publishing House, 1988. xvii + 240 pp. [Contains 21 articles.]

(6) Hejka-Ekins, April. *The Perennial Wisdom: Fundamental Teachings of H.P. Blavatsky.* Los Angeles, California: The Los Angeles Center for Theosophic Studies, 1990. 1 *video* cassette, VHS, 72 minutes. [Video comes with a book entitled *A Study Guide to The Perennial Wisdom,* by April Hejka-Ekins, Jerry Hejka-Ekins, and Brett Forray, same publisher as video, xiv + 146 pp.]

(7) Blavatsky, H.P. *The Key to Theosophy: Being a Clear Exposition, in the Form of Question and Answer, of the Ethics, Science, and Philosophy for the Study of which the Theosophical Society has been Founded.* Pasadena, California: Theosophical University Press, 1987. (First Edition, 1889.) 373 pp. [Contains a 62-page Glossary of Theosophical and related terms.]

(8) McDavid, William Doss. *An Introduction to Esoteric Principles.* Second Edition. Wheaton, Illinois: The Department of Education, The Theosophical Society in America, 1990. ix + 91 pp.

(9) *H.P. Blavatsky to the American Conventions, 1888-1891.* With a Historical Perspective by Kirby Van Mater. Pasadena, California: Theosophical University Press, 1979. x + 74 pp.

(10) Ryan, Charles J. *H.P. Blavatsky and the Theosophical Movement: A Brief Historical Sketch.* Second and Revised Edition. Edited by Grace F. Knoche. Pasadena, California: Theosophical University Press, 1975. (First Edition, 1937) xviii + 358 pp.

(11) Farthing, Geoffrey. *Exploring the Great Beyond: A Survey of the Field of the Extraordinary.* Wheaton, Illinois: The Theosophical Publishing House, 1978. xi + 214 pp.

(12) *Dynamics of the Psychic World: Comments by H.P. Blavatsky on Magic, Mediumship, Psychism, and the Powers of the Spirit.* Compiled by Lina Psaltis. Wheaton, Illinois: The Theosophical Publishing House, 1972. xviii + 132 pp.

(13) *Karma and Reincarnation: A Collation from the Writings of Helena P. Blavatsky*. Los Angeles, California: The Theosophy Company, n.d. 16 pp.

(14) Bendit, Laurence J. *The Mirror of Life and Death*. Wheaton, Illinois: The Theosophical Publishing House, 1967. ix + 199 pp.

(15) Farthing, Geoffrey, comp. *When We Die: A Comprehensive Description, In Outline, of the Processes and Subjective States in the Period Between Lives, with Some Information about Spiritualistic and Psychic Phenomena*. [Compiled from *The Mahatma Letters to A.P. Sinnett*.] London: The Theosophical Publishing House, LTD, 1968. x + 51 pp.

(16) *Spiritual Evolution: Articles by H.P. Blavatsky*. Los Angeles, California: The Theosophy Company, n.d. 39 pp. [5 articles]

(17) *Teachers and Disciples: Articles by H.P. Blavatsky*. Los Angeles, California: The Theosophy Company, n.d. 40 pp. [8 articles]

(18) *The Voice of the Silence: Being Chosen Fragments from The "Book of the Golden Precepts" for the Daily Use of Lanoos (Disciples)*. Translated and Annotated by "H.P.B." Pasadena, California: Theosophical University Press, 1976. (First Edition, 1889.) xiv + 97 pp.

(19) Wachtmeister, Countess Constance and others. *Reminiscences of H.P. Blavatsky and The Secret Doctrine*. Second Edition. Wheaton, Illinois: The Theosophical Publishing House, 1976. (First Edition, 1893) 141 pp.

(20) *An Invitation to The Secret Doctrine*. Pasadena, California: Theosophical University Press, 1988. 112 pp. [Selections from H.P. Blavatsky's *The Secret Doctrine*, reproduced from the original 1888 edition.]

(21) Nicholson, Shirley. *Ancient Wisdom---Modern Insight*. Wheaton, Illinois: The Theosophical Publishing House, 1985. xvii + 198 pp.

(22) Blavatsky, H.P. *An Abridgement of The Secret Doctrine*. Edited by Elizabeth Preston and Christmas Humphreys. Wheaton, Illinois: The Theosophical Publishing House, 1967. xxxii + 260 pp.

(23) Edge, Henry T. *Esoteric Keys to the Christian Scriptures and The Universal Mystery Language of Myth and Symbol*. San Diego, California: Point Loma Publications, Inc., 1974. 42 pp.

(24) Barborka, Geoffrey A. *The Divine Plan: Written in the Form of a Commentary on H.P. Blavatsky's Secret Doctrine*. Adyar, Madras, India: The Theosophical Publishing House, 1964. xxvii + 564 pp. [Highly recommended.]

(25) Murphet, Howard. *Yankee Beacon of Buddhist Light: Life of Col. Henry S. Olcott*. Wheaton, Illinois: The Theosophical Publishing House, 1988. xii + 345 pp. [Formerly published as *Hammer on the Mountain*, 1972.]

(26) Hanson, Virginia. *Masters and Men: The Human Story in The Mahatma Letters*. Quest Paperback Edition. Wheaton, Illinois: The Theosophical Publishing House, 1980. xx + 323 pp.

(27) Osborn, A.W. *The Cosmic Womb: An Interpretation of Man's Relationship to the Infinite*. Wheaton, Illinois: The Theosophical Publishing House, 1969. xiv + 233 pp.

BIOGRAPHICAL SKETCHES

Arundale, Francesca (? -1924), an Englishwoman converted to the Episcopalian Church of England and later to the Roman Catholic Church, Francesca's growing skepticism finally made her leave orthodox religion. She then investigated spiritualism, and upon learning of Theosophy in 1881, she joined the British Theosophical Society. By 1884, Miss Arundale was Assistant Treasurer to the T.S. worldwide. [Consult Francesca Arundale's *My Guest---H.P. Blavatsky* (1932)].

Ballard, Anna, American journalist and life-long member of the New York Press Club. No other biographical information available.

Besant, Annie (1847-1933), English social reformer, Theosophist, Indian Independence leader and one of the greatest orators of her day. Rejecting Christianity, Mrs. Besant joined the National Secular Society in 1874 and became an associate of Charles Bradlaugh, an atheist freethinker. In the 1880s she developed an interest in socialism and worked with George Bernard Shaw in the Fabian Society. Then in March, 1889 she met Madame Blavatsky and joined The Theosophical Society. After H.P.B.'s death, Mrs. Besant became joint outer head of H.P.B.'s Esoteric School along with W.Q. Judge. In 1893 she went to India where in later years, she campaigned for Indian nationalism and founded the Indian Home Rule League (1916). Mrs. Besant was president of The Theosophical Society (Adyar) from 1907 until her death. She was the author of several hundred books including *The Ancient Wisdom* (1897) and *Esoteric Christianity* (1901). [Consult the two-volume biography by Arthur H. Nethercot, *The First Five Lives of Annie Besant* (1960) and *The Last Four Lives of Annie Besant* (1963)].

Brown, William Tournay (1857 - ?), Scotsman with a law degree from the University of Glasgow, Brown became interested in Theosophy while living in London in 1883. In India from September, 1883 to January, 1885, Brown settled in the U.S.A. in 1886. By the next year he had converted to the Christian faith and believed that Madame Blavatsky had "sold herself...to the devil". He wrote two pamphlets on his Theosophical experiences: *Some Experiences in India* (1884) and *My Life* (1885). [Consult H.P.B.'s *Collected Writings*, Vol. VI, pp. 428-430, 31-32.]

Burrows, Herbert (1845-1922), English civil servant. Son of a Methodist parson and educated at Cambridge University, Burrows was a vocal partisan of Secularism, Irish independence, and women's rights. A founder member of the Social Democratic Federation, Burrows was active with Annie Besant in leading the Match Girls' Strike of 1888. He was a Parliamentary candidate in 1908 and 1910.

Cleather, Alice Leighton (1846-1938), English Theosophist, Buddhist, and musician. Joining The Theosophical Society in 1885, Mrs. Cleather became a member of the Inner Group of H.P.B.'s Esoteric School. In 1918, Mrs. Cleather, with her son Graham Gordon Cleather and Basil Crump, went to India, and in 1925, to Peking, China where they met the Panchen Lama of Tibet. At the request of the Panchen Lama, Mrs. Cleather and Mr. Crump republished H.P.B.'s *The Voice of the Silence* (Peking, 1928). She founded the H.P.B. Lending Library (now located at Vernon, British Columbia, Canada) and was associated with The Blavatsky Association of London (1923-1947). Alice Cleather's published works include *H.P. Blavatsky, Her Life and Work for Humanity* (1922) and *H.P. Blavatsky As I Knew Her* (1923). [Consult H.P.B.'s *Collected Writings*, Vol. XIV, pp. 518-521.]

Cooper, Laura Mary (? -1924), the younger sister of Isabel Cooper-Oakley. Laura was a member of the Inner Group of H.P.B.'s Esoteric School. From her pen we have an eyewitness account of H.P.B.'s death: "How She Left Us." In 1899 she married G.R.S Mead.

Cooper-Oakley, Isabel (1854-1914). Born at Amritsar, India, Isabel in 1881 entered Girton College, Cambridge where she met her future husband Alfred J. Oakley. In March, 1884, she joined The Theosophical Society. In 1889, she joined the T.S. staff at Lansdowne Road and also was a member of the Inner Group of H.P.B.'s Esoteric School. Her published works include: *Mystical Traditions* (1909) and *The Comte de St. Germain* (1912). [Consult H.P.B.'s *Collected Writings*, Vol. XII, pp. 730-733.]

Corson, Eugene Rollin (1855- ?), B.S., M.D., son of Professor Hiram Corson. Eugene published H.P.B.'s letters to Hiram Corson in *Some Unpublished Letters of Helena Petrovna Blavatsky* (1929).

Corson, Hiram (1828-1911), American educator and distinguished professor (1870-1903) of English Literature at Cornell University, Ithaca, New York. He was proficient in mathematics and in classical languages. As early as 1874, he avowed his faith in Spiritualism. Professor Corson's writings include *An Introduction to the Study of Robert Browning's Poetry* (1886) and *An Introduction to the Study of Shakespeare* (1889). [Consult H.P.B.'s *Collected Writings*, Vol. I, pp. 450-453.]

Coulomb, Emma, an Englishwoman who first met H.P.B. in Cairo, Egypt in 1872. In 1879, H.P.B. in Bombay received a letter from Emma Coulomb, then living in Ceylon. The next March, Emma and her French husband Alexis arrived penniless at the Bombay Theosophical Headquarters. For the next four years, Emma served as housekeeper and Alexis as general handyman, carpenter and mechanic for the T.S. Headquarters. In May, 1884, the Coulomb couple was expelled from The Theosophical Society for charges of theft, attempted extortion and slander. "Certain crude, unworkable and newly-made trapdoors and sliding panels," writes Theosophical historian, Walter Carrithers, Jr., "were found in HPB's private quarters then exclusively under the care of the Coulomb couple. After a lapse of months, Emma Coulomb contracted to supply the local Christian missionaries with several dozen letters ostensibly in HPB's handwriting. *If genuine*, some few letters and parts of others clearly implicated her in a conspiracy with the Coulombs to produce fraudulent 'occult phenomena.'" [Consult p. 315 of this volume for a list of books on the "Coulomb Case." For an overview, consult Michael Gomes, "The Coulomb Case, 1884-1984," *The Theosophist* [Adyar, Madras, India], Dec., 1984, Jan., 1985 and Feb., 1985.]

Dharmapala, Anagarika (1864-1933), famous Buddhist, born in Colombo, Ceylon. In December, 1884, he accompanied H.P.B. and Olcott to Adyar. H.P.B. encouraged him to study the Buddhist Pali writings. In May, 1891 he founded the Maha Bodhi Society in Calcutta, India. In 1893 Dharmapala spoke at the World Parliament of Religions in Chicago, Illinois, U.S.A. The remainder of his life was spent in promoting Buddhism and working on behalf of the Maha Bodhi Society. [Consult Rick Fields' *How the Swans Came to the Lake* (1981).]

Dick, Frederick J. (1856-1927), civil engineer, Theosophist. Fred Dick was Head of the Harbors and Lighthouse Board for Ireland. He joined The Theosophical Society in Dublin, Ireland in December, 1888. In 1905, Professor Dick went to The Theosophical Society (Point Loma), San Diego, California where he served as professor of mathematics and astronomy at the School of Antiquity. [Consult H.P.B.'s *Collected Writings*, Vol. XI, pp. 571-572.]

Eglinton, William (1857-1933), famous English medium. He was noted for his materialization and slate-writing performances. In late 1881-early 1882, Eglinton visited Calcutta, India where he was the guest of J.G. Meugens, a wealthy Indian merchant. He also stayed with Col. William and Alice Gordon of Howrah, Calcutta. In later life, Eglinton became the editor of the magazine *The New Age* and was a director of a firm of British exporters. [Consult *Encyclopedia of Occultism & Parapsychology*, edited by Leslie A. Shepard, 2nd ed., Vol. I, pp. 392-393.]

Fadeyev, Nadyezhda Andreyevna de (1829-1919), H.P.B.'s favorite aunt, H.P.B.'s mother's sister. Nadyezhda was only two years older than her niece. Miss de Fadeyev corresponded with H.P.B. in the 1870s and 1880s. Her letters are preserved in the archives of The Theosophical Society (Adyar). She died in Prague, Czechoslovakia.

Gebhard, Rudolph Ernst (1857-1935), German Theosophist, son of Gustav and Mary Gebhard of Elberfeld, Germany. He was the fourth oldest of six sons and one daughter. Rudolf went with Col. Olcott to India in October, 1884 and was present at the Theosophical Convention (Adyar, Madras, India) in December, 1884. Madame Blavatsky stayed on two occasions at the Gebhard home in Elberfeld.

Gordon, Alice, English Spiritualist, Theosophist, and wife of Major-General William Gordon (1831-1909) of the Indian Army. A resident of Howrah, India, Mrs. Gordon went in December, 1879 to A.P. Sinnett's house in Allahabad to meet H.P. Blavatsky and Colonel Olcott. In 1890, Mrs. Gordon gave a talk in London on H.P.B. and her occult phenomena. [Consult *Light* (London), Nov. 29, 1890, pp. 575-577.]

Hartmann, Franz (1838-1912), German physician, noted Theosophist and prolific author. He came to live in the United States in 1865. After reading *The Occult World* (1881) by A.P. Sinnett, Hartmann became interested in Theosophy. His books include *Magic, White and Black* (1886), *The Life of Paracelsus*, etc. (1887) and *Occult Science in Medicine* (1893). [Consult H.P.B.'s *Collected Writings*, Vol. VIII, pp. 439-457.]

Hodgson, Richard (1855-1905), Australian psychical researcher. He joined the Society for Psychical Research in 1882. Known for his "exposes" of Madame Blavatsky and the Italian medium Eusapia Palladino, Hodgson investigated the mediumship of Mrs. Leonora Piper of Boston and became convinced that she not only had genuine psychic powers but that deceased persons actually communicated through her. [Consult Hodgson's biographical sketch in Arthur S. Berger's *Lives and Letters in American Parapsychology: A Biographical History*, etc. (1988); for a definitive refutation of Hodgson's charges against H.P. B., consult Adlai E. Waterman's *Obituary: The "Hodgson Report" on Madame Blavatsky* (1963); also see p. 315 in this volume.]

Holloway, Laura Carter (1848-1930), American author and journalist. Her first book *Ladies of the White House* (1870) sold over 100,000 copies. Mrs. Holloway was an associate editor (1870-1884) of the *Brooklyn Daily Eagle*. In the spring of 1884, she met Madame Blavatsky in Paris.

Holt, Elizabeth G.K., no biographical information available.

Johnston, Charles (1867-1931), Irish Theosophist, accomplished Sanskritist and Orientalist. In 1885 Johnston joined The Theosophical Society. In the autumn of 1888 he married H.P.B.'s niece, Vera V. de Zhelihovsky. In 1896 the Johnstons moved permanently to the United States. In later life, Johnston was one of the editors of the *Encyclopaedia Britannica*. He translated several Indian scriptures into English including: *The Bhagavad-Gita* (1908), *The Yoga Sutras of Patanjali* (1912), and *The Great Upanishads* (1927). [Consult H.P.B.'s *Collected Writings*, Vol. IX, pp. 422-426.]

Johnston, Vera Vladimirovna (1864-1923), daughter of H.P.B.'s sister Vera Petrovna de Zhelihovsky. In the autumn of 1888, Vera married Charles Johnston.

331

Judge, William Quan (1851-1896), Irish-born attorney and noted American Theosophist. Born in Dublin, Judge and his family immigrated to Brooklyn, New York in 1864. He studied law and was admitted to the bar in 1872. Judge was one of the three chief Founders of the Theosophical Society. In 1886, he started publishing *The Path*, a Theosophical monthly which he edited till his death. Also in 1886, Judge was elected General Secretary of the American Section of the T.S. In 1888, he assisted H.P. Blavatsky in establishing her Esoteric School. After H.P.B.'s death, Judge became joint outer head of the Esoteric School along with Annie Besant. His writings include *The Ocean of Theosophy* (1893) and *Echoes of the Orient* (3 volumes; 1975-1987). [Consult Sven Eek and Boris de Zirkoff, *William Quan Judge: The Life of a Theosophical Pioneer*, etc. (1969).]

Keightley, Archibald (1859-1930), successful English physician, Theosophist and one of H.P.B.'s most faithful friends. In the spring of 1884, he joined The Theosophical Society. In 1887-1888, Archibald organized (with the help of his uncle, Bertram Keightley, and Countess Wachtmeister) H.P.B.'s household in London. During this same period, Archibald and Bertram prepared H.P.B.'s manuscript of *The Secret Doctrine* for publication. In 1891, Archibald married Julia ver Planck of Pennsylvania. [Consult H.P.B.'s *Collected Writings*, Vol. IX, pp. 427-432.]

Keightley, Bertram (1860-1945), English Theosophist and close supporter of H.P.B. Cambridge-educated, Bertram Keightley became interested in Theosophy in 1883. In the spring of 1884 Colonel Olcott admitted Bertram and his nephew Archibald Keightley into the Theosophical Society. In 1887 Bertram joined forces with Archibald and the Countess Wachtmeister in forming H.P.B.'s household in London. Both Keightleys worked with H.P.B. in preparing the manuscript of *The Secret Doctrine* for publication. [Consult Bertram Keightley's *Reminiscences of H.P.B.* (1931); also H.P.B.'s *Collected Writings*, Vol. IX, pp. 432-435.]

Keightley, Julia Wharton (185?-1915), American Theosophical writer. Daughter of a prominent lawyer and congressman, Julia's first writings were published in *Harper's Magazine* and *Galaxy*. After hearing a talk on Theosophy in 1886, she joined The Theosophical Society. Julia soon became a frequent contributor to W.Q. Judge's magazine *The Path*. In 1891, Julia married Archibald Keightley. [Consult H.P.B.'s *Collected Writings*, Vol. IX, pp. 435-438.]

Kingsland, William (1855-1936), English electrical engineer and Theosophical writer. In 1923, Kingsland and Alice Cleather helped to form The Blavatsky Association to perpetuate and defend H.P.B.'s name and work. His writings include *The Real H.P. Blavatsky* (1928) and *The Gnosis or Ancient Wisdom in the Christian Scriptures* (1937). [Consult H.P.B.'s *Collected Writings*, Vol. X, pp. 419-424.]

Kislingbury, Emily, English teacher, Spiritualist and Theosophist. She became a spiritualist in 1870 and served later as Secretary of the British National Association of Spiritualists. In June, 1878, Miss Kislingbury was elected the first secretary of the British Theosophical Society. In 1890, she became a member of the Inner Group of H.P.B.'s Esoteric School.

Leadbeater, Charles Webster (1854-1934), English clergyman and prominent Theosophical author. C.W. Leadbeater joined The Theosophical Society in 1883. In the ensuing years he became a Theosophical lecturer and writer and collaborated with Annie Besant on several clairvoyant studies (*Thought-Forms*, 1901 and *Occult Chemistry*, 1908). His writings include *Man, Visible and Invisible* (1902) and *The Chakras* (1927). [Consult Hugh Shearman's biographical study *Charles Webster Leadbeater, A Biography* (1980); also the controversial biography *The Elder Brother: A Biography of Charles Webster Leadbeater* (1982) by Gregory Tillett.]

Machell, Reginald Willoughby (1854-1927), English painter, illustrator and Theosophist. Reginald Machell is famous for his mystical paintings such as "The Path." In 1893, he was elected a member of the Royal Society of British Artists. In 1900, Machell left England to reside at and work for The Theosophical Society at Point Loma, California. [Consult H.P.B.'s *Collected Writings*, Vol. XII, pp. 755-757.]

Maitland, Pelham James (1847-1935), English military officer. In 1880-1881, Captain Maitland was Deputy Assistant Quarter Master General (English Intelligence Branch) at Simla. He was Military Secretary (1896-1901) to the Government of India. His writings include *Modern Military Organizations and the British Army* (1906).

Massey, Charles Carleton (1838-1905), English attorney, metaphysician, Spiritualist and Theosophist. In 1878 he was elected first president of the new British Theosophical Society. In 1882, Massey became one of the founders of the Society for Psychical Research (London). He resigned from The Theosophical Society in 1884. [Consult H.P.B.'s *Collected Writings*, Vol. I, pp. 497-499.]

Mavalankar, Damodar K. (1857- ?), Hindu member of The Theosophical Society and devoted disciple of Mahatma K.H. Born in a wealthy family of the Brahmana caste, Damodar joined the Theosophical Society in 1879. Becoming a member of the Theosophical Headquarters staff, Damodar became business manager of the T.S. publications department and assisted in the publication of *The Theosophist*. In the spring of 1885, Damodor left India for Tibet. [Consult *Damodar and the Pioneers of the Theosophical Movement*, compiled and annotated by Sven Eek (1965).]

Mead, George Robert Stowe (1863-1933), Cambridge-educated Theosophist and scholar on Gnosticism and early Christianity. In 1884 Mead joined The Theosophical Society. He first met H.P.B. in 1887 and became her private secretary during the last few years of her life. His writings include *Pistis Sophia: A Gnostic Gospel*, etc. (1896, 1921), and *Fragments of a Faith Forgotten* (1909). [Consult H.P.B.'s *Collected Writings*, Vol. XIII, pp. 393-397.]

Nagnath, Martandrao Babaji, a Hindu Brahmana and member of The Theosophical Society. He was a clerk in the Examiner's Office of Public Accounts, Bombay, India. In the early 1880s, Nagnath was Treasurer of the local Bombay Theosophical Society.

Olcott, Henry Steel (1832-1907), American journalist, editor, attorney, co-founder and first president of The Theosophical Society. Olcott was associate agricultural editor (1859-1861) of the *New York Tribune*. He served in the Civil War and was appointed Special Commissioner (1862-66) in the U.S. War and Navy Departments to investigate corruption and fraud in military arsenals and navy yards. Colonel Olcott practiced law in New York City from 1868 to 1878. In 1875 he was elected President of The Theosophical Society, an office he held for the rest of his life. He worked tirelessly on behalf of the Theosophical Society, traveling throughout India, southern Asia, Australia, Europe and elsewhere. Olcott also worked for the renewal of Buddhism in Ceylon, helping to establish three colleges and 250 schools. His writings include *People from the Other World* (1875), *The Buddhist Catechism* (1881), and *Old Diary Leaves* (1895-1935), a six-volume history of The Theosophical Society. [Consult Howard Murphet's *Yankee Beacon of Buddhist Light: Life of Col. Henry S. Olcott* (1988).]

Old, Reverend B., brother of Walter Old. No other biographical information available.

Old, Walter Richard (1864-1929), English author and professional astrologer. Old wrote under the name Walter Gorn Old and the pseudonym "Sepharial." He was a student of medicine and the Kabala. Old became a member of the Inner Group of H.P.B.'s Esoteric School. His writings include *Second Sight* (1911) and *The Kabala of Numbers* (1913).

Padshah, Sorab Jamaspji, a Parsi poet, journalist and member of The Theosophical Society. A graduate of Bombay University, he was Assistant Recording Secretary to the Theosophical Society in 1880-1881. In the early 1880s, Padshah was the editor of *The Indian Spectator*, an Indian weekly.

Pashkov, Countess Lydia Alexandrovna de, Russian author and traveler. A member of the Geographical Society of France, Countess Pashkov was an author of several books on travel including *En Orient, Drames et Paysages* (1879). In April, 1878 on a trip to New York City, Countess Pashkov visited her old friend Madame Blavatsky. [Consult H.P.B.'s *Collected Writings*, Vol. I, pp. 521-522.]

Pillay, R. Casava, Hindu police officer and inspector at Nellore, India. In 1881, Pillay joined The Theosophical Society. The next year he was the Secretary of the local T.S. Branch in Nellore. [Consult *Report of the Result of an Investigation into the Charges against Madame Blavatsky*, etc., (1885), pp. 87-91.]

Racowitza, Princess Helene von (1844- ?), German princess. She was born Helene von Donniges. In 1864, Ferdinand Lassalle, the German Socialist, fought a duel over her and lost his life. [Consult her *Autobiography* (1910).]

Ramaswamier, S. (? -1893), a Brahmana of high caste. He worked in the English Government service as a District Registrar of Assurances at Tinnevelly, India. Ramaswamier joined The Theosophical Society in 1881. [Consult Geoffrey Barborka's *The Mahatmas and Their Letters* (1973), pp. 320-332.]

Russell, Edmund, a widely-traveled American artist who resided in Paris for many years. No other biographical information available.

Shankar, Bhavani (1859-1936), a Canarese Brahmana and disciple of Master K.H. Bhavani Shankar met H.P.B. soon after she landed in Bombay in 1879. He worked for The Theosophical Society for many years. In the early 1930s, Shankar gave a series of talks on *The Bhagavad-Gita* under the auspices of The United Lodge of Theosophists (Bombay). [Consult his book *The Doctrine of the Bhagavad-Gita* (1966).]

Sidgwick, Henry (1838-1900), English philosopher and psychical researcher. He was professor (1883-1900) of moral philosophy at Cambridge University. Sidgwick was a founding member and the first president (1882-1885) of the Society for Psychical Research (London). His writings include his definitive work *The Methods of Ethics* (1874). [Consult Alan Gauld's *The Founders of Psychical Research* (1968).]

Sinnett, Alfred Percy (1840-1921), English journalist, editor of *The Pioneer* (Allahabad,India), and Theosophical writer. A.P. Sinnett achieved fame as the recipient of *The Mahatma Letters*. Sinnett's *The Occult World* (1881) and *Esoteric Buddhism* (1883) popularized Theosophy. [Consult *Readers' Guide to The Mahatma Letters to A.P. Sinnett*, edited by George E. Linton and Virginia Hanson, (2nd ed., 1988), pp. 349-356; also Virginia Hanson's *Masters and Men: The Human Story in The Mahatma Letters* (1980).]

Smith, John (1821-1885), Scottish-born professor of chemistry and experimental physics. He taught at the University of Sydney, Australia from 1852 till his death. In his later years Smith devoted much of his time to civic affairs and the promotion of education. He joined The Theosophical Society in 1882. [Consult *Australian Dictionary of Biography*, Vol. 6, 1851-1890, pp. 148-150.]

Solovyov, Vsevolod Sergueyevich (1849-1903), Russian novelist and brother of the Russian philosopher Vladimir Solovyov. Vsevolod Solovyov met H.P.B. in Paris in the spring of 1884. At first relations between the two were quite friendly, but Solovyov turned against H.P.B. and wrote a book *A Modern Priestess of Isis* (Russian ed., 1893; abridged English ed., 1895) in which he attempted to portray H.P.B. as a fraud. [Consult H.P.B.'s *Collected Writings*, Vol. VI, p. 446; Beatrice Hasting's book *Solovyoff's Fraud: A Critical Analysis of the Book "A Modern Priestess of Isis"* (1988).]

Stead, William Thomas (1849-1912), English journalist, editor, and spiritualist. In 1883 Stead became editor of the famous London *Pall Mall Gazette.* Then in 1890 he started publishing the prestigious monthly *Review of Reviews.* Becoming interested in spiritualism, psychical research and Theosophy, W.T. Stead founded *Borderland* (1893-1897), a periodical specially devoted to these subjects. Bound for New York, Stead lost his life on the liner *Titanic.*

Tweedale, Violet (1862-1936), English novelist. Mrs. Tweedale, a psychic herself who could see auras, became interested in Spiritualism and attended seances with Lord Richard Haldane (1856-1928), English statesman, and William E. Gladstone (1809-1898), prime minister of England. She wrote almost thirty books, including *Ghosts I have Seen* (1919) and *The Cosmic Christ* (1930).

Wachtmeister, Countess Constance (1838-1910), devoted Theosophist and widow of the Swedish Count Karl Wachtmeister (1823-1871). Investigating spiritualism in the late 1870s, she became interested in Theosophy and joined the Theosophical Society in 1880. Countess Wachtmeister first met H.P.B. in April 1884 on a visit to London. Her book *Reminiscences of H.P. Blavatsky and "The Secret Doctrine"* (1893) gives a fascinating account of H.P.B.'s sojourn (1885-1887) in Wurzburg, Germany and Ostend, Belgium. [Consult H.P.B.'s *Collected Writings*, Vol. VI, p. 448.]

Wiggin, James Henry (1836-1900), American Unitarian clergyman and editor. A Bostonian by birth, Reverend Wiggin moved to New York in 1875 to edit the *Liberal Christian* but returned to Boston the next year. By 1881 he had become an agnostic and had left the ministry. From 1885 to 1891 Reverend Wiggin assisted Mary Baker Eddy (of Christian Science) with the preparation of several of her works.

Wilder, Alexander (1823-1908), American physician, author, editor and Platonic scholar. Wilder received a medical degree in 1850. Wilder was on the editorial staff of several newspapers and was the editor of various medical and philosophical journals. He also held teaching positions at various medical colleges. Wilder wrote many scholarly essays on religious, metaphysical and Platonic subjects. His published works include *New Platonism and Alchemy* (1869) and *History of Medicine* (1901). [Consult H.P.B.'s *Collected Writings*, Vol. I, pp. 531-533.]

Windust, Esther. No biographical information available.

Wyld, George (1821-1906), Scottish physician, Spiritualist and Theosophist. Having received his M.D. degree in 1851, Dr. Wyld took up the study of homeopathy, mesmerism and spiritualism. In 1879 Wyld joined The Theosophical Society, but he resigned from the Society in 1882. He was one of the original founders of the Society for Psychical Research (London) in 1882. His writings include *Clairvoyance* (1883) and *Theosophy, or Spiritual Dynamics and the Divine and Miraculous Man* (1894). [Consult H.P.B.'s *Collected Writings*, Vol. III, pp. 538-539.]

Zhelihovsky, Vera Petrovna de (1835-1896), H.P.B.'s younger sister. She was married twice and had six children. She was a writer of children's stories and a contributor to various Russian magazines. Vera's writings on H.P.B.'s life include: *When I Was Small* (2nd ed., 1894), *My Adolescence* (1893), "The Truth About Helena Petrovna Blavatsky," *Rebus [St. Petersburg],* 1883, and "Helena Petrovna Blavatsky," *Lucifer* [London], Nov., 1894-April, 1895. Vera traveled several times to western Europe in the 1880s to visit H.P.B. [Consult H.P.B.'s *Collected Writings*, Vol. I, pp. 534-537.]

INDEX

Page numbers in bold refer to reminiscences.